The Decline of Comity in Congress

The Decline of Comity in Congress

Eric M. Uslaner

Ann Arbor
THE UNIVERSITY OF MICHIGAN PRESS

Copyright © by the University of Michigan 1993
All rights reserved
Published in the United States of America by
The University of Michigan Press
Manufactured in the United States of America

1996 1995 1994 1993   4 3 2 1

A CIP catalogue record for this book is available from the British Library.

Library of Congress Cataloging-in-Publication Data

Uslaner, Eric M.
    The decline of comity in Congress / Eric M. Uslaner.
        p.   cm.
    Includes bibliographical references and index.
    ISBN 0-472-10456-X (alk. paper)
    1. United States. Congress. 2. Legislators—United States—
Attitudes. 3. Courtesy. 4. Organizational behavior—United
States—Case studies   I. Title.
JK1021.U85   1993
328.73—dc20   93-14861
                                                           CIP

For Avery, with love from Daddy

Preface

The world, and especially the U.S. Congress, is a less pleasant place than it was in the famous era when the norms of courtesy and reciprocity were central to Congressional behavior. It often seems less pleasant than when I began this project about a decade ago.

Some of these impressions are my own doing, or undoing. The project seemed like a natural extension of another long-term effort, my discussion of the politics of energy in the United States and Canada (*Shale Barrel Politics: Energy and Legislative Leadership*, 1989). The nastiness on energy in the early and late 1970s seemed to be spreading everywhere. I then realized that energy was just an egregious example of a trend that had been occurring for a long period of time. In my analysis of energy, I argued that the nation's inability to reach agreement on a national energy policy stemmed not from institutional barriers or "bad" politicians but from a public that had conflicting preferences on what to do. Here I make a similar argument, but the stakes are even larger. Congress is a much less civil place, but neither new members nor structural reforms are likely to make much difference. The bad behavior in Congress reflects a decline of comity in the country.

I thought that this thesis was self-evident, but it turned out not to be. My claims turned out to be rather controversial for a wide variety of reasons, sometimes even eliciting the sort of incivility of which I write. Some objected to the soft evidence I present. Others thought that I made too much of the actual data that were available. Some did not like my use of social choice theory, while many "rat choicers" said no to linking that approach to political culture. Many found my criticism of institutional approaches wrong headed. Some bemoaned my failure to offer a solution to the problems we face. Still others said that things weren't really that bad or that the whole thing depended on economics and not values. Did my framework try to explain everything, or did it fail to account for what was happening elsewhere in the world?

My argument, I now realize, is controversial. Yet, that is how it should be. I press on my students, especially graduate students undertaking dissertations, the lesson: Don't wimp out. Pick a bold thesis and state it unequivocally. Qualify when necessary, but please don't give me a product that, in the unpublished words of Charles O. Jones, amounts to showing that "lots of things are related to lots of things, other things being equal." I think that I finally got it right.

I had help along the way. The support of the Everett McKinley Dirksen Center for the Study of Congressional Leadership and the General Research Board and Scholarship Incentive Award Program of the University of Maryland—College Park is greatly appreciated. Some of the data employed were obtained from the Inter-University Consortium for Political and Social Research, which is not responsible for any interpretations in this book. The same applies to the Roper Center.

I have big debts to a lot of people who tried to set me straight. So many people gave me advice that surely I have forgotten at least a few. A few hardy souls took a great deal of time and labored over the entire manuscript. Charles Stewart III did so not just once but twice and offered frankly brutal advice that only either a good friend or a severe enemy could do. The latter would insist on anonymity. William Bianco, Richard A. Smith, Karol Soltan, and Michael Gusmano each labored through the full manuscript and gave me both constructive and destructive suggestions. I might have been better off if I had taken more of the former. Roger Davidson, Paul Herrnson, Anthony King, and David Lalman have read prior papers and helped me sort out my thesis. Piotr Swistak was an invaluable leaning post on both social choice theory and statistics. Among the others who have shaped my thinking on this project are Richard S. Beth, Christopher J. Bosso, M. Margaret Conway, Lawrence C. Dodd, Patrick Dunleavy, Stephen Elkin, Robert Grafstein, Richard Hall, Susan Hammond, Desmond King, Ronald King, Steven Leventhal, Burdett Loomis, David McKay, Ralph Merritt, Joe A. Oppenheimer, John J. Pitney, Jr., Barry Rabe, Barbara Sinclair, Ronald J. Terchek, Michael Turner, Deborah D. Uslaner, Steven Wasby, Aaron Wildavsky, Rick Wilson, Christopher Wlezien, and Dean Yarwood. They are all more than exonerated. Most of them agreed with most of what they read, but I won't reveal who said what. If I had taken all of their advice, I would have had no book.

Raymond Smock, Richard Baker, Herman Belz, Kim B. Clark,

Linda Kaboolian, and Barbara Romzek provided important bibliographic advice. Smock, the Historian of the House of Representatives, and Baker, the Historian of the Senate, also graciously provided key data. Many graduate and undergraduate students provided key research assistance, most notably Nalini Verma. Mike Wagner's assistance in data analysis was, as ever, both cheerful and extremely helpful. Ann Marie Clark helped keep the manuscript, especially the myriad tables, in good order.

The truly blameworthy are those who read my work, held their fire, and let the project continue. Among the audiences that failed to dissuade me were panelists and panel-goers at the 1987 Annual Meeting of the Midwest Political Science Association, the 1989 and 1990 Annual Meetings of the American Political Science Association, the 1991 Biennial Meeting of the American Politics Group of the Political Studies Association of the United Kingdom, and the 1987 meeting of the same group—which bestowed on my tome its unofficial "longest paper" award. The *British Journal of Political Science* published an earlier cut at the theoretical issues combined with a longer-term historical perspective in January 1991 ("Comity in Context: Confrontation in Historical Perspective").

Patrick Bova of the National Opinion Research Center, Jennifer Bagette of *American Enterprise*, Richard Pazdalski of the Department of Agriculture, and Katherine H. Reichelderfer of Economics Research Service provided important data. Colin Day at the University of Michigan Press was a most hospitable editor.

The greatest impact on my thinking came from Avery Benjamin Uslaner. He graciously (well, not quite) saw fit to shred pieces of paper that did not contain my notes. As he grew older, he tried (sometimes successfully) to mark up the manuscript itself with crayons and felt tip pens. His comments were slightly less decipherable than those of good friends. To get my attention, he threw things at the computer and pounded the keys with a seriousness that dwarfed my own. His keen intellect led him to force me to rewrite part of chapter 6 and make it much better than it intially was. Avery expressed his unhappiness with the earlier draft by throwing his beach ball at the power surge protector and sending several pages into the oblivion of suburban Maryland's electrical supply. In this and other ways, he provided many diversions from this project, demonstrating his keen sense of humor even when it seemed that much of the world had lost its own. Debbie helped me maintain my sense of composure. How she kept hers as I got wrapped up in this seemingly endless journey is a mystery defying both institutional and macropolitical approaches. She and Bo provided the love and sustenance that led me to complete this project after almost a decade, but this one is for my big boy.

Contents

Chapter 1. On Good Behavior 1

Chapter 2. Norms and Normlessness 21

Chapter 3. Five Explanations in Search of Evidence 45

Chapter 4. Values, Norms, and Society 63

Chapter 5. The Decline of Comity in the Nation 103

Chapter 6. Policy-Making in an Era of Resource Constraints 127

Chapter 7. A New Order in the New World? 157

References 171

Subject Index 199

Name Index 203

Chapter 1

On Good Behavior

> America is safe for the legislative way of life as long as it retains its sense of humor; for humor keeps our humility from becoming sticky and makes our friendliness function fruitfully. It punctures vainglory and purifies pretense.
> —T. V. Smith

"Americans were not born to frown," wrote the *Economist*, in its anonymity and graceful style the current Publius (or Bagehot, as it prefers) of the English-speaking world (*Economist* 1987, 11):

> It does not suit them. The quintessentially American characteristics are cheerfulness, optimism and generosity, a general buoyancy of spirit, a belief that tomorrow will dawn a better day. So it may, but suddenly many Americans seem not so sure. They assumed the American Century, born in 1941, would endure a hundred years; now, after fewer than 50, they fear it is on the wane.

American society and its politics have hardened over a period of approximately two decades. Politics is now not just a serious business but a highly polarized one. Give and take has given way to non-negotiable demands. We have lost the collective sense of humor that is so necessary to sustain cordiality and the trust in others that is essential to reciprocity. Without reciprocity, policy-making becomes more difficult and some of the most pressing problems facing the nation go unresolved. Comity, the adherence to a set of norms that includes courtesy and reciprocity, enhances collective action.

Think back to the 1960s and remember Dick Tuck. He was an unofficial Democratic prankster who dogged Republican presidential candidates with what we would now call dirty tricks. Some were harmless, such as making Richard Nixon's whistlestop train take off from the station with the candidate still on the platform making a speech. Others were less tasteful. All were good copy and kept people laughing. By the 1980s and 1990s we took such antics with deadly seriousness. In 1988 Senator Joseph Biden (D—Del.) was almost forced to withdraw from the Presidential campaign because his speechwriter had "plagiarized" a phrase from one of British Labor Party leader Neil Kinnock's addresses. In 1990 the Massachusetts Democratic Party sued a White House aide for "conspiracy to obstruct the individual civil rights of . . . delegates" to the party's convention by organizing a picket line at the convention (Butterfield 1990a). The pickets were organized by a local police union that had endorsed Republican candidates.[1]

Confrontation, not dialogue, dominates when we lose our sense of humor. The policies we adopt will not benefit from reason but reflect the shrillness of demands. The politics of the 1970s, 1980s, and 1990s reflect rising economic uncertainty and changing social mores in the United States. We are no longer so polite to each other. We do not trust each other as much as we once did. Few places show this waning of norms, this decline of comity, as clearly as the U.S. Congress, both the House and the Senate.

What has happened to Congressional norms? Why are there so many loud voices? The answer does not lie within the legislature or in any other institution. Neither the Congressional reforms of the 1970s, divided control of the legislative and executive branches, the media, nor the new members in the legislature is responsible for our problems. Congress behaves poorly because its masters, the constituents, set a bad example. It is not just that Congressional mores have waned. Some core values that underlie American political culture have atrophied, as have the associated prescriptions for action (norms) in the society.

Four important values—individualism, egalitarianism, science (as social engineering), and religion—have waned. One is central to my thesis: an "enlightened" individualism that is the foundation of trust

---

1. Democrats charged the picketers with "striking, shoving, and spitting upon" delegates (Butterfield 1990b), obviously making the situation rather different from Dick Tuck's more harmless pranks. The union denied the charges. If the allegations are correct, they emphasize how conflictual politics have become. If they are not, they indicate just how much we have lost our sense of humor.

in other people. Trust is the basis of cooperation in collective action. The 1950s and 1960s were a more trusting era. Confidence in other people declined sharply in the 1970s and 1980s. We adopted a harsher version of individualism, looking out for ourselves and denying the legitimacy of others' claims. The decline of trust led to the fraying of other values and their associated norms of behavior, including those that promote civility. The result was a more contentious policy environment, with unhappy results.

Ronald Reagan tried to put the old normative order back together, attempting to restructure political alignments in the United States through tax reform. He failed, but succeeded in further polarizing American politics and adding yet another layer of incivility—this time partisan—to the disorder of the late 1960s and early 1970s. The legacy of the 1970s and 1980s is a rather tepid war of each against all, nasty enough to block cooperation on critical policy issues such as the budget and energy and to extort benefits for great numbers (and small groups) of citizens. Yet the battles are not sufficient to polarize the entire society. We are stuck in a rut. We do not cooperate with each other as much as in the past. We stick together just enough to keep the system together but not enough to forge ahead.

The American public is fed up with the Congress and its inability to solve national policy problems. More than two-thirds of Americans in 1992 thought that the way to resolve the mess in Congress was to limit the number of terms legislators could serve (Morin and Dewar 1992). An already skeptical electorate became, by 1991, substantially less likely (than in 1987) to state that the government is run for the benefit of all and that most elected officials care what people think; they were considerably more likely to charge that elected officials in Washington lose touch with the people (Times-Mirror Corporation 1991). The basic problems of American society could be traced to the doorstep of Congress; the legislature's bad behavior was one more manifestation of its uncaring incompetence. The scandal at the House bank, in which the majority of members wrote checks with insufficient funds, further eroded public confidence. In March 1992, three quarters of Americans disapproved of Congressional performance.[2]

The bank scandal and other misdeeds of legislators are not the

---

2. Americans even began to doubt their own representatives. Job approval ratings for "your representative" fell from 71 percent in 1989 to 49 percent (Morin and Dewar 1992).

heart of the problem. Stalemate over policy is. Yet the blame does not rest with Congress—either alone or primarily. Congress is truly a representative institution, perhaps too much so. It receives too many conflicting demands on policy from the folks back home to take bold action. Ordinary citizens might overdraw their checking accounts less often than many legislators. Yet they are hardly role models for comity. Neither term limits nor any other set of "reforms" will make our legislators behave better or solve pressing problems. To get back to a more civil society we need a political realignment. Political sea changes in the past have renewed core American values, yet none is in sight now.

A Civil Body

In the 1960s, when an elaborate system of Congressional norms sustained cordiality and reciprocity, Representative Clem Miller (D—Cal.) observed that "[o]ne's overwhelming first impression as a member of Congress is the aura of friendliness that surrounds the life of a congressman.... The freshman congressman is being constantly made aware of the necessity, even the imperative, of getting along with his fellow congressmen" (Miller 1962, 93). Minority leaders in both houses boasted of how well they got along with their counterparts in the majority. The friendships of Joe Martin (R—Mass.) with Sam Rayburn (D—Tex.) in the House and Everett McKinley Dirksen (R—Ill.) with Mike Mansfield (D—Mont.) in the Senate were particularly warm (Martin 1960, 9; Loomis 1990); House Minority Leader Robert Michel (R—Ill.) and Speaker Thomas P. (Tip) O'Neill (D—Mass.) regularly played golf.

Two decades later the Congress was a much less congenial place. Representative Newt Gingrich (R—Ga.) read into the *Congressional Record* on May 8, 1984, a report highly critical of some fifty House Democrats' record on foreign policy. A week later Speaker O'Neill took to the well of the House to charge that Gingrich had attacked the "Americanism" of the Democrats and that the verbal assault was "the lowest thing that I have ever seen in my 32 years in Congress." Minority Whip Trent Lott (R—Miss.) demanded that the Speaker's words be taken down, making O'Neill the first Speaker since 1797 to be rebuked for his language (Granat 1984b).

In 1985 the Georgian accused Senate Majority Leader Bob Dole

(R—Kan.) of helping to sustain the "welfare state" (Dewar 1985). Three years later Gingrich would file ethics charges against another Speaker, Jim Wright (D—Tex.), leading to Wright's ultimate resignation in one of the most bitter partisan disputes of the twentieth century.[3] In 1989 Gingrich's staff was implicated in spreading rumors about Representative Tom Foley (D—Wash.) in an attempt to prevent him from succeeding Wright. At the very least one would have expected legislators on both sides of the aisle to ostracize Gingrich. For a while they did (Walsh 1985). However, by 1989 he had become assistant minority leader of the House.

In the 1950s and 1960s, the Congress was a civil, if not very open, institution.[4] The House was guided by Rayburn's maxim, "To get along, go along," while the Senate disdained "petty exhibitionism" and extolled reciprocity (White 1956, 117, 56–57):

> To grant to one's opponent in high political discussion and maneuver each and all of the rights that one demands for oneself—this is, uniquely in this country certainly, and perhaps in all the world, a Senate rule.

Friendships regularly crossed party lines (Baker 1980), and until recently members could not even refer to one another by name on the floor. Personal attacks were verboten.[5] The norms of collegiality outlasted the closed "Inner Club" Senate period (Polsby 1971).

By the 1980s the House and the Senate came to resemble day care centers in which colicky babies got their way by screaming at the top of their lungs. An elaborate set of norms emphasizing courtesy and reciprocity that had been in place since at least the 1950s no longer restrained members from making personal attacks on each

---

3. Wright, in his resignation speech, said "All of us, in both political parties, must resolve to bring this period of mindless cannibalism to an end." Minority Leader Bob Michel (R—Ill.) responded "Now it's a catchy phrase, but the distinguished members of the ethics committee ... are neither mindless nor cannibals. I am all for putting an end to bitterness ... but we don't do so by sweeping things under the rug" (Hook 1989, 1289; Alston 1989, 1374).

4. A glaring exception was Senator Joseph McCarthy (R—Wis.); but see chap. 7.

5. The most famous stretching of the limits was the late Speaker John McCormack's remark in a fit of pique, "I hold the gentleman in minimum high regard" (quoted in Ornstein 1983, 199).

other. While the majority of members still spoke in civil tongues, sanctions did not deter legislators who flouted the rules. In some instances the panoply of shrill voices in the Congress led to stalemate. In other cases it led to "bad" policy. Bad policy does not mean decisions that one might dislike. Instead, programmatic arguments are crowded out by nonnegotiable demands that would be rejected in a more deliberative, less hostile environment (see chap. 6).

Rational debate requires sufficient cooperation to give the other side its due, at a minimum a modicum of respect. Comity establishes the basis for reasoned policy-making, not necessarily for the adoption of one's preferred alternative. Deliberation need not be scholarly or even disinterested. Within bounds it can even be raucous, as between partisans in parliamentary systems. Debate must be to the point, to the substance of policy, rather than focusing on nonnegotiable demands from outside groups or the electoral needs of the politicians.

Deliberation depends on breadth of view, on a longer-term perspective that is *communitarian*.[6] The conflict between giving constituents immediate rewards and maintaining the health of the economy is one of many "collective action" problems I shall investigate. Short-term immediate gratification might leave everyone worse off in the longer run, while sacrificing immediate benefits will ultimately make each person well off. The instantaneous profits from self-interest always are higher than those from collaboration. If everyone acts egoistically, the gains dissipate. Cooperation is essential to a regime of comity.

Debate must be civil. Legislators must maintain a sense of respect for others, including the opposition. Discord must not become so severe that members lose all perspective. Serious discourse demands that we *exchange* views with adversaries and give them the respect that we demand of our own ideas. It also requires keeping our sense of humor, often an important element in rhetoric. Comity permits reasoned debate over policy. It makes give-and-take possible and

---

6. There is a growing literature on *communitarianism,* which uses the term differently (and perhaps more appropriately) from the way I do (see Mansbridge 1980). This approach contrasts adversarial democracy, the classical liberal approach emphasizing conflicting ideas and candidates, with a more communitarian alternative, focusing on discussion and compromise. My usage stresses the need to forsake short-term rewards from selfish actions in favor of the longer-term benefits that enlightened self-interest would yield. This is the traditional cooperation problem in rational choice theory.

inhibits the acceptance of nonnegotiable demands. Civility is not the end product; policy based on civil debate is. However, comity is not simply an intervening variable. Without it there can be no regime of reason.

A regime of reason emphasizes breadth of view. Policymakers must take into account the long-range consequences of their alternatives and the effects on others. They must abjure threats and nonnegotiable demands in favor of comity, pure egoism in favor of enlightened self-interest. Toqueville's (1945, vol. 2, p. 122) concept of "self-interest rightly understood" stresses "an enlightened regard for themselves [that] prompts [people] to assist one another and inclines them willingly to sacrifice a portion of their time and property to the welfare of the state."[7] People need not be altruists; they must only recognize that they have commitments to others. Such social obligations arise from a consensus on the central values in a society (Galston 1991, 159–60). The commonality of views establishes a bond within society that provides the tolerance and comity that are essential to breadth of view.

A weakened normative regime is not likely to produce as much good policy as a polity with deeply held beliefs. Even a battered Congress retains some good will and is thus capable of making good policy from time to time. In the 1960s the robust economy provided enough to go around. Issues were not quite so contentious, nor were demands so extreme. When boom and bust cycles appeared over the next two decades, voices became more shrill and people inside and outside the Congress were less willing to compromise. Economic downturns are critical to the emergence of pit-bull politics, but they are not the whole story. The waning of values and norms began during boom times, when new groups with new issues entered the fray, disrupted traditional coalitions, and pressed a reluctant society with confrontational tactics. In the civil rights movement, these strategies were necessary; other groups copied them as a first resort. When uncivil tactics worked in good times, they became common when the economy soured. The policy agenda of good times—the Great Society of the mid-1960s—set the dialectic in motion. The vast expansion of government's role in the economy raised expectations of what the polity could do and should do. Government became the "permanent

---

7. Margolis (1982) contends that people have "dual utility functions," one representing self-interest and the other concern for the larger society.

receiver" for individuals, groups, and institutions in trouble (Lowi 1979). In bad times, everyone flocked to the new savior. They demanded more protection than the society could provide and declared their own claims special and others' demands illegitimate.

The Bases of Comity

Comity is more than simply being nice to one another. It encompasses courtesy and reciprocity within a system of norms. If I am polite to you and you are rude to me, we do not have a regime of comity. There must also be standards of behavior or norms, what is called regular order in the House of Representatives.[8] Courtesy is more than just an external veneer. It symbolizes respect for other people and the recognition that alternative views are legitimate. Reciprocity offers the promise of fair exchange and the keeping of promises. Both norms enhance the development of trust, which is essential for collective action.

We generally think of comity as civility. Most dictionary definitions place gentility first. As with more political accounts, they also highlight reciprocity, often stressing that the two go hand in hand (see n. 8). Comity in both U.S. constitutional practice and international law implies mutual obligations of one sovereign body to another, "full faith and credit": "The term, insofar as it suggests *mere courtesy*, is misleading" (McLaughlin and Hart 1914, 330, emphasis added). Congressional comity has historically referred to both standards of behavior for members and the mutual respect of the two chambers for each others' prerogatives (see Cannon 1935, 806–7 and especially 896; and Brown 1979, 162–64).[9]

Reciprocity is arguably even more central to comity than courtesy. One can "kill" an adversary with kindness. Civility becomes

---

8. Members of the House of Representatives mean two different things when they demand "regular order." Corresponding to "laws and usages" is the procedure for the day, as determined by the calendars, the Rules Committee, and the rules of the House itself (Brown 1979, 167). The *demand* for regular order, however, occurs "[w]hen the House procedure is contrary to the rules, or when it is boisterous or noisy in the Chamber" (Riddick 1949, 306). This second component implies both civility and the rules of procedure. The two aspects of comity follow the definition of the term in *The Compact Edition of the Oxford English Dictionary* (Oxford: Oxford University Press, 1971), 606.

9. This paragraph depends heavily on sources and ideas provided by Richard S. Beth.

sincere only when it is founded on mutual respect and obligations. A regime of comity depends more heavily on reciprocity than civility, although good manners makes mutual deference easier.

Beyond reciprocity and courtesy, comity can encompass a wide range of normative systems. The particular norms of the Congress of the 1950s and 1960s—encompassing courtesy, reciprocity, institutional patriotism, legislative work, apprenticeship, and specialization (see chap. 2)—fit very well a legislative body with weak parties and a commitment to accommodating a wide range of interests. More majoritarian systems, such as Parliamentary regimes or the Congress of the late nineteenth century (Cooper and Brady 1973, 42), employ different conventions. Yet even raucous chambers such as the Houses of Commons in Great Britain and Canada must follow some rules of civility, tempering remarks and insisting that bargains be kept (Searing 1982; Kornberg 1964). The specific norms adopted depend on the nation's or firm's "corporate culture" (Kreps 1990). They can vary widely but must include—and cannot clash with—courtesy and reciprocity for comity to take root.

It is nice to be nice, but is it worth the trouble? The payoff comes in achieving collective action on policy-making. Comity is not cooperation; it enhances the chances for cooperative decision making. Each actor in a world of rational egoists wants to gain as much as possible with few—or no—costs. Everyone fears contributing too much to some common purpose, so that others might gain more. If enough others reciprocate, you will not have to do so. You can reap the gains of cooperation without cooperating yourself. The collective action problem is an N-person Prisoner's Dilemma (PD) (Hardin 1971). The PD highlights the tension between individual and collective rationality.[10] If everyone cooperates, all would benefit. However, each would do best by defecting. So all players have incentives to defect. Two legislators might wish to exchange promises to support each other's bills, but there is nothing to prevent the one whose proposal

---

10. Much of the literature on resolving the PD also presumes (correctly) that there is a cyclical majority, where no alternative can gain a majority against any other (Arrow 1951). In particular, the anything-can-happen result of McKelvey (1976)—in which *any* outcome from a set of alternatives might be selected—is at least as unsettling in the search for a socially preferred outcome as the PD. Yet cycles and the PD are rarely linked together. I have made a stab at the problem in Uslaner (1989, chap. 2).

is voted on first from reneging (Weingast 1979).[11] The opportunities for reneging breed distrust (Murphy 1974, 179).

A commitment to reciprocity, backed by the veneer of courtesy that indicates sincerity, can overcome a reluctance to keep one's word. People who share fundamental values will be more likely to trust each other and ultimately to consummate deals. The decline of comity points to the waning of a system of norms and the larger values that sustain them. People trust each other less and are more willing to defect for personal gain rather than pursue any common objective. Without a common bond of shared values, they look inward and reject others' claims as illegitimate. Collective action is stymied.

Do norms sustain cooperation? Many are skeptical, and most students of collective choice offer alternative views of overcoming the problem of reneging. After all, rogue outlaws often cooperate with each other. Consider alternative accounts of cooperative behavior based on institutions, sanctions, and repeated play. People who seek to avoid risk will create structures to enforce promises (Shepsle 1986). Courts can compel people to keep their word by imposing sanctions against people who violate contracts (written promises). Congressional committees can force the full chambers to accept their bills as written or settle for the status quo through control over the agenda. These panels can demand rules prohibiting amendments and can prevent other committees from considering similar legislation (Shepsle and Weingast 1981).

Institutional accounts fail to resolve a fundamental issue: How can people who don't trust each other to keep their promises agree to establish an institution that will bind them? Why presume that courts are neutral or that Congressional committees with overarching power will behave better than their individual members would?[12] They also fail to account for the decline of comity in a wide range of contexts that have little in common structurally: the California, Michigan, New York, and New Jersey state legislatures; the Westchester County and Suffolk County (New York) legislatures; and the Chicago City Council. The supposedly judicious Illinois Supreme Court, the U.S. Court of Appeals for the District of Columbia, and

---

11. If everyone rationally defects, it matters little what the operative decision rule in a legislative chamber is.

12. This is the "second-order collective action problem." See Taylor 1987, among others.

even the Supreme Court have been marked by rancor (see Walters 1986; Christoff and Bell 1991; Wilkerson 1986; Peterson 1988; Foderaro 1989; Associated Press 1987; Taylor 1987; *New York Times* 1989; Lyall 1991; Kerr 1990).[13]

Institutions appear powerful because they can impose sanctions.[14] Law violators are less afraid of the courts than of the punishments meted out. If we cannot be sure that we can construct external institutions, what can we do? People can—and do—impose sanctions on defectors through voluntary collective action (Ostrom 1991). Punishment may not be the answer. The costs of enforcement are often higher than the benefits from preventing defection (Ostrom, Walker, and Gardner 1990). Retaliation can result in a decline in morale for the entire group and take defectors out of reach of those who are disciplined (Blau 1955, 155). The sanctioners face another dilemma: They will either plunder their colleagues or fail to catch enough defectors. Leaders who chose the first course will not last long; those who take the second will have to make up the collective losses from their own resources (Bates 1988; Hammond and Miller 1990).

Repeated plays of PD games with no set end point can yield cooperative outcomes. Legislatures don't meet, vote, and go home. They stay in session for months at a time, and many members serve together for years. People learn from experience. If you trust someone to exchange votes and you get stung, you withhold cooperation until the other player learns that cooperation is more profitable in the long run (Axelrod 1984). Yet even the optimism of the repeated play result, which has achieved the status of a folk theorem in game theory, must be tempered (Fudenberg and Maskin 1986; Bianco and Bates 1990).

---

13. On the Supreme Court, note the opinions of Justices Antonin Scalia and Harry Blackmun in the Missouri abortion case decided in July, 1989. Scalia stated in his concurrence, "Justice [Sandra Day] O'Connor's assertion that a 'fundamental rule of judicial restraint' requires us to avoid reconsidering Roe cannot be taken seriously." Blackmun's dissent was even sharper: "Never in my memory has a plurality announced a judgment of this Court that so foments disregard for the law and for our outstanding decisions. Nor in my memory has plurality gone about its business in such a deceptive fashion." In an earlier dissent over a civil rights case, Blackmun was only slightly less acerbic: "I can find no justification for the bare majority's apparent eagerness to consider rewriting well-established law" (Taylor 1988).

14. The Japanese sumo wrestler Futahaguro was banned for kicking the eighty-eight-year-old head of his supporter's group and injuring his master's wife. For negligence in supervising the wrestler, the Sumo Association reprimanded the stable master, and for permitting the entire event to have occurred at all, the directors cut their own salaries by 20 percent for three months (Haberman 1988).

The cooperative outcome is but one of many possible equilibria to PD games, and the evidence from experimental studies on the likelihood of achieving coordination is mixed (Rapoport, Guyer, and Gordon 1976; Larson 1986, 26–27). As with institutions and sanctions, the repeated play result at most can tell you how to sustain cooperation once you initially get there; it is silent about how one induces defectors to take risks in the first place.

Enter values and norms. Shared values create social obligations to cooperate. People seek to develop reputations for trustworthiness. In time, cooperation based on reputation becomes self-enforcing (Kreps 1990, 103). In the Senate, "[n]onconformity is met with moral condemnation, while senators who conform to the folkways are rewarded with high esteem by their colleagues" (Matthews 1960, 116; cf. Muir 1982, 159 [on the California legislature]). In contrast to accounts that stress institutions, sanctions, or repeated play, a normative thesis presumes that at least some people are predisposed toward cooperation (Axelrod 1986; Bendor and Swistak 1991; Calvert 1991; Frank 1988). Betting that others will cooperate is a rational gamble when trust is widespread (Bates 1988, 398). Critics charge that this argument is circular (Krehbiel 1986, 543), while defenders such as Kreps (1990, 107) state simply, "[I]t works because it works."

If people adopted just any set of norms, the argument might well be circular. Yet, selecting standards of behavior is not the same as putting a quarter into an amusement park game and taking whatever prize comes out. There is a hierarchy of beliefs, with values (in the United States individualism, egalitarianism, science, and religion) at the top, norms of behavior beneath them, and preferences over alternative policies further down. Norms derive from more enduring values, which in turn are shaped by a nation's history. Values and norms change over time—and sometimes they fall apart altogether. Comity declines when there is conflict among the fundamental values; the system of norms atrophies and people have less in common. They are less willing to cooperate with each other on policy-making. Pressing problems go unresolved. Specifying the values, the norms, and how each changes removes any circularity.

"Self-interest rightly understood" is the American value that is central to cooperative behavior. It is an "invisible hand" that promotes cooperation through reciprocity and a gentle veneer (courtesy).

Enlightened self-interest together with a system of norms leads to comity. Trust is essential for reciprocity, which in turn is critical to maintaining social cohesion (Gouldner 1960, 171, 174; Larson 1986, 1; Becker 1990, 80). People can get by without courtesy, as thieves who cooperate do, yet incivility sends a message to be on guard. Long-term trust cannot flourish in an atmosphere of belligerence.

A normative account leads to a more pessimistic outlook than any of the alternative explanations of collective action. Supporters of voluntarily imposed sanctions and repeated play explanations are always optimists, but they offer no theses for why people cooperate sometimes and not other times. Institutionalists believe that we can alter structures to produce better outcomes (Bolling 1965; Clark 1964; Shepsle 1984; see also chap. 3).[15] Americans have long believed in social engineering and its ability to make our political order work better (Ranney 1976; Diggins 1984, 66–68). An account that stresses norms and especially values offers less hope. As difficult as it might be to change institutions, it is even more of a task to shift the values and norms of a nation.

Everything New Will Be Old Again

Nastiness isn't new. We've been there before. American politics runs in cycles (Huntington 1981) that correspond to the breaking up of traditional coalitions that define party systems (Burnham 1970; Sundquist 1973). What we think of as "normal politics" are relatively quiescent periods when there is widespread agreement on fundamental values and the norms that translate ideals into behavior. When people agree on values, they have a greater sense of community and are more likely to trust each other. In turn, they adhere to norms such as courtesy and reciprocity, the fundamental bases of comity. When there is consensus on individualism, egalitarianism, science, and religion, people both inside and outside the legislature are willing to compromise with each other to initiate new legislation.

In the weak American party system, cooperation across partisan lines is common, especially in the mature party systems that help to

---

15. Representative John Dingell (D—Mich.), chair of the Energy and Commerce Committee, is an unreconstructed institutionalist: "If you let me write procedure and I let you write substance, I'll screw you every time" (quoted in Barry 1990, 84).

socialize conflict (Schattschneider 1960). Both values and party systems age and get cranky. So do people. The life span of a party system is approximately one generation—thirty years (Burnham 1970). Some of the aging process is generational. Younger people do not share the same emotions toward the old coalitions as their parents, who grew up strongly identifying with one party or the other. Young people do not always have the same values either. Toward the end of systems of values and parties, old attachments wane before new ones form. Advocates of alternative visions of what the country should be choose up sides; the old coalitions fray and so do tempers. New issues emerge that cut across the old ones; new actors come into the political battle. All of a sudden, the values no longer seem consistent. Nor is it clear where the traditional parties stand on the new issues and, most critically, on questions of fundamental values. Trust in others declines, as does confidence in government. Policymaking becomes more difficult. Congress gets stuck in a rut at the trough of the cycle of values and partisan attachments (Dodd 1986). So does society, which Congress well reflects (Dodd 1981).

Then something happens to shake up the old order. The new issues begin to cohere into clear approaches to the central values of individualism and egalitarianism (see especially Huntington 1981) and science and religion. So do party cleavages. Ultimately a flash point occurs during an economic crisis. A new interpretation of the core values emerges victorious and carries into hegemony the political party that is associated with the regime of ideals. It is more than a generation passing by; real conversion of partisanship—and values—occurs (Erikson and Tedin 1981). For a while the winners rule in a majoritarian fashion. Political realignments bring about widespread policy innovation without party cooperation (Brady 1988). Soon the new value system catches on and becomes consensual. Value conflicts and partisanship subside and we return to normal politics. The cycle starts anew.

Incivility occurs both at the trough of an old alignment and at the zenith of the new, yet these points are fundamentally different. After a realignment, the winners invite the losers in, and the offer is generally accepted. It is a heady time of policy innovation. The nadir of a system of values is a period of despair. The old norms have withered, and no rescue is in sight. No one wants to cooperate with others, and policy-making is stymied. Comity gives way to nonnegotiable demands.

Realignments bring about bursts of policy innovation because they bring about *both* a new normative order and strong partisan cleavages in the electorate. Clear lines of division on policy questions only occur when a coherent value system reigns or is about to ascend. Realigning eras clear the deck and establish a dominant value system. Occasionally a renewed party system—such as the Democrats in the early 1960s—will also find a congruent value system mixed with partisan polarization in the electorate.

Coherent values don't imply partisan or ideological polarization on issues, as the 1950s demonstrated. When ideals are congruent, civility is more likely. Crazy-quilt preferences over policy may lead politicians to compromise in a regime of comity (cf. Miller 1983). Reciprocity and courtesy can help achieve concessions, but only when the vast majority of players share a common set of values. When there is conflict over core ideals, there will almost certainly be multiple sources of discord over policy questions. There may not be enough civility to reach accommodations; when there is, the accords will represent commitments to the most strident groups in the electorate and thus will add up to bad policy.

The story of sturm und drang comports well with how Congress has behaved in the troughs of realignment cycles and how social tensions developed in the larger society (see chaps. 2, 4, and 5). If so, why be pessimistic? If we wait, things will improve. We have been waiting. Previous realignments have come almost like clockwork. Our dialectical timepiece has broken down. We should be approaching the end of the post–New Deal alignment, but it never arrived. Our values have been in decline for more than two decades, but there has been no triggering event to induce a new alignment. We might even be beyond a reshuffling of our partisan and value attachments, stuck in a not-so-benign purgatory.

For a while it seemed as if we would get there. The 1964 election renewed the New Deal coalition without the trauma of the trough. An era of sustained legislative activism seemed possible, but racial conflict, the war in Vietnam, Watergate, and the rise of new actors in American politics all contributed to the waning of the old order. The late 1970s seemed to constitute a new low, with the 1980 election marking the beginning of the long-sought realignment, yet not even Ronald Reagan could reshape American politics. Trust in others failed to rebound, except briefly in 1980 and 1984, and we remain stuck in neutral.

The Search for Regular Order

My puzzle begins with Congress but moves on to the rest of the society before returning to Congressional performance. The route might seem circuitous, but it has a logic. As in a whodunit, we first must visit the scene of the crime—the incivility in Congress (chap. 2). Is there enough to moan about? If so, let's round up the usual suspects and scrutinize them. Potential culprits for the increased nastiness include the legislative reforms of the 1970s, divided control of the legislative and executive branches, the impact of television on Congress, the changing membership of Congress, and the emergence of a liberal majority that owed little to the old set of norms. None of these accounts, nor one based on the rise of many new interest groups, satisfactorily explains the decline of comity (chap. 3).

We have the body and have eliminated most of the contenders in the lineup. Next we solve the puzzle. To account for voluntaristic cooperation, we must focus on values. Some core American values— American exceptionalism, individualism, egalitarianism, religion, and science—have all come under assault from the late 1960s onward. We don't trust each other as much as in the 1960s. When we doubt that the future will be better than the past, we lose faith in the social engineering that underlies our faith in science; our view of America as the new Canaan also comes under attack. Atrophying values lead to waning norms. The norms of Congressional behavior have direct counterparts in the larger society. Among other changes, Americans have become less tolerant of themselves and less charitable. These maxims have waned among the American people as well as among their representatives. Decreasing support for these norms can be traced to conflicts among the core values (chap. 4).

What shook up these values? The social turmoil of the 1950s (civil rights) and the 1960s (protests over the war in Vietnam) led to an era of confrontational politics. The boom years of the 1950s and 1960s led to rising expectations. The energy crises of the 1970s and the corresponding wide economic swings that have buffeted the

American economy ever since have dashed them with a vengeance. These unmet anticipations added to the incivility of civil rights and Vietnam protests. People sought protection against increasing economic uncertainty, and they looked to Washington to guarantee that they would not face undue hardships. As people demanded more and more, governmental resources became stretched. Groups seeking benefits for themselves attacked the legitimacy of others' demands, in a direct slap at the enlightened individualism that is so fundamental to American political culture. The economic turbulence of the 1970s disrupted the regular order of American political and social life, fraying the norms along the way (chap. 5).

The 1980s, however, brought hope to many. The Reagan administration restored many Americans' faith in government (if not in themselves). Reagan attempted to engineer a political realignment to reestablish some regular order. This was a novel attempt, but it failed during his first administration. We were left with the same old conflicts that had emerged during the 1970s and disrupted traditional coalitions. They were overlaid with new partisan barbs within the Congress that Reagan's advance guard, including Gingrich, aimed at Democrats in the attempt to reforge party ties. By the end of Reagan's first term, there was even less regular order than at the beginning. The beginning of his second term saw a new, and bolder, attempt at political engineering: Realignment would occur through a specific issue, tax reform. Yet taxes did not grab the public's attention. By the time Congress finally enacted the Tax Reform Act of 1986, the bold new politics of ideas had fallen prey to many interest groups. The legislation was too complex to forge a new political alignment, and most Americans thought the new tax system was at least as unfair as the one it replaced (chap. 5).

The mystery is closed, but nonfiction demands a "so what?" that bedtime reading does not. In a world of frayed norms, policy-making in Congress becomes more contentious. The loud voices and incivility inside and outside Congress have made deliberation more difficult. The most complex and controversial issues, with many diverse groups pressing claims, wind up in stalemate. This has been the case with energy and the federal budget deficit. Where there has been less organized opposition, groups have nevertheless demanded ever more generous government support, as in agriculture, and attacked the legitimacy of their opponents, as on the environment. These latter cases lack civility. The process is debased and bad policy results. Declining trust in other people has led to increased budget deficits, higher agricultural price supports, and fewer major laws enacted by Congress (chap. 6).

The lessons of the past do not give room for optimism. Conflicts in the 1850s, 1890s, and 1930s all led to a decline of comity in Congress, but each heralded a party realignment. The present discord is not unique, but there are no signs of an imminent change now. While trust in government has bounced up and down and has rebounded somewhat from the low levels of the 1970s, confidence remains low. More critically, support for the communitarian values that sustain cooperation has dropped virtually monotonically since the 1970s. No rebound is in sight. We might well be beyond realignment (chap. 7).

An Eclectic Topic, An Eclectic Approach

This is a bare bones outline of my general argument. It is complex, covering a wide spectrum. The evidence for my thesis comes from a variety of sources. Much is impressionistic, but it is voluminous and virtually all of it points in the same direction.[16] Other evidence is harder, specifically quantitative. My thesis will be controversial not just for my eclectic data base but also because my approach is unusual. My argument draws from both rational choice and political culture, two ways of thinking that don't usually mix well. Rational choice takes preferences as given. It doesn't matter what you believe as long as your behavior reflects—in some consistent way—your values. For political culture, it matters very much what you believe. Almond (1991, 49) likens rational choice theory to "the blank tile in Scrabble [that] can take on the value of any letter." By focusing on individual choice, this approach ignores the context in which values are formed. Rational choice theorists, on the other hand, find arguments from norms circular (Barry 1970, 51–52, 97–98). Culture, in

---

16. Henry David Thoreau was certainly correct when he said, "Some circumstantial evidence is very strong, as when one finds a trout in the milk." From his *Journal* (November 11, 1850). Quoted in *The Oxford Dictionary of Quotations*, 3d ed. (Oxford: Oxford University Press, 1979), 550. The qualitative evidence is largely from the 1980s and 1990s. This reflects my research agenda—when I began collecting these observations—rather than when comity began to wane.

effect, denies the very element of choice that is central to cooperation problems.

This is not a shotgun marriage. If one denies that institutions are central to achieving cooperation, culture is the major (if not the only) alternative. I see values as resolving the collective action problems posited by rational choice theory. Both sides in the debate are partially right and mostly wrong about each other.[17] Rational choice theorists correctly stress self-interest as a fundamental motive. Students of political culture are correct when they maintain that different societies have alternative ways of resolving conflict. Rational choice approaches do not have to reject inquiries into values. Culture does not have to be self-explantory ("we do things this way because we are Americans") or valid for all time (Barry 1970, 50).

There is a rather odd payoff to a cultural approach. It makes one less optimistic about a resolution to the problem of the decline of comity. I offer little solace to people who see political or social reform as the solution to the decline of comity. Reformers have proposed all sorts of redesigns, from changing our system to a parliamentary one to imposing "politically correct" civility on misbehavers. None will work. People who want to violate norms will do so. If you force them to obey, they will take their views underground—or repackage them. Rational actors will almost always find ways to get around constraints. The message ahead is not sanguine.

---

17. There are some rational choice theorists who stress culture. See Bates (1988), Calvert (1991), and Kreps (1990). Other analyses, as noted above, at least implicitly make cultural assumptions (Axelrod 1986; Bendor and Swistak 1991; Frank 1988).

Chapter 2

Norms and Normlessness

> The general discussion in Congress ... is an animated exchange of arguments of every caliber and degree, of contradictory resolutions mixed with applauses and hisses, of exaggerated eulogies and brutal invectives. A stranger who finds himself suddenly thrown into the midst of this hubbub is confounded and stupified; he thinks himself present at the primeval or the final chaos, or at least the general breaking up of the union. But ... we see here the realization of the *Forum*, on an immense scale, the *Forum* with its tumult, its cries, its pasquinades, but also with its sure instincts, and its flashes of native and untaught genius.
> —Michel Chevalier

The six norms of Congressional behavior—reciprocity, courtesy, institutional patriotism, legislative work, apprenticeship, and specialization—did not all crumble at once. To varying degrees they all persist. To speak of the waning of the normative regime and the decline of comity in Congress, one does not have to posit a shooting war. Most people are still polite to each other. Members share stories in the House and Senate gyms; they make deals on the pork barrel across party lines. Yet life is neither as uniformly civil nor as pleasant as it used to be. Tempers flare more often. Personal relations spill over onto the House and Senate floors. Members impugn the motives of each other and occasionally go even further. The trust that is essential for cooperation is in short supply. Waning norms are part of a realignment cycle, and previous shake-ups of party systems reveal even greater incivility.

The Congress of the 1940s through the 1960s was clubbish. During the reign of Speaker Rayburn, key business was conducted over bourbon in an unmarked hideaway office. The major players were committee chairs and the leaders of appropriations subcommittees, dubbed the College of Cardinals. Leading Senators also made policy in their private offices. Power was concentrated in the chairs of appropriations subcommittees, who tended to be the leaders of other standing committees. By the 1980s this had all changed. Senator Ernest F. Hollings (D—S.C.) noted:

> There is no longer any senatorial club.... You do not get to see the other Senators.... You have five breakfasts and eight dinners and seven other things, and by the time I finish my speech here I have to get back to the staff because they have four appointments waiting in the office. So the collegial relationships are a thing of the past. (*Congressional Record* 1989a)

Members of the House and Senate today do have friendships, but such patterns are highly idiosyncratic and often not enduring (Baker 1980, 41).

Two aspects of norms stand out in the contemporary Congress. First, adherence to folkways has declined. While there are still standards of acceptable behavior, fewer members are willing to be bound by them. Second, there are few sanctions and even fewer rewards for obeying the folkways. In the old Congress there was a fairly straightforward system of rewards: Proper behavior led to an early appointment to a key committee. Seniority advanced one along the ladder to power. Only by conforming to the norms could one be accepted into the realm of the power brokers.

There is no longer a simple path to power. Junior members, often untested in any previous forum and with no clear ties to those who hold formal leadership positions, get on important committees. Once on a committee there is no guarantee that longevity will suffice to become its chair. Committees no longer control the agenda. In the Senate every majority party senator chairs at least one subcommittee; about two-thirds of House Democrats do likewise. The 1970s brought to the Congress a large number of policy-oriented members (Uslaner 1978; Loomis 1988, 28). Their emphasis on issues has put a damper on the compromise that is at the core of the normative system, especially that of reciprocity.

The decline of comity in Congress dates from the 1970s. There is no clear trajectory from any single starting point to the present. The 1980s marked a new turning point with the election of Ronald Reagan. Reagan and his Congressional supporters sought a party realignment that would end a half century of Democratic dominance. To get there they needed to capture the public imagination. Conservative Opportunity Society (COS) members argued that the cooperative leadership that had been the hallmark of Republican leaders had fostered what Jones (1970) called a "minority party mentality." They began guerilla warfare against the Democratic leadership in the early 1980s, interrupting House sessions, demanding roll calls on unpopular measures, engaging in uncivil discourse, and using special orders after the House had adjourned to address a small but interested national audience on the cable network C-SPAN (Walsh 1985; Pitney 1988a).

The uncivil war of the 1980s was largely partisan, but it was full of internecine rivalries as well. Flailings crossed party and even ideological lines. Even with a scorecard it was difficult to predict who would next attack whom. The House and Senate often appeared to lack any sort of "regular order," or indeed any order at all. Legislators took to the floor and to the press to mourn the sad state into which they had fallen. Senator Arlen Specter (R—Pa.) remarked:

> In a sense, the Senate is disintegrated or has disintegrated, because without comity and courtesy the United States Senate simply cannot function, and that is our status today. (*Congressional Record* 1988)[1]

Legislators such as Senator Nancy Landon Kassebaum (R—Kans.), former Senator Gary Hart (D—Colo.), and House Republican Leader Bob Michel have written op ed articles lamenting the decline of comity (Kassebaum 1988; Hart 1989; Michel 1984 and 1989). Senators David Pryor (D—Ark.) and John Danforth (R—Mo.) were so concerned with the decline of comity that they established a working group dubbed the "Quality of Strife" caucus (Peterson 1985). How, then, has comity declined? I turn now to a review of the evidence—all collected by others. It is, as the English would say, a dog's dinner, a mix of soft survey data from a limited number of junior members at three time points, even softer anecdotes, and some harder data on

---

1. Specter was protesting the "arrest" of Senator Bob Packwood (R—Oreg.), who was boycotting a late-night session in an attempt to deprive the Democratic leadership of a quorum on a cloture vote.

changing behavioral patterns in the House and Senate. While behavior is not a foolproof indicator of norms (Rohde 1988), it is hard to figure out how the changes I shall detail here could have occurred without a shift in legislators' values. The data base is both soft and eclectic, yet the overall picture is clear. The evidence on courtesy is the least systematic, but it all points in one direction. The behavioral indicators of Congressional norms are more direct, but they constitute a brief time series. Nevertheless, the impacts of societal values and norms on legislative behavior are strong (see chap. 4) and most pronounced on those norms that are most directly tied to those maxims that underly reciprocity.

Reciprocity

The two norms that are central to comity are courtesy and reciprocity. Rohde, Ornstein, and Peabody (1985) found reciprocity alive and well in the early 1970s. The norm quickly began to wither as name-calling became more common. When people express themselves uncivilly, they violate both courtesy and reciprocity. The COS is hardly unique in abjuring reciprocity. Some senators see mean-spiritedness everywhere they look. Consider the following quotes. Senator David Durenberger (R—Min.) spoke of a collective action problem: "If you sacrifice one day for the collective will, you do it knowing that somebody else will refuse to do the same thing the next day. So you're reluctant to make the sacrifice" (Ehrenhalt 1982, 2177). Former Senator Thomas Eagleton (D—Mo.) commented similarly, "What's in it for me as Senator X is first and foremost, not what's in it for the party, or what senatorial custom dictates" (Broder 1986b, A1, A5).

Senator Joseph Biden (D—Del.) remarked on reciprocity in 1982:

> There's much less civility than when I came here ten years ago. There aren't as many nice people as there were before. . . . Ten years ago you didn't have people calling each other sons of bitches and vowing to get each other. The first few years, there was only one person who, when he gave me his word, I had to go back down to the office to write it down. Now there's two dozen of them. As you break down the social amenities one by one, it starts expanding geometrically. Ultimately you don't have any social control. . . . We end up with 100 Proxmires here.

One... makes a real contribution. All you need is 30 of them to guarantee that the place doesn't work. (Ehrenhalt 1982, 2176, 2181)

Packwood came to a strikingly similar number of less than trustworthy senators four years later:

Some senators, if they give you their word, stick with it, even if three months later they wish they hadn't. Everybody in the Senate knows who the unreliables are. There are five that you just can't trust and probably twenty nervous Nellies who are never quite sure what their vote will be. As for the other 75, their word is good. (1986, 97)

Trust is in short supply in the House as well.

Asher (1973) and Loomis (1988) interviewed freshman Representatives in 1969 and 1976 and asked how important some of Matthews's norms were to them. Loomis reinterviewed the freshmen of the Class of 1974 in 1980. The data in Table 2.1 give the percentage of Asher's respondents who believed that the norms were "important" and the percentage of Loomis's interviewees who said that they were "very important" (as compared to only "somewhat important" or "not at all important"). In 1969 almost three quarters of the freshmen said that they would be willing to trade votes with other members. By 1976 and 1980 just about half of the members agreed that the ability to compromise was important (see table 2.1). The number of defectors

TABLE 2.1. Norm Acceptance Among House Freshmen (in percentages)

Norm	1969	1976	1980
Personal cordiality	100[a]	63	37
Ability to compromise	72[a]	50	49
Specialization	73	54	44
Expertise	90[a]	77	72
Apprenticeship	57	19	8
Seniority	—	21	26
Hard work	—	—	74
Institutional patriotism	—	—	5

Sources: Asher 1973, 503; Loomis 1988, 48.
[a]Question wording differs for 1969. Personal cordiality: friendly relations important. Ability to compromise: likely to trade votes. Expertise: important work done in committees.

dramatically affects the possibility for cooperation (Axelrod 1984 and 1986; Frank 1988). Once a threshold is reached, collective action collapses and is not easily restored. For any group to sustain cooperation, a majority must be predisposed to cooperate (Bendor and Swistak 1991). A simple majority appears to be the minimal amount of consensus necessary to establish a culture. If the freshman data are representative of the whole House, the chamber is at the edge of anarchy.

The Senate's archaic procedures permit those who would abjure reciprocity ample opportunity to do so. Any member can hold up floor action through unlimited debate. Senators became increasingly frustrated with Southern filibusters over civil rights legislation and in 1975 changed the rule for cloture from two-thirds of the entire Senate to 60 percent of the full Senate. Of the 245 cloture votes from 1917 to 1987, 58 percent occurred after the rules change (Calmes 1987). There were more filibusters between 1964 and 1980 than from 1841 to 1969 (Kilpatrick 1985). The number of filibusters per Congress increased from .67 per Congress in 1955–60 to 12.3 in 1981–86; the trajectory was straight up during the entire period. Since 1971 there have been four and a half times more cloture votes than in the entire period of 1919–70. In the 100th Congress alone (1987–88) there were almost as many such roll calls (forty-three) as in 1919–70 (forty-nine) (Ornstein, Mann, and Malbin 1990, 163).

The fine art of delaying was perfected by Senator James B. Allen (D—Ala.), who, during his tenure from 1969 to 1978, became "a legislative nihilist" for whom any "addition to government action ... was as worthy of obstruction as another" (Ehrenhalt 1982, 2180). Allen was a master of Senate rules and "invented" the "post-filibuster filibuster" in which legislators offered scores of amendments after cloture had supposedly cut off debate. Yet he observed many of the Senate's other norms, especially courtesy. His "courtly politeness [and] bland, somewhat hesitant speaking style" made Allen's tactics largely an annoyance to other senators, rather than a harbinger of things to come (Barone, Ujifusa, and Matthews 1980, 2).

The "new filibuster" no longer occurs on civil rights bills; it is found on all types of legislation, including special interest provisions for some senators' constituencies—which ought to have been accepted on the grounds of universalism (Sinclair 1989a, 94–95). Can we attribute the increase in filibusters to the rules change? The logic is hardly compelling, since the change in the procedure was supposed to make cloture easier to achieve. The spread of the filibuster to all sorts of new issue areas suggests that the increase is part of a larger trend in the decline of comity.

Legislators in both the House and the Senate were increasingly likely to offer amendments to bills, especially those originating in committees on which they did not serve. Amendments sponsored by nonmembers were also more likely to pass—especially in the House. Committees were expected to defer to each other under the reciprocity norm of the 1950s and 1960s. Each panel was a source of both expertise and hard work. By the 1970s this norm had clearly waned. Trends for the behavioral indicators of ten norms are presented in figures 2.1 and 2.2: overall amending activity in the Senate, representatives and senators sponsoring amendments to bills from committees on which they do not serve, percent of noncommittee amendments that pass in the Senate and House, amending activity by first and second term members in the House and Senate freshmen, amending activity by third and fourth term House members, number of generalists in the Senate, and percent generalists among freshmen.[2]

The spurt in amending activity occurred in the 91st Congress (1971–72) for the Senate and two years later for the House. The percentage of Senators offering amendments outside their committees virtually doubled between the mid-1960s and the early 1970s. The growth in the House was slightly more delayed: Not until the mid-1970s did half of the legislators sponsor amendments to bills originating in committees on which they did not serve. The success rate for such amendments increased somewhat in the House in the mid-1970s before taking off later in the decade; the Senate pattern is somewhat more erratic, owing to the high enactment rate in 1955–56, but violations of reciprocity were clearly higher in the 1970s than in the 1960s. By the end of the 1970s, committees had far weaker control of their agendas.[3] Policy activism had replaced committee reciprocity.

---

2. I break the data up in these figures so I do not create any more of a blur than is necessary. Putting all of the House data on one figure (and the Senate on another) would be more convenient, but there are problems of scale values.

3. The committees that were particularly hard hit were the "control committees" dealing with expenditures and revenues and those panels dealing with particularly controversial legislation (Foreign Relations, Armed Services, and Energy and Commerce in the House). See Smith (1989, 139–44, 177–83).

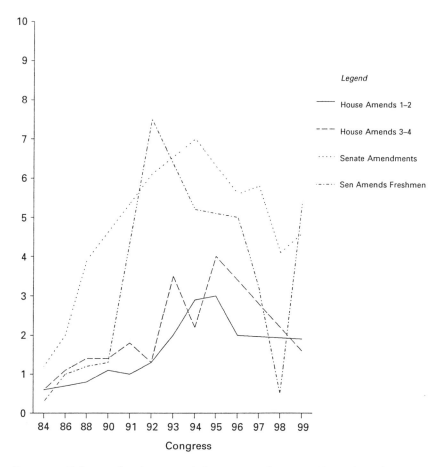

Fig. 2.1. Behavioral indicators of Congressional norms (I), 84th–99th congresses. (Data from Sinclair 1989a, 82, 84, 86–87, 123; Smith 1989, 136, 144–45.)

By the 1970s each member had access to a large staff, vastly increased support agencies, and interest groups and experts who hawk their policy recommendations all over Washington (Smith 1989, 175). "Every legislator," wrote Ornstein (1983, 198), "had the opportunity and the ability to track every issue area and to introduce timely amendments to all bills as they hit the floor." With every member now claiming expertise, the case for reciprocity is weaker.

The surge in amending activity led to a loss of leadership control of the floor in the 1970s. In the 1950s and 1960s key House com-

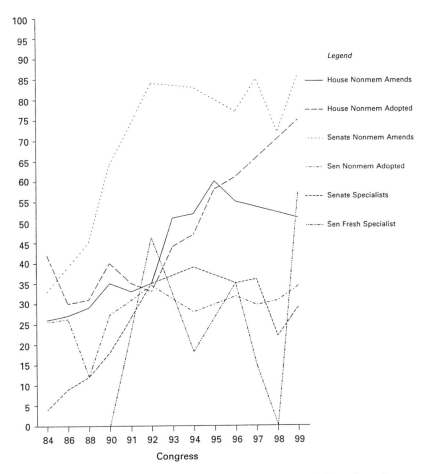

Fig. 2.2. Behavioral indicators of Congressional norms (II), 84th–99th congresses. (Data from Sinclair 1989a, 82, 84, 86–87, 123; Smith 1989, 136, 144–45.)

mittees—especially Ways and Means—had their legislation protected on the floor by rules that either prohibited or greatly restricted amendments. By the 1970s these rules were rare. The flood of amending activity made leaders hostages to any legislator willing to take the few seconds to hand a sheet of paper to the parliamentarian. By the late 1970s and early 1980s the House returned to using closed and restrictive rules, largely to contain the amending activity of conservative Republican activists who were deliberate "norm-busters" (Smith 1989, 75).

The waning of reciprocity was exacerbated by the budgetary problems that have dominated American politics since the mid-1970s. In an era of fiscal stringency, legislators will look out for their own projects and attack those of other members. Universalism took a hard hit as presidents looked to cut the pork barrel for both economic and political reasons and legislators found it more difficult to cooperate with each other.

Jimmy Carter and Ronald Reagan did not accept the idea of universalism. Carter effectively blocked the enactment of water legislation (a key pork barrel program) during his administration, legitimizing presidential objections to the pork barrel (Skowronek 1984). The new chair of the Water Resources Subcommittee, Daniel Patrick Moynihan (D—N.Y.), sided with the president (Sinclair 1980). For Reagan, universalism was an anathema. Not only did it provide for wasteful government spending, but the bipartisan coalitions that sustained it stood in the way of the distinctive identity the Republicans required to forge a realignment.

Congress overrode Reagan's vetoes of major water and highway legislation in 1987, but some of the foundations of reciprocity were shaken. In the previous year many Democrats joined with conservative Republicans to strip local projects from a housing bill (Greenhouse 1986). The Clean Water Act enacted over Reagan's veto required state and local governments to share project costs with the federal government for the first time. The pork barrel was no longer spared any cost considerations; since 1969, environmental impact assessments were required by all federal agencies, including the Army Corps of Engineers, which builds the water projects (Stanfield 1986b). In 1987 the Interior Department's Bureau of Reclamation announced plans to scale back the number of large dams it would construct (Shabecoff 1987a).

From 1981 to 1987 federal spending rose by more than 18 percent, adjusted for inflation, while spending for pork barrel projects dropped significantly. Expenditures for water and power projects fell by 13 percent (in real terms), while grants for pollution control dropped by 30 percent and for community development by 37 percent (Blustein 1988). Military bases were a traditional source of pork barrel. Congress had prohibited the Pentagon since 1977 from closing any large installations, yet in 1988 a bipartisan accord recommended closing about two dozen bases (Rasky 1988).

Not only has there been an absolute decline in funding for the pork barrel, but the reciprocity needed to sustain universalism has been undermined. Legislators now challenge the legitimacy of each other's projects. Traditional legislative allies from New Jersey fought over expenditures for the proposed Westway highway in New York City in 1985 (Oreskes 1985b). In 1988 the Sunbelt and Northeast-Midwest Caucuses exchanged monographs charging that each region received more than its share of federal grants (Elving 1988). The next year saw an interstate battle between Representative Butler Derrick (D—S.C.) and the other members of his delegation over a sewer line that would be paid for with funds from other districts' projects (Phillips 1989a). Representatives Robert Mrazek (D—N.Y.) and Jim Jontz (D—Ind.) overpowered a bipartisan Western coalition in 1990, as Congress restricted private access by loggers to the national forests (Egan 1990).[4]

Many attacks were made by legislators who did not sit on the relevant committees. Representative Richard Armey (R—Tex.), a COS member who proposed the successful cutback in military installations, did not serve on the Armed Services Committee. Two years later Jim Slattery (D—Kans.) launched a campaign to rescind a dozen pork barrel projects, including one helping a North Dakota town commemorate Lawrence Welk's birthplace. Slattery made his assault on the pork barrel even though he recognized that other members would retaliate; his prophecy proved correct when the Senate Appropriations Agriculture Subcommittee chair Quentin Burdick (D—N.D.) threatened a plant science center at Kansas State University (Yang 1991).

Reciprocity has hardly disappeared from the two houses. Members still make deals with each other, but the smaller pie has set off a competition for benefits that undermines universalism. There have been salutary outcomes, such as the trimming of pork barrel costs. Yet, like with conflicts on other policy areas (see chap. 6), restrictions on the pork barrel rarely arose from a wide-ranging debate over what national policy should be. Some projects died because they faced legislative stalemate. Other concessions were made lest the entire system on which they were based collapse for budgetary reasons. The pork barrel is the lowest common denominator of compromise

---

4. A leader of the pro-logging bloc, Les AuCoin (D—Oreg.), once threw Jontz out of his office (Egan 1990).

in American politics. When dissension reigns over universalism, coordination on larger issues of public policy appears unreachable.

Courtesy

The evidence on courtesy is almost exclusively impressionistic, but again the signs seem to go in one direction. There were many incidents of verbal confrontation between and within the parties in both houses of Congress since the late 1970s. Rohde, Ornstein, and Peabody (1985, 172-73) report that courtesy was still an important norm in the Senate of the early 1970s. However, the energy crises lit the fires of hot rhetoric (Uslaner 1989) and voices continued to rise thereafter. Legislators impugned each others' motives during the debate over the impeachment of President Richard Nixon in 1975 and especially in the confirmation fights over Robert Bork's nomination to the Supreme Court and John Tower's as Secretary of Defense in the late 1980s.

In the House, COS members were irate when O'Neill directed in 1984 that cameras pan the nearly empty chambers during special orders. Republican House members, led by Michel, walked out en masse in protest over the outcome of a vote on a disputed electoral contest in Indiana the next year (Plattner 1985). They stood on the steps of the Capitol singing "We Shall Overcome" and proclaiming a "unanimous declaration of war" (Associated Press, 1985). COS activist Robert Dornan (R—Calif.) called the seating of Democrat Frank McCloskey a "rape," while Michel said it represented "autocratic rule" (*Congressional Record* 1985a and 1985b). Minority members staged a variety of other protest strikes. In 1985 they boycotted the Energy and Commerce Committee to protest what they considered unfair party ratios on subcommittees (Davis 1985). Minority Whip Dick Cheney (R—Wyo.) called Wright "a heavy-handed son of bitch [who] will do anything he can to win at any price" in a dispute over legislative procedure on a tax bill (quoted in Pitney 1988b, 1).

Senate Republican leader Bob Dole (Kans.) confronted then Democratic leader Robert Byrd (W.Va.) on the procedures for debating legislation imposing sanctions on South Africa, Tom Harkin (D—Iowa) on farm legislation, and Hollings over the Tower nomination (Dewar 1986; Fuerbringer 1986). In 1990 he charged Majority Leader George Mitchell (D—Maine) with "gagging" the GOP and treating its members "like a bunch of bums" (Dewar 1990b). After a sharp exchange over whose personal attacks were more bitter, Dole suggested what seemed to be an old-style playground brawl:

> I say to my friend from South Carolina, I will be glad to discuss this with him privately, or maybe he wants to go out and make that statement when not protected by speaking from the Senate floor. (*Congressional Record* 1989b)

In 1985 such a fracas did take place in the House as Dornan grabbed Representative Thomas Downey (D—N.Y.) by his tie and accused him and other Democrats of being weak on national defense (Shapiro 1985). Three years later Capitol police carried Packwood feet first into the chamber after "arresting him" for boycotting a Senate session to deprive the Democrats a quorum on a cloture vote (Dewar 1988). In 1990 Walker and Representative Craig Washington (D—Tex.) had to be restrained from battling over intemperate remarks by Representative Henry Hyde (R—Ill.) addressed to Barney Frank (D—Mass.) (Kenworthy 1990).

It is neither sheer partisanship nor even ideology that has driven the current outbreak of confrontational politics: Republican Whip Alan Simpson (Wyo.) attacked his predecessor Ted Stevens (Ark.) over transition rules for the tax reform bill of 1986 (*Congressional Record* 1986), while Republican liberal Lowell Weicker (Conn.) called his moderate colleague John Heinz (Pa.) "devious" and "an idiot" (Sinclair 1989a, 89). Senator Jesse Helms (R—S.C.) has gotten into confrontation with virtually every other member of the Senate (Greenberger 1986), while Michel and former Representative Jack Kemp (R—N.Y.), now Secretary of Housing and Urban Development, took to insulting each other over Contra aid (Evans and Novak 1987). In 1990 Guy Vander Jagt (R—Mich.) likened his challenger for the chair of the National Republican Congressional Committee, Don Sundquist (R—Tenn.), to Iraqi dictator Saddam Hussein (Dionne 1990).

These anecdotes are bolstered by the data in table 2.1. In 1969 every freshman interviewed stressed that "friendly relations are important." Personal cordiality was cited by just 63 percent in 1976 and by 37 percent in 1980.[5] The centrality of interpersonal relations

---

5. Despite the differences in question wording, the importance of this norm suggests that the data can reasonably be compared.

in an increasingly individualistic Congress has declined. There are now few incentives for representatives or senators to hold their tongues. Even leaders now regularly join the fray.

Specialization

The weakening of reciprocity, specialization, and apprenticeship go hand in hand. As Smith (1989, 139) argued:

> By serving apprenticeships in the work of their committees, members developed expertise, earned the respect of their colleagues for matters under their committee's jurisdiction and presumably gained special influence in the policy fields in which they specialized. Apprenticeship, specialization, and committee deference were inseparable, permitting overburdened members to set their priorities wisely and endowing the institution with a division of labor essential to managing a large workload.

Senators never specialized as much as House members because they served on more committees. In the 1970s and 1980s, however, these norms became uncoupled. Expertise is still valued, even as specialization no longer serves as a norm (see table 2.1).

Multiple referral of House bills more than doubled (from 6 to 14 percent) from 1975–76 to 1985–86, eroding the link between specialization and expertise. The already fragile bond in the Senate was not further weakened by this procedure, which actually declined in that chamber (Davidson, Oleszek, and Kephart 1988; Davidson 1989). Multiple referral also placed strains on committee reciprocity, especially on highly contentious issues. Many panels had jurisdiction over energy, and they often used multiple referral to block legislation rather than to broaden its scope (cf. Uslaner 1989, chap. 6).

In 1955–56 only four senators offered amendments to bills from four or more committees; just six senators proposed alterations on three or more of six issue areas. By 1971–72 there were approximately forty generalists on each measure, a number that held relatively constant for the next decade and a half (see table 2.2). New forms of organization emerged to salvage legislation that crossed jurisdictional boundaries. Wright established task forces, composed of members of many committees with interests in legislation as well as nonmembers, to expedite the passage of complex bills. Over 40 percent of all Democratic members of the 95th Congress (1977-78) served on these task forces (Sinclair 1983, 143; Garand and Clayton 1986, 416-17). Junior members were particularly active on task forces. Members of the House and Senate had established over ninety caucuses by 1985 (Kernell 1986, 28-32). These special interest bodies cut not only across committee jurisdictions but often across chambers. Unlike the task forces, caucuses had no ties to legislative party organizations. They explicitly fragmented decision making in Congress.

Old forms of organization adapted as well. Conference committees between the House and Senate grew larger. From the 84th Congress (1955-56) to the 99th, three decades later, the average size of Senate contingents more than doubled while their House counterparts more than tripled (Smith 1989, 210). As Ornstein (1983, 198) stated, "... specialization is still considered theoretically desirable and still has meaning to many members. But ... it has little effect on actual congressional behavior."

Legislative Work

No norms were as widely held among younger members as expertise and legislative work (see table 2.1). Hard work retains its importance in both the House and the Senate, but there is now a difference. In Matthews's Senate, adherence to this norm meant putting in long hours behind the scenes in the drudgery of legislative drafting. Members

TABLE 2.2. The Decline of Seniority: Activities by Freshmen

	Congress (Years)		
	89th (1965-66)	91st (1969-70)	94th (1975-76)
Managed major bill or amendment on floor	0	—	37
Offered floor amendments	12	40	86
Offered committee amendments	24	—	96
Served on conference committee	6	17	69
Made "major" floor speech	30	—	72

— not asked for 91st Congress.
Source: Loomis 1988, 40.

could expect some publicity for their efforts, but they were expected to be "work horses" rather than "show horses" (Matthews 1960, 94–95). The new Senate and House are very different. Legislators now actively seek publicity. They believe that diligent work and media coverage are compatible (Loomis 1988, 28; Cook 1989, 9, 123; Langbein and Sigelman 1989).

Some representatives still toil behind the scenes. Representative Vic Fazio (D—Calif.) wins plaudits from his colleagues for his work on ethics legislation, while John P. Murtha (D—Pa.) excels at bringing the party's right and left flanks together on budgetary matters (Toner 1990; Towell 1989). This role has largely disappeared in the Senate. Ehrenhalt (1982, 2180) refers to senators elected in the 1970s as "without old-fashioned institutional loyalties." Reaching out is now considered a critical component of leadership.

Current leaders—Senate Majority Leader Mitchell (D—Maine), Speaker Thomas Foley (D—Wash.), House Majority Leader Richard Gephart (D—Mo.), House Majority Whip Bill Gray (D—Pa.), and especially House Minority Whip Gingrich—were selected for their television skills as well as for organizing coalitions (Oreskes 1989). The accession of Gingrich to the GOP leadership points to the weakening of this norm: The Georgia Republican never gained a reputation for expertise on any policy area; he attained his fame by being brash.

Apprenticeship

Legislators elected in the 1970s were young men and women in a hurry. Fewer than a quarter of them accepted apprenticeship, a folkway that had been in decline since the 1950s. When Lyndon Johnson became senate majority leader in 1955 he established the "Johnson Rule" that guaranteed every Democrat, regardless of seniority, a major committee assignment. Democrats gained thirteen Senate seats in 1958, and the corps of activists (and norm violators) grew. Senior senators and representatives imposed few sanctions for violating apprenticeship (Smith 1989, 134). Nevertheless, junior senators still were specialists until 1971. By the mid-1980s a larger percentage of freshman senators were generalists than any other cohort; since 1971 newly elected senators offer about as many amendments as their more senior colleagues (table 2.2; Sinclair 1989a, 87–88). In the House junior members have remained less active than their more senior colleagues, but the gap began to narrow dramatically in 1973. At the same time, the House began to accept junior members' amendments at rates similar to their senior colleagues.

By the 94th Congress (1975–76) freshmen had largely overturned the apprenticeship norm. Table 2.2 presents data (from Loomis 1988, 40) demonstrating just how active new members had become. Seventy percent or more served on conference committees, made major floor speeches, and offered amendments on the floor. Almost all proferred amendments in committees. Just six years earlier fewer than half offered committee amendments and just 17 percent served on conference committees. A decade earlier freshmen were much more restricted: Fewer than a third made major floor speeches, a quarter offered committee amendments, and only a handful served on conference committees or proposed floor amendments. None managed legislation on the floor; by the 94th Congress more than a third of new members did.

While specialization declined as a norm in both houses, apprenticeship collapsed (Rohde, Ornstein, and Peabody 1985, 175–77). Not only do new members hit the ground running, but they are assiduously courted by the leadership. The gerontocracy that used to run the Congress has itself been replaced by younger officers. At sixty years old, Foley was the youngest legislator to assume the speakership since Rayburn. Many current or recent leaders assumed their posts before reaching fifty: Gingrich, Majority Leader Richard Gephardt, Majority Whip Gray, former Majority Whip Tony Coehlo (D—Calif.), and former Minority Whips Cheney and Trent Lott (R—Miss.).

Not only did the informal norm vanish, but its formal counterpart fell on hard times as well. Seniority as a formal criterion for selecting committee leaders was abolished in the early to mid-1970s, although the principle continued to reign, even if not supreme. In 1975 House Democrats ousted three aging Southern committee chairs. In that Congress thirteen members were passed over when new chairs were elected, the largest number of uncompensated violations of seniority since 1891. In 1985 and 1987 the seniority of twelve members was violated, almost equal to all such actions—excluding 1975—from 1946 to 1987 (Cox and McCubbins 1989, table 6-1; Polsby, Gallaher, and Rundquist 1969, 794).

The apprenticeship norm did more than establish a pecking order for leadership positions. It helped to socialize members into cooperative behavior and fostered the policy expertise associated with specialization. The waning of this maxim led to a decreased policy-making capacity in Congress as legislators became "instant experts" on a multiplicity of subjects in an incessant drive to protect constituency or personal interests. As socialization became less important, so did the self-restraint that is essential for collective action (Dodd 1981, 408).

Institutional Patriotism

The final norm, institutional loyalty, is a catchall: It emphasizes commitment to the chamber and its honor, but its scope is much broader. It encompasses aspects of reciprocity, which is essential for maintaining respect. Leaders and followers alike now respond to the coalitions of the moment. The institution and its customs command far less obeisance. In 1980 only 5 percent of the 1974 House freshmen cited this norm as critical (see table 2.1). Regular order, including the order of succession on committees, may be redefined as political conditions change.

Each house traditionally defended its honor vigorously and largely ignored the other. House members were required to call the Senate "the other body." In 1987 representatives were finally able to use the term *Senate*, although references to individual members or quotations from Senate proceedings remained taboo (*Congressional Quarterly Weekly Report* 1986). In 1988 forty-nine House Democrats took the extreme step of writing to the speaker to complain about the Senate's slow pace in enacting legislation. Representative Mike Synar (D—Okla.) called the upper house "a mess," while Dan Rostenkowski (D—Ill.) blamed the Senate for the bad reputation of the entire Congress (Hook 1988; Franklin and Werfelman 1988).

The norm of institutional patriotism reflects respect for the traditions of each house. It represents a feeling of being at home in one's environment. When members no longer know each other well, loyalty to the institution will diminish. In the 1970s legislators worked to develop reputations distinct from that of their less popular institutions. Constituents came to value their own legislators highly even while remaining critical of Congress. In turn members ran *for* Congress by running *against* the Congress (Fenno 1975).

A more direct, though not so comprehensive, indicator is senators' ambition. Matthews (1960, 101, 110) argued that senators are "expected to be a bit suspicious of the President" and that "a man who entirely adheres to the Senate folkways has little chance of ever becoming President of the United States." Hibbing and Thomas (1990, 143) found that administrative assistants in 1987 respected senators who adhere to traditional values *or* who run for president. Sinclair (1989a, 100) agrees that senators now frequently run for the White House without condemnation from their colleagues, making this norm "defunct." Even Senate leaders (such as Majority Leaders Howard Baker [R—Tenn.] and Dole) now make the race for the presidency and use whatever loyalty remains in the institution to harness the backing of other members of their party.[6]

There is also less loyalty to the parties and leadership. In the 1970s party leaders, including the speaker, were regularly challenged, even if few contests were seriously contested. Senate Democrats, unlike their Republican counterparts, rarely upset sitting leaders. In 1969, however, Edward Kennedy (D—Mass.) upset Russell Long (D—La.) as whip; in turn, Byrd defeated Kennedy just two years later. In 1989, after several challenges, Byrd finally relinquished his position as Democratic leader.

The late 1960s and 1970s were marked by unprecedented numbers of party switchers. Most did so for ideological reasons. By the late 1980s some legislators threatened to bolt their party if they were not awarded better committee positions: In 1986 Senator Edward Zorinsky (D—Nebr.) threatened to join the Republicans (and hence threaten possible Democratic control of the Senate) if he did not remain ranking member of the Agriculture Committee. Three years later Representative Arthur Ravenal, Jr. (R—S.C.) pitted Democratic and Republican party officials against one another over a slot on the Merchant Marine and Fisheries Committee; he ultimately stayed with his own party (Calmes 1986; Phillips 1989b).

The waning of the central norms of Congressional behavior has policy consequences beyond the pork barrel. Coalitions have become much more difficult to build across a whole range of issues, from the

---

6. This norm weakened some time ago. Matthews (1960, 110) noted that Lyndon B. Johnson (D—Tex.), Robert Taft (R—Ohio), and William Knowland (R—Calif.)—all Senate leaders—ran for the White House but had little chance of winning. Aside from this incorrect prediction on Johnson, now Senate leaders often begin as leading candidates.

budget to agriculture. There are loud voices everywhere. The new world of policy-making is somewhat paradoxical: Much of the time coalitions implode on themselves as members turn against each others' interests, yet sometimes the pressures from the blaring cries from constituency groups are so strong that legislators cave in and reward groups far out of proportion to either need or political strength. In an era of budgetary constraints, this forces either retrenchment elsewhere or spiralling deficits. Ultimately, the short-term winners will face challenges from others in a spiral of tumult. With little sense of institutional loyalty, personal power struggles—often in the name of constituency interests—inhibit collective action (Dodd 1981, 409).

Cycles of Comity

The contemporary Congress seems rather tame compared to the chamber during earlier realignments, especially the one preceding the Civil War. At the trough of realignment cycles, there is little regular order either in Congress or in the larger society.

In the years of the Republic, brawls and duels were common. In 1789 Representatives Matthew Lyon (Vt.) and Roger Griswold (Conn.) battled each other with a cane and a fire tong. Four years later Representative John Stanley (N.C.) challenged former Representative Richard Spaight to a duel and killed him. Incivility reached a fever pitch in the antebellum period, when there were seventeen recorded breaches of comity, including violence between 1831 and 1860, accounting for 40 percent of all recorded incidents between 1790 and 1956.[7] Representative William Graves (Ky.) killed Representative Jonathan Cilley (Maine) in a duel in 1838; the House refused to punish Graves but reluctantly passed a bill banning dueling in the capital; nevertheless Representatives Samuel Inge (D—Ala.) and Edward Stanly (Whig—N.C.) battled in 1851 (Haynes 1960, vol. 2, 948–49).

The most famous breach of comity occurred in the Senate in 1856 when Senate leader Charles Sumner (R—Mass.) delivered a

---

7. Computed from compilations provided by the Historians of the House of Representatives (Raymond Smock) and of the Senate (Richard Baker). See United States House of Representatives Office for the Bicentennial (N.D.) and United States Senate Historical Office (1988). These documents also provide information on some of the incidents cited here.

strongly worded abolitionist speech, "The Crime Against Kansas," attacking Senator Stephen Douglas (D—Ill.) as a "noisome, squat, and nameless animal [who] is not the proper model for an American Senator" and Senator Andrew Butler (D—S.C.) as a liar (Donald 1967, 286–87; Potter 1976, 209). Representative Preston Brooks (D—S.C.), a distant cousin of Butler, entered the Senate chamber after adjournment on May 22, 1856, and beat Sumner with a cane until the leader fell to the floor bleeding and unconscious. Sumner was not to return to the Senate for four years. No senator made any attempt to stem the assault. The Senate established a committee with no Republican representation to investigate the affair, but the panel decided it had no jurisdiction. The House could not muster the two-thirds vote to expel Brooks and Representative Laurence M. Keitt (D—S.C.), who entered the Senate chamber with him. Brooks escaped unpunished except for a $300 fine for assault in a District of Columbia court.

The antebellum Congress "was beginning to lose its character as a meeting place for working out problems and to become a cockpit in which rival groups could match their best fighters against each other" (Potter 1976, 67). A content analysis of the *Congressional Globe* in 1850 and 1860 showed that almost 30 percent of references to Senate norms such as courtesy, specialization, institutional patriotism, apprenticeship, and a proscription against personalization of issues constituted violations (Yarwood 1970). In the House, the rise of third parties and splits within Democratic and Whig ranks meant that neither party could organize the chamber at times, leading to new records for contested elections in 1849–58 and especially 1859–68 (Galloway 1962, 48; Polsby 1968, 164). The House was unable to select a speaker for periods ranging from two weeks to three months in 1839, 1849, 1855, and 1859.

Comity was restored by the late nineteenth century when the Congress was once again "a clubby and often casual institution" marked by the friendliness of the small town (Keller 1977, 300). In the prerealignment decade of the 1880s, unlike that of the antebellum years, party conflicts increased. House Republicans, under Speaker Thomas B. Reed, forged a strongly partisan order. The relatively even balance between the parties made minority obstructionism possible (Strahan 1990); the number of contested elections reached new peaks (Polsby 1968, 164). The Democratic minority filibustered for almost two months in 1881 until two Republicans resigned, permitting the Democrats to organize the chamber (*Congressional Quarterly* 1976, 82).

The triggering mechanism for disorder in the late 19th century was a contested election contest that the Republican minority called up on January 29, 1890 (Robinson 1930, 213; *Congressional Quarterly* 1976, 42–43; Josephy 1975, 260; Treese 1990, 3).[8] Democrats sought to block a decision on the case by refusing to answer quorum calls and demanding roll calls over and over again. Reed ignored them and simply counted Democrats in the chamber to ensure that a quorum was present. Representative Richard P. Bland (D—Mo.) called Reed "the worst tyrant that ever ruled over a legislative body." The *New York Tribune* reported that "the House resembled a perfect bedlam" and the *Washington Evening Star* noted that the proceedings were "more like . . . a riot than . . . a parliamentary body" as the House remained in tumult for three days. Congressional problems were compounded by repeated charges that the unelected Senate was an unrepresentative body. Public confidence in legislative institutions was at a low ebb (Rothman 1966, chap. 9).

The next realignment brought more incivility to the halls of Congress. The 1896 party system began to weaken in the 1920s. Democrats were torn between a revived Northern bloc that sought to nominate New York Governor Al Smith in 1924 and the party's large Southern wing, which could not tolerate a Catholic at the top of the ticket. Republican divisions between traditional conservatives and Midwestern Progressives deepened. In 1925 the Senate Republican Conference voted to deny GOP committee positions to senators who had backed Robert LaFollette's third-party presidential bid. In 1930, President Herbert Hoover urged Senator James Watson, who aspired to be majority leader, to permit Progressive Republicans to join with Democrats to organize the Senate; that way, he argued, the opposition party could "convert their sabotage into responsibility" (*Congressional Quarterly* 1976, 88).

The two parties were closely divided in Congress at the start of the decade. Progressives held the balance of power after 1922, and they held up the election of a new speaker until they could force

---

8. I am grateful to Joel D. Treese of the United States House of Representatives Office of the Bicentennial, and to its director, Raymond Smock, for preparing Treese (1990) for me.

reforms. The environment of the 1920s was far less hostile than that of the antebellum and turn-of-the-century Congresses, yet several observers (Haynes 1960, 387–88; Josephy 1975, 310) pointed to the sharp tongues of this era. Would-be pugilists were common in the 79th Congress, but most were deterred by their colleagues. Nevertheless, Speaker Nicholas Longworth (R—Ill.) received the gloves Jack Dempsey and Gene Tunney used in their heavyweight championship fight, with the sender noting that "they are a necessity in the halls of Congress" (Riddick 1949, 72).

The Sources of Comity

The ups and downs of comity follow a realignment cycle. The antebellum era, the late nineteenth century, and the 1920s all show increases in incivility at the nadir of party systems. Following a realignment comes a period of sharp partisanship and majoritarian government. A more restrained politics ensues, marked by norms of courtesy and reciprocity (among others) between and within parties. The rancor of the antebellum years gave way to a more agreeable body, but only after a highly partisan and contentious Reconstruction. The 1930s realignment first led Franklin D. Roosevelt to majoritarian tactics ranging from redefining national priorities on the role of government to attempting to pack the Supreme Court. Democratic cohesion waned late in the decade, and the extant system of norms emerged.

The 1970s through the 1990s is a period of incivility in Congress and turbulence throughout the larger society (chaps. 3 and 4). If realignments occur about once each generation (Burnham 1970), the early years of the present discourtesy are on track. The New Deal party system had aged and was due for a challenge. The waning of norms occurred on schedule, but the realignment did not.

How did the Congress get into this mess? As in previous realignments, the culprit is the larger society. The waning of Congressional norms reflects changing values in the larger society. The direct link between Congressional norms and value change comes in chapter 4. But first we must dispose of some more prominent suspects.

Chapter 3

Five Explanations in Search of Evidence

> The reverse Houdini consists of a politician tying himself up in knots and then going before the public and saying, "Gee, I wish I could help you, but I can't because I'm tied up in knots." This concept is frequently embodied in legislative rules that contain various devices by which it can be made to appear that many legislators are being restrained by someone from doing something that they have absolutely no interest in doing.
> —Representative Barney Frank (D—Mass.)

If comity has declined in the Congress, what is the reason? What has changed in the contemporary era from the 1950s and 1960s? Four prominent explanations focus on (1) the Congressional reforms of the 1970s; (2) divided control of the legislative and executive branches; (3) the impact of membership change on the Congress, especially the emergence of a liberal majority in the 1960s; and (4) the impact of the media, especially television. The first three focus on the internal politics of Congress, the fourth on an external factor. Each account has been offered, often by members themselves, as leading to the weakening of the traditional norms of the House and Senate. A fifth story, based on the growth of interest groups, puts us on the right track even if it does not quite get us all the way.

If we can trace the waning of Congressional norms to factors such as reform, divided control, or the media, we might see a ray of hope. Proposals to restructure Congress, to change the electoral system, or to enhance the media's role abound. Might Congress benefit from further structural tinkering? On the other hand, the influx of new members with new priorities, the rise of interest groups, and the waning of values in the larger society present few opportunities for setting things right. Optimists and structuralists would focus on reform. It is my first stop too.

Congressional Reform

It is by now commonplace to refer to the contemporary Congress as *postreform*. Some of the most prominent reforms included the Legislative Reorganization Act (1970), which permitted a committee majority to move legislation when the chair refused to do so, restricted the number of committees and subcommittees that members of both houses could serve on or chair, opened committee hearings to public attendance (and television), required members to vote openly in committees, and changed House voting procedures so that teller votes would be recorded. The Subcommittee Bill of Rights (1973) effectively transferred power in the House from full committees to subcommittees by granting the latter considerable autonomy over rules, staff, and budgets. Both parties in each house relaxed the strict seniority rules for the selection of committee and subcommittee leaders in the early 1970s, though Democrats in the House went furthest.

Structural reforms led to a decline in comity by opening up the decision-making process. Shepsle and Weingast (1987, 941–42) argued that the reforms of the 1970s "affected the norms of apprenticeship and specialization," which in turn led to the spurt in amending activity that characterized the decade (see chap. 2). Junior members were frustrated not only by the informal norms against activism but also by rules of procedure that effectively gave control to committee leaders (Smith 1989, 234–35; Sinclair 1989a, 64–68). Their activity level took off after the House adopted one such reform, electronic voting in the Committee of the Whole.

Changes in institutional design did not directly cause the heightened decibel level in the Congress. The impact was more circuitous, through reciprocity. The structural changes disrupted the longstanding system of norms by attacking the chief instrument of reciprocity in the Congress, the committee system. Committee power depended on "full faith and credit" in the autonomy of each panel's recommendations. Weakening committee autonomy spurred a new pattern of amending activity in the Congress, especially the House, according to institutional accounts. As reciprocity waned in the postreform Congress, so did courtesy. With few obligations to respect each other's jurisdictional concerns, members engaged in a free-for-all that turned into a war of each against all. Smith (1985) argued that the reforms of the 1970s changed Congress from a decentralized body to a collegial one. Collegial decision making can lead to a cooperative body of equals or to a chamber of bickering members, each jockeying for position. The current Congress is much closer to the second pole. Institutional reform could change the structure of incentives, making civility count for less.

Of the procedural changes, electronic voting was the great emancipator in terms of time. After it was introduced in 1973, amending activity sharply increased, not only from committee members but from outsiders as well (Smith 1989, 28–35). As action shifted from committees to subcommittees in the House, decision making became much more segmented. Peterson (1990, 107–8) found that as Congress became more decentralized in the post–World War II era, the legislature became more hostile to presidential legislative initiatives. Consensus was replaced by an unwillingness to bargain.

The new structures made it possible for legislators to act out more long-standing frustrations. How well do changing Congressional norms track the reforms of the 1970s? The four behavioral indicators of House norms (amending activity for members in their first and second terms, amending activity for members in their third and fourth terms, amendments offered by non–committee members, and percent of nonmember amendments adopted) show sharp rises beginning in the 93rd Congress (1973–74), after the introduction of electronic voting (see figs. 2.1 and 2.2).[1]

Reform seems to matter, but the Senate findings temper enthusiasm. Of the six indicators for the Senate, one (overall amending activity) began increasing in 1963–64, another in 1967–68 (nonmember

---

1. These data are based on small sample sizes ($N = 11$ for the House and $N = 10$ for the Senate). They are thus not conclusive, but the overall picture is clear. I rely on graphical displays of the data in the text, but the results are confirmed by statistical analysis. The statistical technique employed is generalized least squares. Generalized least squares is a statistical technique for time series analysis. Time series data tend to trend independently of any real movement. This trend will affect the residuals, the errors in prediction. Standard ordinary least squares regression assumes that the residuals from one time to the next are uncorrelated. Time series data often violate this assumption. Generalized least squares corrects for this "autocorrelation." The predictors are dummy variables. For the 93rd Congress, the dummy was set at zero for all observations prior to the 93rd and at one thereafter. (I also experimented with a variety of counter variables.) The best model was selected by the equation with the lowest standard error of the estimate. For House nonmember amendments adopted, the 94th Congress model performed slightly better than the 93rd model.

amendments), and the rest (amending activity by Senate freshmen, number of generalists, percent of freshman generalists, and percent of nonmember amendments adopted) in 1971–72 (figs. 2.1 and 2.2). The Senate trends largely resembled the House ones—except that they occurred in a chamber that did not undergo such extensive structural reform and they came first.[2] The patterns do not differ substantially between those norms that are fully or partially based on reciprocity—overall amending activity in the Senate, nonmember amendments offered or adopted in both chambers, and the number of Senate generalists—and the behavioral indicators linked to other maxims.

If reform led to the House changes, why did the unreconstructed Senate, which barely had microphones and could not countenance computerized voting, change as well? The House, it seems, was playing catch-up with the Senate. Both chambers were responding to changes in the larger society, including the energy crisis, environmental regulation, and other heated issues of the day that made life in Congress more contentious. Smith (1989, 181, 236), who focuses on the role of electronic voting, acknowledges these agenda changes as contributing to the breakdown of the behavioral indicators of Congressional norms. The Senate results suggest that we reverse the order of priority: The larger forces were central, the structural changes secondary. At most, reform expedited the avalanche of participation that would have come anyway.

There has also been a decline of comity in a wide variety of unreformed settings cited in chapter 1. They range from Chicago's city council to judicial bodies. A more convincing account would treat both the reforms and the decline of comity as stemming from the same set of larger societal forces, so that the direct relationship between these two variables would be spurious.[3] Institutions are not exogenous, nor are reforms imposed by a deus ex machina or with no rhyme or reason. To say that reforms change an institution only

---

2. The Legislative Reorganization Act of 1970 was a consequential reform, but its provisions were not nearly as comprehensive as the 1973 and 1974 reforms in the House. See Congressional Quarterly (1971, 449–50) for a discussion of the act's changes in Senate procedures. The major Senate committee reforms came after (1977) the behavioral indicators shifted (see Parris 1979).

3. We often presume that structural reforms cause changes in outcomes when there are larger societal forces that are behind both. For a similar account in another context (party nomination reforms), see Reiter (1985).

answers part of the question, why the reforms occurred at a particular point in time, and not the most interesting part.

If reform were the culprit, then countervailing tinkering should undo the damage. This view has many adherents within the Congress. The Quality of Strife working group proposed a series of structural reforms that would expedite scheduling: the imposition of a two-hour debate limit on motions to proceed to legislation, eliminating filibusters before a bill is introduced, enforcing the fifteen-minute time limit on roll calls, requiring bills on the floor to be amended section by section so that some regular order of business could be established, and barring "sense of the Senate" resolutions (with no binding effect) unless they have twenty cosponsors (Hook 1987). Smith (1989, 248–49) suggests some of the same reforms and advocates the use of extraordinary majorities to protect the House minority against restrictive rules and to restrict filibusters in the Senate. Senator David Boren (D—Okla.) goes even further: He would drastically cut staffs, reduce the number of committees, bar nongermane amendments, restrict the number of quorum calls, and restructure campaign finance rules (Boren 1991).

The rationale behind the proposals is that tempers fray when members abuse procedure. Structural tinkering is not going to restore the bonds of friendship—or even camaraderie—in the legislature. It might change some of the incentives. Extraordinary majority rules might make stalemate more likely, inducing legislators to become more cooperative at the outset. Once people get in the habit of cooperating, they might even become more civil.

Manipulating rules is not a panacea. Structural changes are often codifications of what has already become common law (King 1991): Congressional committee restructuring occurs after the panels have either seized new jurisdictions or given up old ones. Alternatively, wily politicians will find ways to circumvent the new strictures. The Legislative Reorganization Act of 1946 tried to reduce the number of committees in Congress, only to wind up with an even more disorderly subcommittee system. Several attempts at budgetary reform, from the 1946 package to the 1974 Budget Reform Act to the 1985 Gramm-Rudman-Hollings automatic cuts have failed to reduce the deficit (Davidson 1990; Yang 1989). Even a scheduling reform designed to placate senators failed to entice them to the floor (Johnson 1990).

The reforms of the 1970s are just as much dependent variables in need of explanation as the waning of the canons of behavior. Why was the House thoroughly reorganized, indeed so much so that we now speak of the new or postreform Congress, in the 1970s and not in the 1950s or 1960s? Institutionalists would focus on the changing incentive structure within Congress, which in turn reflects the members' preferences on issues. A macropolitical focus would emphasize more deep-seated values. The showdown will come in the next chapter. The central point is that we must move beyond simple structures.

Divided Control of the Legislature and the Executive

Most of the harangues in recent years have been partisan. Democrats and Republicans on Capitol Hill have taken sharp aim at each other. Partisan fire intensified during the Nixon administration, when the president attempted to circumvent disagreement with the legislative branch by impounding funds, harassing the bureaucracy, and defying Congressional mandates on both domestic and foreign policy (cf. Nathan 1975). After four less turbulent years, the fever pitch resumed at an ever higher rate during the Reagan administration.

Sundquist (1988, 75) argues:

> When government is divided . . . the normal and healthy partisan confrontation that occurs during debates in every democratic legislature spills over into confrontation between the branches of the government, which may render it immobile.

Legislators yearn for the more predictable regular order of single party control—the old order. From 1900 to 1952, one party controlled both the legislative and executive branches for forty-four years. In the forty years since 1953, only fourteen have not been marked by divided control. Moreover, from 1854 to 1954 only two incoming presidents confronted Congresses controlled by the opposition; since 1956, six presidential terms began with at least one house held by the opposition (Fiorina 1992; Sundquist 1986, 77).

Divided control clearly plays some role in the recent decline of comity. The COS has been an important actor in the assault on Congressional norms, yet the picture is far more complex. Split government has no measurable impact on the size of the budget deficit or the level of agriculture price supports (chap. 6). Neither does it inhibit passage of the president's program or even heighten legislative-executive conflict (Peterson 1990, 133). Divided government has no effect on the behavioral indicators of Congressional norms.[4] Mayhew (1991, 177) found that split government from 1947 to 1990 did not block major policy innovations. My reexamination of his data from 1955 to 1988 suggests that divided control does matter but yields *more* activist government.

Divided control might heighten partisanship, but much of the acrimony that has occurred over the past two decades has taken place within parties. The Carter administration had its share of Congressional brouhahas. They were simply less structured along partisan lines than were those of the Nixon, Reagan, and Bush eras. Divided control does not automatically lead to acrimony. Rancor depends less on which party controls each branch than the willingness of the president and Congressional leaders to compromise.

In the Nixon era day-to-day domestic politics was hardly cordial, but it was not matched by the fever pitch of the Reagan and Bush years. The Eisenhower administration provides a stunning contrast to more recent split governments. For all but the first two years of Eisenhower's two terms, Democrats held both houses of Congress. While the president had sharp policy differences with Congressional Democrats, he recognized that he needed their help to get anything passed. The president went out of his way to be courteous to the two Texans (Hardeman and Bacon 1987, 392). In turn, they pursued their own agenda "with unbroken civility," refusing to humiliate the president of the United States in "this eight-year period of large-minded generosity on both sides." Politicians might even prefer divided government. Eisenhower found Democratic control of Congress a useful counterweight against his party's own right wing (Hardeman and Bacon 1987, 392).

Divided government might promote, not inhibit, compromise and cooperation. Players must put aside partisan differences if they hope to enact any legislation. This is a classic collective action problem in which there is a high temptation to defect for potential electoral

---

4. The correlations are all positive (averaging .22) for the House, suggesting that more amending activity takes place there under unified party control. Five of the six Senate correlations are negative, but they average only −.17. None of the ten are statistically significant.

advantage. Compromise depends on people's faith in each other, and legislators' willingness to make deals reflects their larger environment. When the public is deeply split over issues (and more fundamental values), there are few incentives for legislators to alienate their followers and seek cooperation with the enemy. When there is greater consensus among constituents, people are less likely to perceive their adversaries as betrayers of the public faith.

Divided control is not the cause of incivility and the waning of the courtesy norm. Courtesy and especially reciprocity flourished during earlier periods of split control. Since 1981, divided government has contributed to the problem of incivility by adding a sharper partisan edge to the already widespread waning of Congressional norms. Democrats in the Congress and Republicans in the executive branch refuse to cooperate with each other, lest each lose face in a battle for electoral predominance. The House Republicans, especially the COS, have been at the forefront of the battle. COS members believe that confrontation will publicize their agenda, persuade the electorate, and ultimately lead to a Republican Congressional majority. The COS pressures the White House not to capitulate; Congressional Democrats follow suit tit-for-tat. Elites have become more polarized along partisan lines, while voters have not. Political leaders have engaged in a battle for the electors' souls. Republicans have exploited their perch in the executive branch and Democrats theirs in the legislature to proclaim their own legitimacy and the opposition's apostasy.

Each party condemns divided government as an easier target than the voters who anoint each party with just part of the prize. No one forces Americans to anoint Democrats in Congress and Republicans in the White House, yet they seem persistent in their willingness to do so. Citizens do not blindly go to the ballot box and accidentally impose divided government on themselves. Americans want split control; many polls from the early 1970s onward find considerable majorities favoring divided government.[5] Americans have saddled

---

5. Sundquist (1986, 87) summarizes polls from 1972 to 1984, noting that after the electorate chose a united government in 1977, it expressed support for single-party control. More recently, see NBC News (1990a and 1990), where 63 and 67 percent, respectively, favored divided government. Even 56 percent of Republican identifiers—the very group that COS members must rely on to build a Republican Congressional majority—favor divided control.

themselves with a collective action problem: They want lower taxes (from Republicans) and more spending (from Democrats), they know how to get both (through split control), and they seem not to want either side to back off (Jacobson 1990). They do not trust either party to control the government, so many split their tickets; yet people do not want the stalemate that stems from the inconsistent preferences underlying divided government. Rather than looking inward to their own values, they blame the institutions for policy failure and demand organizational tinkering.

Structural reforms to move the United States toward a parliamentary system with automatic unified party control would not restore comity. The Committee on the Constitutional System has proposed forcing voters to select candidates for the White House and Congress as a partisan team and giving the president's party bonus seats in Congress (Sundquist 1986, chap. 4). An electorate that prefers divided government is unlikely to approve such a radical reform—or to respond to less provocative ones such as requiring each state to offer a party ballot. Split government itself is not the problem; unwillingness to compromise and the inability of voters to realign themselves are the difficulties.

The Media Factor

An alternative explanation focuses on the impact of the media, especially television. The "Inner Club" of the 1950s projected only shadows. The television cameras now reflect the glare of a watchful public, and the new media-oriented members of Congress do their best to play to the crowds. The House has televised its proceedings since 1979, the Senate since 1986. These broadcasts have provided the forum for COS members to flay the Democratic leadership and gave Gingrich a platform from which he could launch his bid for Minority Whip. The "Watergate babies" of 1974 were perhaps the most conspicuously television-conscious legislators (Loomis 1988, 87–88).

Many in Congress worried that the media—indeed, even the cameras covering the legislature—would draw substantial attention to legislators who played to the camera. The media would focus on the loudest members, not the workhorses toiling behind the scenes to forge compromises. The locus of legislating would shift to the floor from (sub-)committees as publicity-seeking legislators used the media to shape public opinion. Members would communicate less with each other, and the norms fostered by frequent contact would wither (Fenno 1989; Ehrenhalt 1986).

In fewer than twenty-five years, the Washington press corps has nearly quadrupled (Ornstein 1983, 200–201). Network newscasts have expanded from fifteen minutes to half an hour, the Cable News Network operates two cable channels devoted almost exclusively to news, and local stations now send correspondents to the nation's capital. As Polsby (1981, 28) argued, "From the crime hearings of Estes Kefauver to the impeachment vote of the House Judiciary Committee, whenever television has covered Congress there has been lightning in the air waiting to strike, making an instant celebrity out of an everyday politician." McDowell (1986, 146) wrote of the normlessness of the contemporary Congress: "television is not just one of the developments but the driving force behind all the others."

Congressional campaigns are now media events. The more open Congressional environment invites coverage by the press (Sinclair 1989a, 64–68). Technology more broadly understood begat the new style of legislating and campaigning. The requisite electronics now includes WATS telephone lines that facilitate communications between legislators and their districts, air travel that permits members to make trips back home with greater frequency, and electric typewriters at first and then computers that have led to a 600 percent increase in the volume of Congressional mailings from the early 1960s to the mid-1980s (Broder 1986a). Ranney (1983, 144) links the decline in trust in government—and the general malaise in values—to the rising power of television.

Technology is not the culprit. There has been increasing rancor in institutions not so dramatically affected by either the new media or the new technology (among them, the New York and Michigan legislatures, the Chicago City Council, and the Supreme Court). While there is a strong correlation between the rise of television in the late 1960s and the 1970s and the decline in trust, the relationship went precisely the other way in the 1980s as a master of the media (Ronald Reagan) presided over a nation in which trust was increasing (*Gallup Report* 1985) and cable television was experiencing its strongest growth patterns.

The press and television do not give the average legislator much attention: They concentrate on party and committee leaders in the

House and the Senate—even more now than in the past (Cook 1989, chap. 3; Hess 1986). Even as media-oriented legislators tailor their investigatory hearings to the television cameras, such behavior is hardly novel—in the Civil War era, members of Congress believed that these same activities could transform their careers into national figures. Their medium of choice was newspapers (Bogue 1989, 108, 145–46).

Media-type explanations presume that the content of the message is determined by technology rather than the other way around. This perspective cannot account for how tastes in media and politics change. The press of the nineteenth century mirrored the issues of the time, as does contemporary television. A media-centered account does not tell us why some eras are marked by bitterness and others by a more forgiving spirit. Expectations of media impact can reflect the hopes and fears of the observer as well. Television coverage of the Senate has had modest effects on the conduct of the chamber's business (Rundquist and Nickels 1986).[6] The minimal impact of television on the Congress and the Commons should not be surprising. The pace of legislative life is too slow and the number of actors too large to make for good viewing (Toner 1989).

Television can magnify or even, like a mirror in the circus, distort reality. It does not create reality. Piore and Sabel (1984, 5) cogently argue:

> Industrial technology does not grow out of a self-contained logic of scientific or technical necessity. Which technologies develop and which languish depends crucially on the structure of the markets for the new technologies' products.... Machines are as much a mirror as the motor of social development.

The media-conscious legislator thus portrays an image that the public

---

6. When television finally came to the British House of Commons in November, 1989, most observers worried (or hoped) that such coverage would reduce boisterousness in that chamber. Indeed, one member of Parliament mistakenly argued that televised sessions had been civilizing for the Congress. Early readings suggested a similar lack of effect in Great Britain (Frankel 1989; Toman 1989). Hetherington, Weaver, and Ryle (1990, 11–13) argue that there might be some tendency toward restraint in the Commons, but the main effect of television has been to educate the public about why the chamber is so rowdy.

wants to see. The images of Congress and of legislators on television are reflections of the larger society. If the viewing public of the United States (or anywhere else) wanted discourses on grand issues of public policy, the three networks (and many cable stations) would drop "Roseanne," "LA Law," and "Designing Women" to present debates from the Oxford Union.

Yet they do not, and this irks people who would restructure the media's role in elections. Some prominent reforms offered by the Markle Commission on Media and the Electorate (1990, 6–8), among others, include requiring the networks to offer free air time during election campaigns, demanding that broadcasters and publishers investigate the veracity of candidates' claims, and training journalists to stress substance rather than style or "horse race" news. NBC News chief Tim Russert, in a "physician heal thyself" introspection, promised to implement such an agenda in 1992. No one can enforce such a pledge. NBC did not make good on it. CBS promised that it would run no candidate statement of under 30 seconds in 1992. It experimented with the format for a few weeks before the sound bites began shrinking once more. Would anyone watch "more serious" coverage? Even if television news did shift gears, would the candidates follow?

The media can hardly undo all the social changes that have occurred in the United States (and elsewhere) in the past four decades. Television has brought these changes to our lives more dramatically than any other medium has—or could. It has not caused them. There must be more to the story than the media.

New Members, New Values

Another account that looks inward to the institution focuses on membership change. There are two versions of this, one popular among legislators, especially those who have left the chamber, and another more scholarly. The first emphasizes the impact of turnover and the junior members' rejection of the old norms and the camaraderie of the 1950s and 1960s. The second account focuses on turnover but emphasizes the changing values of the membership. The system of Congressional norms served the interests of the conservative committee barons who ran the House and the Senate. The dominant bloc suffered a triple whammy in 1958, 1964, and 1974, when liberal landslides changed the face of Congress. The new members tossed out the norms because the maxims did not serve their interests.

Consider the simple "new members" account first. When there is high turnover, institutional memory is lost (Clines 1981). If membership change is rapid, bonds of friendship will become more difficult to form and the new legislators will be less readily socialized into the existing regime of norms. In the 1970s the retirement rate was comparatively high (Cooper and West 1981), and many incumbents lost their seats in highly volatile elections from 1958 to 1982—only 76 of the 274 Democrats serving in the 98th Congress (1983–84) had served before 1975 (Granat 1984a, 498).

The new members have been at the forefront of the explosion of amending activities in both houses (Sinclair 1989a; Smith 1989). They benefited from the decline of the norm of apprenticeship and have taken up their new status as full participants with zeal. They are less tied to the traditional folkways. Loomis (1988, 28) specifically traces the decline of comity in Congress to the election of a large number of new representatives and senators in 1974.

Turnover is an unlikely culprit since it is rather low (for the House) by historical standards (Clubb, Flanigan, and Zingale 1980); the percentage of legislators without prior public office similarly fails to impress (Canon 1989, 69). The evidence from two state legislatures where comity has declined is also not supportive. In California there was a slight drop, by now strongly reversed, in the percentage of legislators who sought reelection from 1968 to the early 1980s; there was no change in the extremely high reelection rate for those who sought new terms. In New York members now run for reelection at slightly higher rates but win significantly more often (Jewell and Breaux 1988, 499, 501). Most critically, changes in the behavioral indicators of norms do not track the share of new members in the House (where the average correlation is .37) or the Senate (where the average correlation is .02).[7]

Looking solely at turnover is too simplistic. The new members of Congress were different from their predecessors. They were more liberal. Foley (1980, 161–69) posits a direct relationship between policy coalitions and norm adherence (Foley 1980, 161–69). Legislators accept norms strategically. Noll and Weingast (1991, 248) argue

---

7. Two of the Senate correlations are negative. None of the ten relationships is statistically significant.

that "norms and conventions... are linked to the purposeful intent of political leaders," specifically to politicians' policy preferences. Reciprocity and courtesy permitted the conservative old guards in the House and Senate to make deals among themselves (Foley 1980, 133). Together with apprenticeship, specialization, and institutional patriotism, these prescriptions kept the outnumbered liberals in their place. Most liberals had little hope of upsetting the establishment, so they went along hoping to effect policy at the margins. The exceptions, the norm violators, were often the most liberal members who simply refused to tolerate right-wing domination of the chamber—Senators William Proxmire (D—Wis.), Paul Douglas (D—Ill.), and Wayne Morse (Oreg.), and the House Democratic Study Group. Did the large-scale liberal victories in 1958, 1964 (largely reversed in 1966), and 1974 lead to the decline of Congressional norms?

A policy-based approach would look to the early 1960s in the House and the late 1950s in the Senate, when Conservative Coalition support on roll calls began to decline, as the turning point for norms. A macropolitical perspective, in contrast, views the Great Society as a communitarian period in which norms should be maintained. The more hostile environment of the late 1960s onward does stem from a change in the policy agenda (see chap. 5), but mere preferences are not sufficient to upset norms. Preferences over outcomes rank below norms (and far below fundamental values) on the scale of beliefs.

Some impressionistic evidence suggests that the apprenticeship norm had fallen on hard times by the early 1960s (Smith 1989, 133–34; Sinclair 1989a, 32). Behavioral measures are less supportive of the preference thesis. Junior senators offered fewer amendments than their senior colleagues throughout the 1960s (Smith 1989, 136). While amending activity gradually increased in the House until 1972 (Smith 1989, 16), the big splurge did not occur until the early 1970s. Neither liberals nor conservatives forsook specialization until the mid-1970s. The reciprocity norm, measured by filibuster frequency, declined in the Senate of the 1960s. The tripling from the 1950s to the early 1960s was matched by yet another three-fold increase in the 1970s. The percentage of contested Senate bills increased steadily throughout the 1950s and 1960s, but the explosion came in the 1970s. The same pattern holds for the success rate of amendments, both overall and by legislators not on committees. The pattern of amending activity by conservative senators shows no clear trend until the mid-1970s. Liberals did not become more active until the late 1960s (Sinclair 1989a, 88-122). Sinclair (1989a, chap. 3) is correct in rejecting the "new members" thesis.

An ideological account leaves us wondering why new policy positions did not produce new norms, why prescriptions for behavior do not occur in cycles. Neither the growth of liberalism in the late 1950s nor the rise in conservatism in the Congress in the late 1970s and especially the 1980s (when the GOP controlled the Senate) produced a new normative era. Congress became *more* contentious during the liberal reign in the mid-1970s, the conservative period of the early 1980s, and the renewed liberal majorities of the late 1980s and the early 1990s. "Mere" preferences have little to do with norms. I shall present a fuller test of the preference versus values account of norms in the next chapter, but for now it is sufficient to note that the behavioral indicators of Congressional norms respond to changes in societal fundamental values (and norms) and not to swings in legislators' ideology.

The "new members" explanation has something to tell us, even if not quite what we expected. Massive and rapid turnover occurs only during realignments (Canon 1989). Such party shake-ups reflect fundamental value shifts in society. American values and norms atrophied in the late 1960s and early 1970s, but no new set of values emerged to supplant the old ones. Turnover was high in only one Congressional election: 1974. The new members, like the rest of society, rejected many traditional values and norms (Loomis 1988). The electorate was not ready to offer a clear mandate to any set of ideals or to any party. Its unease over traditional norms nevertheless filtered through the legislature even as the membership remained stable. The "Class of '74" sent a signal to members already there.

A New Environment

If the decline of comity cannot be traced to institutional forces, does the external environment provide a more compelling explanation? Sinclair (1989a, 5) maintains that the Congress of the 1980s "found itself subjected to a huge increase in the demands made upon it." The explosion in the number of interest groups and the emergence of new, contentious issues produced an environment by the 1970s that was "more open, less bounded, and less stable . . . characterized by a much larger number and greater diversity of significant actors, by more fluid and less predictable lines of conflict."

The old "iron triangles" of legislators, interest groups, and bureaucrats that banded together to produce universalistic outcomes (Freeman 1965) are gone. By 1980 over 70 percent of for-profit and citizen public interest groups perceived other groups that opposed them (Gais, Peterson, and Walker 1984). The number of registered lobbyists increased from 628 in 1942 to 1,180 in 1947-48 and to more than 1,900 in 1981; more than 5,000 corporations and membership interest groups had located in Washington. Citizen groups experienced their greatest growth since 1960 (Salisbury 1984; Walker 1983). The 608 political action committees in 1974 grew to more than 3,500 a decade later (Jacobson 1985). The new participatory environment and the rise of citizen movements opened up the political process to a much larger segment of the American population. New actors who had been shut out of decision making in the "good old days" now came into the system. The new era was decidedly more democratic than the old. Old issues faced different coalitions and new issues finally got on the agenda.

Moral issues such as prayer in schools, abortion, drugs, and gun control became political dynamite. Activists on each side rejected any type of compromise, and often there simply was no ready solution. The new public interest movements that emerged in the 1960s, often with encouragement and even financial support from Great Society programs (Walker 1983), found such tactics as litigation, boycotting, and picketing inviting (Vogel 1989, 99-100). The new open environment in Congress also fostered stalemates. Leaders on the left and especially the right brought hot issues to the floor, even when committees and subcommittees tried to bury them. In a more contentious environment the reward structure for legislators changes. External groups now demand that senators and representatives take up their causes. Legislators depend more on campaign contributions from interest groups. The Congress is now on public display all the time. The incentives for cooperation in the PD are weaker than they were in the 1950s and 1960s (Sinclair 1989a, 21-22, 79).

An interest group explanation seems attractive. It makes intuitive sense, and it links the Congress with larger forces, yet it remains incomplete. Congress reflects more than just the interest group environment. Like the reforms of the 1970s, the new interest groups did not just suddenly descend on the sleepy Southern town that was the nation's capital. These groups could not take full responsibility for disrupting a set of norms in Congress that otherwise still typified the rest of American society. We must look at the bigger picture.

The prospects for reform are not encouraging. Not a restructured Congress, an electoral system designed to prevent divided control, or a chastened media is likely to make Congress a more pleasant place. Congress mirrors society. Value and norm changes did not occur in a vacuum. The social and economic turbulence of the late 1960s onward led to the waning of American values and norms and attempts to restore them largely failed (see the next two chapters). As a representative institution, Congress could hardly be unaffected. The critical link is the decline of the same norms in both settings.

Chapter 4

Values, Norms, and Society

> As a society we don't trust anybody anymore. All the priests you don't know are hypocrites, all the teachers you don't know are incompetent, all the politicians you don't know are corrupt. There's a tremendous belief that none of our institutions is working.
> —Representative Al Swift (D—Wash.)

Congressional norms reflect societal norms. As the consensus on standards of behavior within Congress waned, so did agreement on these same precepts within the larger society. Norms are prescriptions for behavior that derive from underlying values. A cultural approach must specify not only key beliefs of a society but also how these ideas evolve and devolve. The fragmentation of American culture, trickling down to norm adherence, provides the key to understanding the decline of comity in Congress.

I begin with two basic premises. First, no nation or society is based on a single, enduring set of values. Every culture is a quilt of multiple values, at least some of which appear to contradict others (Thompson, Ellis, and Wildavsky 1990). The average person is not bothered by such contradictions, nor would even admit any inconsistencies at all. Cultures change as seemingly contradictory ideas joust for supremacy with each other during realignments. Ultimately one side in the fight will prevail and a new political (and social) alignment will emerge and persist for some time. Outside of these periods of "creedal passion" (Huntington 1981), most people believe strongly in all of the conflicting values. Second, the values of a society lie at the top of a pyramid. When they are in some rough state of equilibrium, norms arise to dictate appropriate behavior. Norms are the concrete manifestations of the more abstract cultural values; they provide the regular order in everyday life. When the tenets of a society fall out of equilibrium and into conflict with each other, norms themselves come under challenge.

How have the values and norms in American society changed since the 1960s? I first trace the waning of four ideals in American society and trace their decline to the fraying of more concrete norms, the same ones Matthews (1960) identified as maxims for behavior in Congress. Then I link trends in one value—enlightened self-interest—to the behavioral indicators of Congressional norms, setting the stage for further discussion of the relationship between communitarianism and policy outcomes in chapter 6.

Ideas and American Political Culture

Comity in the United States depends on a central idea and two dimensions of values. These beliefs are part of, but not necessarily all of, American political culture.[1] American exceptionalism, the central idea, holds that the United States is not just a distinctive society but also one uniquely blessed by seemingly unlimited resources. It is the one place on earth where, in the words of that distinctly American phenomenon Huey Long, every man is a king.

The first, and arguably more critical, dimension is that of individualism and egalitarianism. American politics is often seen as a conflict between them. Hartz (1955, 62) refers to the "atomistic social freedom" of individualism as "the master assumption of American political thought." Huntington (1981) sees American politics as a battle between the "ideas" of equality and the "institutions" based on individualism that so often thwart these lofty goals, yet as Wildavsky (1991, 5) argues, the uniqueness of American political culture is the belief that these two ideas "are (or can be) mutually reinforcing."[2] Americans place a strong value on individual achievement and freedom from intrusion by big institutions (business, labor, or government), yet they also believe, in the words of the Declaration of Independence, that "all men are created equal."

The second dimension encompasses science and religion. Science

---

1. I believe that these tenets are the core of American political culture. However, my thesis does not depend on demonstrating this.
2. Cf. Shafer (1991a, 18), where the same caveat applies.

incorporates two interrelated ideas: the inevitability of progress and the use of technology (including social engineering) to secure a better future. We glorify American ingenuity. Similarly, a nation without an established church nevertheless emphasizes grace. The bountiful land the immigrants came to is a gift from God. Both the scientific and religious aspects of American culture promise a better tomorrow, one through technology and social engineering, the other through divine guidance.

American exceptionalism and the four values combine to provide an answer to collective action problems. Any society that values individualism runs the risk that self-interested actors seek their own advantage and thus make everyone worse off. American history has many examples of plunder, ranging from robber barons to the sorry history of racial discrimination. Yet Americans have stressed a more tempered set of goals encompassing all the key values.

The distinctly American response is Toqueville's idea of "self-interest rightly understood." Americans stress individual achievement with the full cognizance that this can lead to collective action dilemmas. Yet they also forge out of their very diversity a sense of community as an alternative to coercion by the state. As Bryce (1916, 790) commented:

> In works of active beneficence, no country has surpassed, perhaps none has equalled, the United States. Not only are the sums collected for all sorts of philanthropic purposes larger relatively to the wealth of America than in any European country, but the amount of personal effort devoted to them seems to a European visitor equal to what he knows at home.

Homesteaders helped each other on the frontier, rolling each others' logs to build cabins. The spirit of community is the invisible hand that resolves collective action problems in America.

But some vague notion of a spirit of community will hardly do to explain such a remarkable outcome. Here the central values come into play. Americans value individual initiative. The myth of the "yeoman farmer" who through true grit feeds the country and makes a good living for himself typifies support for individualism (Hofstadter

1955a, chap. 1).³ Americans also believe that there ought to be some limits to wealth (Hochschild 1981). Self-interest must be tempered with a sense of restraint, a view of community.

Religion has always played a central role in promoting community spirit, charity, and social reform. American Protestantism emphasized the personal attainment of grace, putting the faith squarely behind the idea of social equality (Lipset 1967, 185–86). Science's part is straightforward: It will provide the know-how to solve our problems, be they physical, biological, or social. The final link is the tenet of American exceptionalism, that of an unlimited bounty. If there are more than sufficient resources to go around, sharing no longer remains a problem. "Self-interest rightly understood" resolves the collective action problem by faith, hope, and charity.

While enlightened self-interest lies at the heart of comity in the American context, the other values are also important. All four values contribute to the ideal of exceptionalism. Exceptionalism promises a better tomorrow; optimists are more likely to adhere to enlightened self-interest than to its selfish counterpart. Egalitarianism is often seen as antithetical to individualism, as science is to religion. Americans—and, no doubt, many others—do not accept these antinomies most of the time. In good times they see all four as compatible. In bad times the conflicts among the values lead to major political conflicts and even realignments. When people are pessimistic about the future, conflicts will likely emerge among these values. The clashes among the ideals signal deeper divisions in the society; they also point to the waning of norms of behavior that derive from the values. Even though only one value plays a starring role in the story, the others are far from peripheral.

To understand value change in contemporary American society, we must have a deeper understanding of each of these tenets. I shall first discuss the central idea and the two dimensions and then consider how each value has lost support since the mid-1960s, the turning point in contemporary American politics.

---

3. Eighty-three percent of Americans in 1990 agreed that "it's important to allow people to make as much money as they legally can because that's what makes the country's economy grow." This result comes from the October, 1990, *Washington Post*-ABC News poll on equality in America. It was provided by Richard Morin, director of polls for the *Washington Post*.

American Exceptionalism

Many of our forebearers came to these shores believing that the streets were paved with gold. Their offspring were not taught the academic theory of American exceptionalism, which stresses why there is no socialism in the United States (Lipset 1967). Yet "[n]othing in all history had succeeded like America, and every American knew it" (Commanger 1950, 5). Potter (1954, 80), better than anyone else, has detailed the idea that Americans were a "people of plenty." In the United States, immigrants could "dwell like kings in fairyland" in a vast expanse, an uninhabited frontier where anyone, no matter how lowly his origins, could claim free land and establish a homestead. The unparalleled bonanza of natural resources—the fertile farms, the many rivers, the timber, the metals, and the energy supplies—made America wealthy (Potter 1954, 80).

More important than the bounty itself were the promises that things would get even better and that the benefits would be attainable to anyone who would work for them. In a land of unlimited resources, people could do better by cooperating among themselves than by resorting to divisive strategies such as class warfare (Potter 1954, 118). For most, the dream did come true. As excluded groups protested, they were serially invited in as the economy expanded (Wiebe 1975, 143–44). Each new entrant provided reassurance to those left behind that the pie could expand sufficiently to include everyone. The presumptions of American exceptionalism that resources are unlimited and that growth is inevitable reassures the excluded that they too will ultimately share in the nation's bounty (Hanson 1985, 362). Despite many good reasons not to expect a rosy future, the less affluent buy into the American creed (Hochschild 1981).

If we are not there yet, we shall get there. Social engineering is the key. The *Economist* (1987, 12) stated, "Optimism, not necessity, has always been the mother of invention in America. To every problem—whether racial bigotry or putting a man on the moon—there has always been a solution, if only ingenuity and money were committed to it."

Individualism

The heroes of the exceptionalist ideal are individuals, not institutions. The yeoman farmer, Horatio Alger, and Johnny Appleseed all are free spirits. Americans distrust authority. Self-made people cannot flourish in just any environment. Freedom in the economic, political, and religious realms is a prerequisite to prospering through merit (McCloskey and Zaller 1984, 113).

While Americans value independence, they do not honor either eccentrics (as the British do) or those who tilt at windmills. The United States had one revolution, which quite suffices. Afterwards, Americans expect conformity, at least to basic values (Hartz 1955, 55). When individuals share similar beliefs, they can trust each other and thus resolve collective action problems. The voluntaristic basis of cooperation is reflected in our national motto, *E Pluribus unum*, one out of many (cf. Heclo 1986, 185). We honor diversity, but within clear boundaries.

Egalitarianism

Americans are distinctive because they blend individualism with egalitarianism (Wildavsky 1991, 5). Myrdal (1964, 8-9) asserts that liberty and other individualistic values in the "American creed" derive from equality.[4] The American commitment to equality has less to do with economics than with social life. As Bryce (1916, 813) argued:

> There is no rank in America, that is to say, no external and recognized stamp, marking one man as entitled to any social privileges, or to deference and respect from others.

The American revolution was a battle against a highly stratified class system in Europe. Support for an egalitarian social ethic stemmed directly from this confrontation (Wildavsky 1989, 284). Two hundred years after the Revolutionary War, 74 percent of Americans agreed that national values preclude teaching that some kinds of people are better than others (McCloskey and Zaller 1984, 66).

Social equality plays a large role in the communitarian spirit that underlies "self-interest rightly understood." The absence of class cleavages in the colonies led to feelings of both liberty and cohesion

---

4. Myrdal (1964, 9) quotes the Declaration of Independence and adds his emphasis: "All men are created equal *and from that equal creation* they derive rights inherent and unalienable, among which are the preservation of life and liberty and the pursuit of happiness."

(Hartz 1955, 55). Immigrants escaping social, religious, and economic discrimination could unite as free people in a new society. As equals with a common sense of purpose, they felt obliged to help each other.

American values meld individualism and egalitarianism. Pole (1978, 119) argues that friction between them constitutes "the central tension of American political consciousness." Not until the twentieth century was there considerable public support for governmental intervention to reduce income disparities (Verba and Orren 1985, 24). Optimism for the future in American exceptionalism, religion, and science sustains "self-interest rightly understood" and the belief that equality of opportunity will eventually produce more just distributions of income.

Bryce (1916, 875–76) praised America for its civility—or comity—and attributed this good will to its particular mix of enlightened individualism and egalitarianism:

> [Americans] are a kindly people. Good nature, heartiness, a readiness to render small services to one another, an assumption that neighbours in the country, or persons thrown together in travel, or even in a crowd, were meant to be friendly rather than hostile to one another, seem to be everywhere in the air, and in those who breath it. Sociability is the rule, isolation and moroseness the rare exception. . . . humour in Americans may be as much a result of an easy and kindly turn as their kindness is of their humour.

The American belief in equality, especially in contrast to the polarizing class divisions of Europe, make for the "pleasantness of American life" (Bryce 1916, chap. 119).

Religion

The roles of religion and science in American political culture stem directly from exceptionalism and its emphasis on growth and progress. Bell (1991, 14) remarked:

> Those like [Thomas] Jefferson, who were deists, saw America as God's design worked out in a virgin, paradisical land. But others, such as [Benjamin] Franklin, more worldly and skeptical, saw

nonetheless the possibility of the United States as being exemplary, and thus a hope for the future.

The Puritans in the colonial period saw the New World as the New Canaan. Claiming they were fulfilling prophecy, Puritans regarded settlement of the territory as the "last stage of the world-wide work of redemption" that would progressively produce an unlimited bounty (Berkovitch 1981, 8–17, especially 10).

While one's primary responsibility was to God, the divinely inspired Declaration of Independence also bound people to their communities and to the government (Pole 1978, 52). The religious spirit was both deep and widely shared. Tocqueville (1945, vol. 1, 314) stated:

> ... all the sects of the United States are comprised within the great unity of Christianity, and Christian morality is everywhere the same. ... There is no country in the world where the Christian religion retains a greater influence over the souls of men than in America.

The United States has no state religion. Yet American life is filled with religious symbols. More than 80 percent of Americans declare themselves "religious" and over 90 percent believe in God (Gallup 1972, 2174; Inglehart 1990, 190).[5] Selfishness is tempered by one's obligations to God and fellow citizens. The same discipline that inheres when one submits to God makes people set aside selfishness in daily life to achieve "self-interest rightly understood" (Tocqueville 1945, vol. 2, 126).

No denomination had the strength to push for dominance, so each praised (at least in theory) the toleration that distinguished the New World from the Old. God bestowed grace directly on the individual, not through an "elect" (Lipset 1967, 185). Support for capitalism further cemented the ties between religion and individualism. Religion was also strongly committed to egalitarian ideals. The requirement of charity (often including tithes) stemmed from the equal dignity of all mankind (cf. Myrdal 1964, 11). Most of the great thrusts

---

5. These figures together make the United States the most religious nation of those surveyed.

toward greater equality in American history had strong ties to religious movements: the Revolution, the antislavery movement before the Civil War, the free silverites and Social Gospellers in the late nineteenth century, and the civil rights movement in the 1950s. Religious forces have also aligned themselves against egalitarianism, as in nativist movements.

Religion and egalitarianism share a zeal lacking in either individualism or science. The solitary individual motivated by self-interest is rarely moved by fervor. Neither is the social or technical engineer. "Self-interest rightly understood" requires, in David Hume's words, both passion and reason.

Science

A people so convinced of inevitable progress could not help but lionize science. Progress went hand in hand with democracy. Tocqueville (1945, vol. 2, 46) stated:

> If the democratic principle does not, on the one hand, induce men to cultivate science for its own sake, on the other it enormously increases the number of those who do cultivate it.

Hindle (1956, 191) wrote, "Praise of useful science echoed and re-echoed through the colonies."

The Founders were convinced that social and technical engineering would make America both wealthy and happy (Hindle 1956, 381–85). They even enshrined this role in the constitution. Article I, Section 8 reads, "The Congress shall have Power ... To promote the Progress of Science and Useful Arts, by securing for limited times to Authors and Inventors the exclusive Right to their respective Writings and Discoveries." This copyright protection might be covered in simple legislation, were the value of inquiry not so great (Nisbet 1980, 203).

By the mid nineteenth century the scientist had become "the modern hero" (Woodlief 1982, 358). "American national culture tends to regard movement and change as virtues," wrote Lafollette (1990, 127). "Never content with any boundary they reached, scientists continually redefined the edge, pushed forward, and, in consequence, discovered new things." Technology promised a better tomorrow, making it easier for people to solve collective action problems. With the bounty promised by science, people can afford to be communitarian.

Democratic science captured the imagination of Americans. There was a boom in scientific tinkering from colonial times onward. Fifteen percent of leading scientists in the mid nineteenth century were amateurs, receiving no income at all from their work. Scientific exhibitions drew huge crowds; even the circus advertized itself as an education in natural history (Wright 1957, 226; Bruce 1987, 135; Buchanan 1987, 33, 143–47). Americans were far more skeptical of organized science. It is too remote and complex and is antidemocratic. Andrew Jackson and William Jennings Bryan plied their populist messages with large doses of antiintellectualism (Lafollette 1990, 176–77; Hofstadter 1963, 154–56, 198).[6]

As long it stressed technology and social engineering, science was essential to American values. When it strayed from that course, it risked isolation from the public and the religious leaders who supported it. The religious leadership always was split. Some saw science as divinely inspired and others as a threat (Hofstadter 1963, 55). Overt conflicts were rare in colonial times and the early years of the republic. Science and religion were natural allies in fighting superstition. Virtually all scientists expressed a belief in God, arguing their mission was to confirm religious truths. As late as the mid nineteenth century one of every six leading scientists was the son of a clergyman (Bruce 1987, 120).

The Values in Conflict

The values are seen as consistent during periods of normal politics in American politics, when a growing economy sustains both the prevalent party system and the belief that the future will bring even greater progress. They are in equilibrium when Americans express strong support for all. Values clash and party systems crash when the economy reels. In periods of economic distress, conflicts between the promise and the reality of egalitarianism dominate political discourse. The parties take more clear-cut stands on issues that divide individualism and egalitarianism, with one side ultimately prevailing in a partisan realignment (Huntington 1981; Sundquist 1973).

---

6. Bryan, long after his popularity waned, was the lawyer defending Tennessee's assault on evolutionary theory in the *Scopes* trial.

Average citizens will not be pulled into one or the other camp at the outset. People will not split into warring camps until political leaders choose up sides and it is clear that one side will prevail and the other will lose, even if the identity of the winner is uncertain. Many people will simply lose faith in both sets of competing values. When the economy revives, a new equilibrium among the four values and a renewed faith in the exceptionalism will emerge.

Party systems begin with cohesive blocs of supporters. Conflicts inevitably develop among elites, and identifiers of *both* parties become less loyal. A crisis, almost always economic, leads to domination by one party and a new party system. Realignments are about more than cross-cutting issues. They revolve around shifts in larger values about what the American polity should be. The decline of an old order reflects a loss of confidence in the inevitability of progress. The most prominent examples of clashes between individualism and egalitarianism and between religion and science occur in prerealignment eras (the 1850s, the 1890s, and the 1920s).

In each realignment the conflict between individualism and egalitarianism is central. Before the Civil War, national debate was focused on slavery. The Populists were the precursors of the 1890s realignment, with their demand that government act to rescue the ailing rural economies. Even as they were routed by the party of Eastern capital, the egalitarian forces regrouped in the Progressive movement, temporarily capturing the Democratic party as Woodrow Wilson promoted his "New Freedom" agenda, and ultimately prevailed in the Democratic realignment of the 1930s.

The roles of science and religion—and particularly their interrelationships with individualism and egalitarianism—are less familiar. Science rode high during boom times. In the mid nineteenth century, home tinkering was very popular. Before the economic collapse of the late nineteenth century, twenty-seven million people flocked to the 1893 fair in Chicago to see demonstrations of scientific and industrial progress. At pre- and post-Depression World Fairs, crowds marvelled at a working television set and the miracle fiber Latex. Scientists produced breakthroughs in public power and irrigation, as well as air conditioning, faster trains, coast-to-coast airline service, and all sorts of new things made of plastic (Nisbet 1980, 204; Kelves 1978, 269). Science and religion shared beliefs in progress and hard work. Their intellectual foundations differed. Science and individualism are rationalistic, shunning the zeal of egalitarianism and religion. Yet science was often linked with egalitarian movements. The most prominent were Progressivism and the left wing of Social Darwinism that believed evolution would lead to the perfectibility of the human spirit (Hofstadter 1963, chap. 8 and 1955b, chap. 5).

Science and religion clashed during periods of intense political and social conflict. The revivalist movement in the 1850s was profoundly antiintellectual. Many scientists advocated equality of the races, and Southern church leaders attacked them. The late nineteenth and early twentieth centuries saw renewed battles, especially over evolution. The *American Catholic Quarterly* published an article in 1907 arguing that "the new spirit of scientific inquiry . . . looks upon religion much as a cat does upon a dog, as its natural enemy" (quoted in Buchanan 1987, 12).

Charles Darwin's *Origin of Species* led to further conflicts between church and laboratory over racial superiority and evolutionary theory more generally. The 1925 *Scopes* trial over the teaching of evolution in Tennessee took place as science came increasingly under assault by religious leaders. Criticism of science in popular magazines almost tripled from 1920 to 1930; one-third of all articles on science dealt with the conflict with religion. The Great Depression led to further tensions; many clergymen argued that they had been mistaken to place such faith in social engineering.[7]

When people find it reasonable to believe in exceptionalism, they will adhere to all four values. In an ever-expanding economy, people are more likely to temper self-interest with a concern for the less fortunate. Those who have fared less well will see prospects for betterment without a radical redistribution of resources. People will see science and religion as working—either together or at least independently—to make life better. During economic downturns, when the promise of a better tomorrow no longer seems guaranteed, tensions among the tenets will occur. There will be renewed demands for equalization of resources and equally strong pressures to resist them. Support for all four values and for exceptionalism has eroded since the 1970s.

There has been neither an economic collapse nor a realignment.

---

7. The sources for the preceding two paragraphs are Bruce (1987, 258); Lafollette (1990, 141, 152); Hofstadter (1963, 88); Woodlief (1982, 358); and Kelves (1978, 237–38).

The economy has reeled from multiple shocks and recoveries have been uneven. Party ties have atrophied. The economic worries and the strongly ideological tone of the 1980 election raised conflicts between individualism and egalitarianism. The politicization of fundamentalists brought religious issues—from abortion to prayer in schools to the teaching of evolution—front and center in American politics and often in conflict with science. Americans have less faith that the future will be better than the past, and they are stuck in the midst of a partisan realignment that offers no ready resolution to the conflict in values.

American High, American Low

The United States came out of World War II in what O'Neill (1986, 291, 4) called an "American High," a faith that "given enough effort, anything could be accomplished" and that "this was the greatest and freest country on earth, with a mandate, possibly of divine origin, to uplift the rest of the world." Americans felt exceptional. Not only were they optimistic about the future, but they also trusted the government and their fellow citizens. And they had every right to be so upbeat: For the next two decades, the United States had a boom that lifted living standards to levels that went far beyond initial promises (O'Neill 1986, 7, 291).

The 1970s and 1980s brought an end to our great expectations. Widespread economic dislocations and two major energy crises ended the boom, and America was no longer preeminent in the world. The "Reagan recovery" of 1981 proved short-lived, as the worst recession since the Great Depression occurred the very next year. Struggles over the economy were just part of the story, which I shall tell in the next chapter. Trends in public opinion support much of a "declinist" argument even though survey data on the values are scarce prior to the 1960s.[8]

---

8. When I compare surveys over time I am making an (implicit) assumption that people are no more (or less) likely to lie to survey researchers now than they were in the past. I do not view respondents as strategic actors who fibbed in the past to maintain some veneer of communitarianism but now feel free to admit their true feelings. An alternative interpretation—in the opposite direction—is that the waning of values reflects a less sophisticated citizenry. Since levels of education have increased, I doubt this account. I also recognize (see below) that the measures I have are imperfect indicators of fundamental values and norms. Better measures should produce higher levels of consensus.

There is an unease about the future, compared to the past. Almost three-quarters of the public in 1939 believed that American industry would lead to expanded opportunities in the future. Over 60 percent believed that life would improve in 1940, 1947, and 1962 surveys. At no point since the late 1970s—not even during the Reagan recovery—did a majority of Americans express such optimism. By 1990 less than a third believed that life would get better. As many now believe that it is likely that they will become poor as those who think they might become rich. By 52 percent to 42 percent, a 1989 sample held that their children would not have good opportunities.[9] Even in the euphoria after the liberation of Kuwait in March, 1991, only 36 percent expected the next generation to have a better life (Toner 1991).

Not only is the future not guaranteed, but America no longer is a role model for the world. Overwhelming percentages of Americans saw their country's influence in the world on the rise throughout the 1960s. The trend reversed itself in 1974, when just 29 percent perceived increasing power and half saw a decline. The numbers seesawed for the rest of the decade but never approached the peak years of the early 1960s. By 1990 less than a quarter saw U.S. influence on the rise. Only 15 percent saw their country as the leading economic power in the world, about the same share that believed the United States was no longer an economic leader.

On a range of issues from illiteracy to drug abuse to education to crime to homelessness, Americans saw themselves as no better than average among the nations of the world; only in the arenas of military power and individual freedoms did as much as 30 percent believe that the United States led the world (*Public Opinion* 1980; CBS News 1990a; NBC News 1990a and 1990b). Twice as many people name Japan as the world's dominant economic power as cite the United States, and they expect the future to be much like the present (Times-Mirror Corporation 1989, 14). While Americans express pride in what they have accomplished and give obeisance to their form of government, there is an unease that goes beyond the

---

9. See *Public Opinion* (1984, 22); Erskine (1964, 524–25; CBS News (1990d); and data from the October, 1990, *Washington Post*-ABC News poll on equality in America. The latter survey indicated that 53 percent of Americans believe that more Americans are becoming rich, while 44 percent hold that there are now fewer wealthy people. On opportunities for the future, see Yankelovich, Clancy, Shulman (1989b).

Values, Norms, and Society

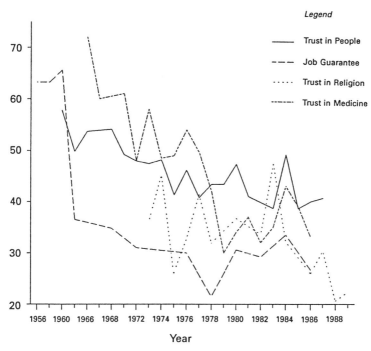

Fig. 4.1. The core values over time, 1956–89.

crisis of the moment.[10] Americans still have great admiration for their country, but they no longer exude the optimism that is the hallmark of exceptionalism.

The Waning of American Values

Support for the four values declined in the 1970s and thereafter. Figure 4.1 shows the trend for indicators of these tenets. The percentage of Americans responding "most people can be trusted" (as opposed to "you can't be too careful") is my measure of enlightened individualism.[11] There is no satisfactory measure of egalitarianism over time,

---

10. The figures are 42 percent believing the American system is a match and 37 percent saying that it is not a match. Toner (1991) reports that two years later 43 percent expected Japan to be the dominant economic power in the twenty-first century compared to 39 percent for the United States. By a more than two-to-one margin (66 to 26), Americans held in March, 1991, that Japan is currently a stronger economic power. Only 7 percent were more pessimistic about the U.S. role thirteen months earlier. See NBC News (1991a).

11. This question was first asked in 1960 by Gabriel Almond and Sidney Verba (1968). The 1964, 1966, 1968, 1971 (Quality of American Life study), and 1974

but the Survey Research Center/National Election Studies time series on support for federally guaranteed jobs is, with appropriate caveats, serviceable. Egalitarianism is, especially since the New Deal realignment, associated with the belief in redistributing wealth (Thompson, Ellis, and Wildavsky 1990, 89). Since the New Deal, Americans have accepted federal government intervention in the economy; the Civil Rights movement further legitimized a governmental role on issues of equality. Trust in religion and science are taken from General Social Survey (GSS) time series beginning in 1973. The trust in science series does not trend downward, so I shall pay less attention to it than another series: Harris polls on trust in medicine (Lipset and Schneider 1987, 48–49) show the same downward movement over time as trust. Medicine is hardly all of science, but it is a practical one. Had the science series begun earlier—the Harris polls start in 1966—we might see a similar decline.[12] Values for all five series are presented in table 4.1.

The four time series in figure 4.1 sharply decrease from the 1960s to 1989. If society needs a majority of cooperators to sustain collective action (Bendor and Swistak 1991), the United States has lacked the requisite share of enlightened individualists for most of the past three decades. Only three times in the time series (from 1960 to 1989) did a majority trust other people; only three times since 1974 was the trusting share even within sampling error of a majority. The three majorities all occurred in the 1960s; since 1975 the figure has hovered closer to 40 percent. Although there are no time series to compare, the pilot for the 1989 American National Election Study presents ominous findings for "self-interest rightly understood": Only 31 percent agreed that "people should care less about their own success and more about the needs of society," while 61 percent held that

---

questions were asked by the Survey Research Center. The General Social Survey (GSS) asked the question in 1972, 1973, 1975, 1976, 1978, 1980, 1983, 1984, and 1986–88. These data were made available by the Inter-University Consortium for Political and Social Research. The 1979 question was asked by the Temple University Institute for Survey Research (made available by the Roper Center). The 1981 data point is reported by Inglehart (1990, 438) as part of the World Values Study. The data reported exclude volunteered intermediate responses and "don't know" respondents, both of which were minimal in every case. I checked the trends for possible "house effects" since the entries were taken from various sources; none were found.

12. The plots (and correlations) of trust in science and trust in medicine over time are very similar after 1973, when the GSS series begins; the drop in confidence in medicine begins earlier.

TABLE 4.1. The Core Values Over Time (Data)

Year	Trust in People	Job Guarantee	Trust in Religion	Trust in Science	Trust in Medicine
1956	—	63.3	—	—	—
1958	—	63.3	—	—	—
1960	57.8	65.6	—	—	—
1964	49.8	36.5	—	—	—
1966	53.7	—	—	—	72.0
1967	—	—	—	—	60.0
1968	54.1	34.8	—	—	—
1971	49.2	—	—	—	61.0
1972	47.9	31.0	—	—	48.0
1973	47.4	—	36.1	40.8	58.0
1974	48.2	30.5	45.2	50.4	48.0
1975	41.3	—	26.0	37.5	49.0
1976	46.1	30.0	32.7	48.6	54.0
1977	—	—	41.4	44.5	49.0
1978	40.8	21.5	31.9	39.5	42.0
1979	43.4	—	—	—	30.0
1980	47.3	30.6	36.7	45.9	34.0
1981	41.0	—	—	—	37.0
1982	—	29.2	33.6	38.8	32.0
1983	38.7	—	47.4	44.4	35.0
1984	49.2	33.5	32.2	47.4	43.0
1985	—	—	—	—	39.0
1986	38.6	26.7	26.0	41.3	33.0
1987	40.0	—	30.4	45.0	—
1988	40.7	—	20.6	42.1	—
1989	—	—	22.4	44.2	—

"people should take care of themselves and their families and let others do the same" (Markus 1990).

Support for government guaranteed jobs also drops sharply, though this time the turning point is 1964, when egalitarian norms were presumably quite high.[13] Backing for this government initiative fell from an overwhelming majority to about a third of the population, where it remained, with some blips, throughout the 1970s and 1980s. The decline in egalitarianism long preceded the Reagan administration, but it further atrophied during that era. In 1975, 40 percent of

---

13. The data from 1956 to 1978 come from Miller, Miller, and Schneider (1980, 172). Later figures were computed from National Election Studies data by Martha Bailey. The question wording changed in 1972; the impact on the trend is minimal.

GSS respondents believed that the federal government had a responsibility to improve the standard of living of poor people, as opposed to believing that people should take care of themselves. By 1983, the figure had fallen to 32.9 percent, where it stayed with minor fluctuations through 1989. More critically, those who strongly agreed with governmental assistance fell by almost half: from 30 percent to 17.5 percent in 1983 (again, with minor fluctuations after that).

Ideological activists on the left and right fought over such issues as racial and sexual quotas, but few people got deeply involved in the debate. Americans remained convinced that it was important to help minorities. At the same time they did not want to violate individualism by giving anyone an unfair advantage. As these values clashed, people lost some faith in both.[14] The hope of the 1960s that the economy could create enough new wealth so that Americans did not have to play Robin Hood faded, along with the dreams that society would quickly become color blind and that liberalism would unite individualism and egalitarianism. As incivility has reduced the trust of individualism, so the tenor of debate has put egalitarianism on the defensive.

The American High years were also boom times for religion. Church membership rose from 64.5 million in 1940 to 114.5 million in 1960. The percentage of Americans belonging to a church rose from 50 to 63. Congress responded by adding "under God" to the Pledge of Allegiance (O'Neill 1986, 212). The time series in figure 4.1 fluctuates from its inception in 1973 until 1984, when it dropped sharply. Indicators other than trust in organized religion show earlier and more pronounced declines. Seventy-five percent of Americans said in 1952 that religion was very important in their lives; only five percent called it unimportant. Seventy-four percent believed that religion's influence was increasing in 1957, compared to only 15 percent who saw it declining （*Gallup Report* 1987; *Public Opinion*, March/May, 1979, 34). Eighty-one percent of a 1952 sample prayed once or more a day; ten years later two-thirds believed the Bible to be the actual word of God (Niemi, Mueller, and Smith 1989, 257).

---

14. The opposition of Reagan and Bush to preferential treatment for minorities did seem to affect public opinion. As late as 1985 Americans were equally divided on preferences in hiring for minorities that had been discriminated against; in 1990 only 32 percent favored such preferences, while 52 percent opposed them (Appelbome 1991).

By the 1970s support for religion had fallen considerably. Slightly more than half of Americans now said that religion was very important to them, a figure that has remained virtually constant. The share of Americans who believe that religion's influence has been increasing has fluctuated from a low of 15 percent in 1969 and 1970 to a 1970s high of 45 percent (1976).[15] At no point since 1962 have more Americans believed that religion's clout is on the rise. Only 55 (1978) to 60 (1985) percent prayed daily, while just about a third of Americans saw the Bible as the literal word from the 1970s through the 1980s (Gallup 1985).

The postwar period began with a surge in public confidence in science. The Manhattan project had led to the development of weapons far more terrible than could ever be imagined, but they helped the Allies win the war. Yet nuclear physicists ranked no higher than fifteenth in occupational status. By the early 1960s they had surged to third, behind only Supreme Court Justices and physicians (Kelves 1978, 391). American faith in science was bolstered by the field testing of Jonas Salk's vaccine against the dreaded killer polio, shaken again by the Soviet Union's *Sputnik* satellite in 1957, but renewed by the success of the American space program in the 1960s, culminating in the moon landing in 1969.

Americans have long held science in high regard and to a considerable extent continue to do so. Ninety-one percent believe that scientific research, more than any other factor, has made the United States great. Two of the next four reasons were also based on social engineering: industrial know-how (80 percent) and technological genius (73 percent). Americans were even more enamored of science than religion. Only 57 percent said "deep religious beliefs" made the United States exceptional.[16] Americans expected major breakthroughs in energy, earthquake prediction, cures for cancer, and desalination

---

15. Since the 1960s the percentage believing that religion's influence has been decreasing has fluctuated with no clear trend until 1988, the same year that confidence in organized religion plummeted (see below). The greatest decline occurred from the late 1950s to the early 1960s, the boom years of the American High. From the late 1960s to the early 1970s there was a significant decline in the percentage of Americans who attend services every week, a trend that has since leveled off. See *Public Opinion* (1990, 97, 100).

16. Right behind industrial know-how were rich natural resources, reflecting a belief in American exceptionalism, and hard-working people. These factors were tied at 79 percent.

of sea water within a quarter century (National Science Board 1981, 337-38). Science would also make our lives better by improving health care, reducing pollution, reducing crime, preventing drug addiction, improving crop yields, and advancing education.[17]

Do Americans still hold science dear? While trust in science shows no trend, there is a sharp decline in confidence in medicine in the early 1970s and again later in the decade.[18] Americans see scientific inquiry as more intrusive than they did in the late 1950s. Even as Americans largely trusted scientists, the percent believing that "scientists always seem to be prying into things they really ought to stay out of" increased from 25 in the late 1950s to 34 in 1988, while the share holding that science breaks down notions of right and wrong jumped from 25 to 32 percent. Even as a plurality (49 to 44 percent) doubted science's ability to solve social problems such as crime and mental illness in the late 1950s, three-quarters of Americans did so in 1988 (Withey 1959, 387-88; National Science Board 1989, 396). Only 42 percent in 1982 held that "scientists can solve any problem if they are given enough time and money"; 55 percent disagreed (National Science Board 1983, 147). People not only worried about science in general. They feared what had happened to American science. In 1981 pluralities held that science in the United States was only equal to or worse than that in West Germany, Japan, and the Soviet Union (National Science Board 1983, 147). Japan passed the United States a decade later, a two-to-one margin of Americans said (Toner 1991).

Challenges to science on several fronts in the 1970s and 1980s decoupled the link between confidence in science and belief in American exceptionalism. Environmentalists questioned the idea that resources were unlimited. They took on objects of progress such as the nuclear breeder reactor in the early 1970s. Pesticides were now identified as pollutants and likely sources of cancer. The promise that

---

17. Respondents were asked whether science could make a major contribution or little or no advance in these areas (National Science Board 1977, 179). The responses, respectively, were 65 to 3, 56 to 4, 51 to 19, 48 to 7, 44 to 5, and 42 to 12.

18. In some years Harris did more than one survey. I averaged the results reported by Lipset and Schneider for those years. The GSS also asked about trust in the leaders of medicine (Lipset and Schneider 1987, 48-49). However, both visual inspection and tests for house effects indicate that the GSS and Harris measures are not comparable.

science could cure all diseases, especially cancer, waned as more and more everyday things were said to be carcinogenic. Even the vaunted National Aeronautics and Space Administration, which had for so long captured the public's imagination, fell into disfavor especially when the Challenger space shuttle exploded in 1986. The nuclear accident at Three Mile Island in 1979 shook confidence in technology.

Values and Norms

The waning of values matters because it has consequences for norms and behavior. The six Congressional norms of the 1950s reflect similar tenets in the society. These maxims, in turn, derive from the values of individualism, egalitarianism, religion, and science. As belief in the values declines, so does adherence to the norms that stem from them.

The two norms that are central to comity are reciprocity and courtesy. In the United States, the basis of reciprocity is individualistic. Bryce (1916, 876, emphasis added) described life on the frontier as neighbors borrowed ploughs from each other and helped one another roll logs to build houses: "It is much pleasanter to be on good terms with these few neighbors, and when others come *one by one*, they fall into the same habits of intimacy." Reciprocity implies fair exchange, so there is a subsidiary egalitarian basis. The religious basis of "self-interest rightly understood" and the historical role of churches in American philanthropy (Bryce 1916, 790) highlights the importance of religious beliefs in fostering reciprocity. Reciprocity is the basis of enlightened self-interest and communitarianism. Communitarianism requires, at a minimum, that people play by the rules of the game, accept the outcomes, and treat each other with respect. If any—or all—are missing, people will be tempted to turn away from enlightened self-interest and the reciprocity norm encompassed in it.

Courtesy reverses the equation of reciprocity. Egalitarianism is fundamental, individualism secondary. Social equality made life more tolerable and improved manners as "people meet on a simple and natural footing, with more frankness and ease than is possible in countries where everyone is either looking up or looking down" (Bryce 1916, 872–73). An individualistic ethic, which downplays group or class identifications, makes social intercourse easier. Each person deserves respect regardless of background. American manners stress the dignity of every individual. When people believe strongly in both egalitarianism and individualism, courteous behavior makes people more willing to grant favors and to reciprocate.

Institutional loyalty in the larger society is a catchall norm, reflecting devotion to long-standing beliefs such as God, family, and community. Hard work encompasses all four values. America's Calvinist heritage and the Protestant ethic more generally stressed enterprise (Merelman 1989; Hofstadter 1955a, chap. 1). Individual effort was central to hard work, but labor was also "the great social equalizer" (Hartz 1955, 219; Vidich and Bensman 1958, 42). Science also demands diligence (Austin 1977).

Seniority and specialization, as in Congress, developed later and somewhat differently than the other values. Apprenticeship evolved in Congress in the late nineteenth century but never took root in the more egalitarian larger society (Elbaum 1989). Instead, a more egalitarian seniority system developed—along side specialization—as a system of property rights (to secure employment) in the workplace marked by the division of labor (Piore and Sabel 1984, 113). Both were "technical" (scientific) solutions to workplace problems (Mosher 1982, 73). Seniority, emphasizing the social equality of workers, derives from egalitarianism, while specialization highlights the contribution of individual workers.

The Waning of the Norms

If there is a connection between norms and values, the maxims for behavior should atrophy in much the same way as the values that underly them. And they do. The communitarian foundation of reciprocity has been particularly hard hit. People trust each other less in a multiplicity of ways. Americans are unhappy with themselves. Over 70 percent said they were dissatisfied with the nation's honesty and standards of behavior in 1987; in 1958 the figure stood at 58 percent. Not since 1973, in the midst of the Watergate crisis, had so many people been so concerned (McLoughlin with Sheler and Witkin 1987). And no wonder. Almost a third of college freshmen admitted cheating on tests, an increase of nearly 50 percent since 1966 (Deutsch 1988, 26). The Treasury Department estimated that tax evasion more than doubled from 1976 to 1981, from an estimated $42.6 billion to $90.5 billion (Church 1986).

In the corporate world, twenty-five of the one hundred largest defense contractors were found guilty of procurement fraud from 1983 to 1990. Few were punished at all, and none were barred from future government contracting (Stevenson 1990). Workers also find less support from their supervisors. The percentage saying that it is "very true" that their superiors are "very concerned about the welfare of those under him/her" fell from 44.8 percent in 1969–70 to 41.1 percent in 1972–73 and to 34.1 percent in 1977 (Quinn and Staines 1979).

Voices are increasingly shrill. The abortion debate in the Maryland legislature in 1990 was marked by antisemitic and anti-black epithets (Tapscott and Shen 1990). John Cardinal O'Connor of New York has threatened Catholic politicians who take pro choice stands with excommunication from the church (Lynn 1990). Even groups with no direct ties to an issue get caught up in the fray: Antiabortion groups have threatened to boycott environmental organizations that do not adopt pro-life positions (Ignatius 1989).

Reciprocity requires that people accept their opponents as legitimate. Even if their arguments are not convincing to us, legitimate actors have the right to persuade decision makers and even to prevail. Giving the other side its due means accepting some decisions as final, at least in the short run. Contemporary politics and social life are less and less marked by reciprocity. When people do not get their way through the legislative process, they are increasingly likely to take their nonnegotiable demands to other forums. Referendum voting is exploding in California (Reinhold 1988). Aggrieved groups often circumvent the electoral process entirely, relying on the courts to do what the legislature will not do (Melnick 1983). Ordinary citizens, not just political activists, increasingly use the legal system. The litigation crisis has hit doctors particularly hard: Malpractice claims in 1989, although 30 percent lower than in 1985, remained at twice the pre-1981 level (Glazer 1991).

Direct action against targets is becoming common. The *National Boycott News* has traced more than 200 boycotts against American and foreign companies for sins ranging from importing coffee beans from El Salvador to running sexist advertizing for jeans (Ramirez 1990). The strategy of blacklisting products has changed from the civil rights era. As with filibusterers in the Senate, boycotters do not restrict themselves to great national issues. Any moral outrage will do. More and more seem to qualify: The number of protests increased almost fivefold from the mid-1980s to 1991. The targets are not quite so selective, either. Groups now punish not just others who disagree with them but entire states and cities where legislative bodies adopt unacceptable policies (Duke 1991).

Sometimes these tactics can backfire (Mansbridge 1986, 130–32). Just often enough they are successful, so that it rarely pays any actors to restrain themselves on behalf of any collective good. Even self-proclaimed extremist organizations such as ACT-UP can claim policy successes; the group is credited with changing Burrough Wellcome's decision to reduce the price of the acquired immunodeficiency syndrome (AIDS) drug AZT (Zidovudine) (Crossen 1989). Groups claiming to represent the elderly forced the Congress in 1989 to repeal a catastrophic health care bill that it had enacted the year before.

Extremist groups are a distinct minority of the population. They can hardly be charged with the entire decline of comity in the nation. Strong-arm tactics spread rapidly, like a contagious disease. If not restrained, nasty actors can dominate the nice majority. Once norm-busters reach a critical mass, those who seek to maintain mores must punish not just defectors but those who tolerate them (Axelrod 1986). When there are relatively few nonconformists, they can be tolerated, as the Senate did with Proxmire, or largely ignored, as the House did with curmudgeons such as Gross. Retribution becomes more important as the number of defectors grows. When the share of trusting persons falls below a majority—as it has since the 1960s—it is much more difficult to police defectors.

A key behavioral indicator of reciprocity is individual charitable giving. Seventy percent of Americans contributed to charity in 1988–89, and 41 percent volunteered for charities or social service organizations (Teltsch 1989), yet charitable contributions by individuals as a percentage of gross national product has declined from the mid-1960s through the late 1970s (see fig. 4.2).[19] There was a slight rebound after that, followed by a sharp jump upward, though hardly to the level of the late 1940s and the 1950s. Throughout the postwar years (data from 1948 to 1957 is not shown), the level of contributions var-

---

19. The data on charitable contributions are from Nelson (1986, 6, 65). The 1983 and 1984 figures are estimates. I am grateful to Professor Ralph L. Nelson for providing me with this and other publications. The gross national product figures come from the *Economic Report of the President 1986* (Washington: Government Printing Office, 1986), 252.

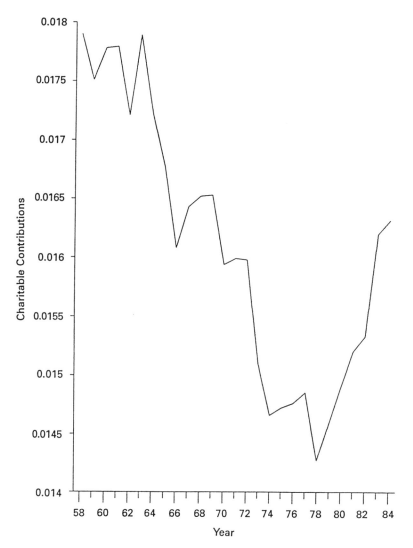

Fig. 4.2. Patterns of charitable contributions over time, as percentage of GNP, 1958–84.

ied little, but the more rancorous mood of the late 1960s took its toll on reciprocity. The spurt in the early 1980s reflected a change in tax laws easing charitable deductions—the only major legislative initiative in the 1948–84 period (Clotfelter 1985, 32–33)—rather than a rise in communitarian sentiments. There is a similar trend in personal contributions to Protestant churches. Giving as a share of income fell from 3.05 percent in 1968 to 2.62 percent in 1989. While real personal income has risen by 237 percent since 1921, the level of giving has fallen by 15 percent. Religious charity dropped during the Depression, picked up in the postwar years, and rose particularly during the 1950s and 1960s before decreasing (Ronsvalle and Ronsvalle 1991, 8, 17).

The evidence on courtesy is softer, but it is consistent. People do not seem to be as nice to each other as they used to be. The *New York Times* devoted a front-page story in 1988 to the "year when civility really took it on the chin." The airwaves boasted "shock radio" and "shock television" (especially Morton Downey, Jr., and Geraldo Rivera), and the movies even gave us "attack comedy." Some considered it acceptable to employ epithets about women and African-Americans, not to mention less popular groups such as gays (Williams 1988). From 1974 to 1989 assaults against young women increased 48 percent (Dewar 1990a).

In turn target groups demanded restrictions on what to them was obnoxious speech. Students at Yale University even protested a Public Broadcasting System program designed to teach French through a soap opera format: Feminists charged that women characters were portrayed primarily as sex objects, lesbians charged that the series focused exclusively on heterosexual relationships, Moslems objected to drinking wine with meals, and Hindus to the repasts themselves, which were feasts for carnivores (Schwartz 1990). Political correctness rules on many campuses. Its advocates disrupt classes, shout obscenities, and demand the ouster of faculty members deemed out of sync with an appropriate world view (Adler 1990). The Colorado state legislature in 1991 passed a bill—ultimately vetoed by the governor—that would permit fruit and vegetable farmers to recover damages against anyone who maliciously disparaged their produce (Associated Press 1991b).

Political activists pursuing such causes as antiabortion, environmental protection, and gay rights increasingly resort to violence. A member of Earth First, which has engaged in sabotage against developers and loggers, argues, "There is a need for an extreme element" (Bishop 1990). A leader in ACT-UP, an AIDS activist group, said of his group's guerilla tactics, "This is about constantly sticking it in the face of every single person you can stick it in" (Crossen 1989, A1). The Kettering Foundation's focus groups in 1991 found political and social life in contemporary America as "battles" demanding adversarial tactics (Kettering Foundation 1991, 36).

Even more conventional politics has been affected. Political campaigns have become increasingly nasty. An estimated 50 percent of Senate campaign ads in 1984 were negative (Taylor 1986). Voters believe by a margin of 59 to 37 percent that negative advertising provides them with useful information (Yankelovich, Clancy, Shulman 1990a, 30). About seventy organizations now rate members of Congress on roll call voting (Whalen 1986), providing the fodder for negative campaigns.

Contemporary society seems inured to loud voices and even violence. Juvenile incarceration rates have increased dramatically since the 1970s (Diesenhouse 1990). Fans at sporting events have become much more abusive (Klein 1989). Advertisers in the 1950s argued that their products were better than those of "Brand X." Now it is Coke versus Pepsi, Colgate versus Crest, and virtually every make of car against others. As in political campaigning, advertising firms find that attack ads work: They increase a product's market share (Harrington 1989; Mitchell 1990).

Two-thirds of Americans who shift from one merchant to another do so because of poor service (Swisher 1991, 22). A similar percentage holds for restaurants (McGill 1989). Diners rate restaurant service positively by just a 55 to 44 percent margin (ABC News 1990c). Customers have been so frustrated with poor service that they have taken to striking back, quite literally, at unhelpful clerks (Schwadel 1988). Younger people are more self-centered and less willing to take on collective action. Three-quarters of 1986 freshmen thought that it was "essential or very important" to be well off financially, as compared to just over half ten years earlier. In contrast, the promotion of racial understanding declined from 35.8 percent to 27.2 percent (*New York Times* 1987).[20] No wonder Miss Manners has lamented

---

20. See additional evidence in Braungart and Braungart (1988, 55), who report a 22 percent increase in the number of freshmen who want to be very well off in

the decline in courtesy throughout much of American everyday life (Martin and Stent 1991).

Hard work remains an American norm, but it has lost some of its sheen. An overwhelming number of people would continue to work even if they did not need to for financial reasons. Almost 90 percent believe that it is important to work hard (Hamilton and Wright 1986; Lipset 1990). People still expect hard work to lead to success, yet fewer (59 percent) believe this now than did as recently as 1981 (two-thirds) (*Public Opinion* 1984, 27; Clymer 1981; CBS News 1988). The linkage is no longer seen as inevitable: In 1968, 58 percent of the public agreed that "hard work always pays off if you have faith in yourself and stick to it." A decade later the figure dropped to 44 percent and by 1983 it fell to 36 percent (Yankelovich and Immerwahr 1983, 17).[21] From 1987 to 1991 the share of Americans who agreed that hard work offers little guarantee of success jumped from 29 to 44 percent (Times-Mirror Corporation 1991, 33).[22] An index of job satisfaction dropped sharply from 1969 to 1977 (Quinn and Staines 1979, 220).

Americans lost faith in a wide range of governmental and public institutions, including both business and labor (Lipset and Schneider 1987). There was a widely held perception of a nation adrift, of a people constantly seeking something better, be it homes, jobs, or marriages (Yankelovich 1979, 11). The loss of social trust produces a "loosely bounded culture" in which "group characteristics no longer inform people about what to expect of others" (Merelman 1984, 12, 30).

The society is more heterogeneous, and people interact with each other less frequently (Bellah et al. 1986, 175). People do not go downtown any more. Instead they frequent impersonal malls, which 78 percent of Americans visit once a week and almost all Americans trek to at least twice a year (Reid 1985). The divorce rate has increased, doubling from 1950 to the 1980s (*World Almanac and Book of Facts* 1984, 907). Forty percent of households fit the mold

---

1987 compared to 1968 and declines of 27 percent in wanting to be involved in an environmental cleanup and 44 percent in seeking to develop a philosophy of life.

21. Their inferences have some basis in fact: Most new jobs created in the early 1980s paid low wages (Bluestone and Harrison 1986, 5-6).

22. Some of the increase is clearly attributable to the 1991 recession, yet the data also show a sharp increase (to 36 percent) by 1990, when confidence in the country and the economy were higher.

of the traditional family, with a father, mother, and one or more children in 1970; by 1990, only 26 percent did (Associated Press 1991a).

The fault lines in our polity show cracks. Much that was familiar is now strange. Banks and savings and loans, among the more highly ranked institutions, are no longer pillars of the local community. The spread of interstate banking and the crumbling of the savings and loan industry replaces the friendly neighborhood banker with an executive from who-knows-where. Even the American icon Coca-Cola briefly vanished, only to reappear as "Coke Classic." Americans are no longer loyal to the three television networks, which now account for about two-thirds of television viewers (Farhi 1990).

Much that is traditional in politics has also changed. The strength of party identification has weakened; Americans are not so much hostile to one party or the other as neutral toward both (Wattenberg 1986a). Americans do not value their political institutions. They increasingly take political decisions out of the hands of their legislatures and subject them to referenda. As more people believe that government is run by a few big interests than at any time since pollsters began asking the question (Oreskes 1990), voters in California, Oklahoma, and Colorado threw the rascals out permanently by enacting term limitations on their state legislatures in 1990.

People are more likely to abstain from voting. Turnout in presidential elections has declined from 62.6 percent of those eligible in 1960 to 50.1 percent in 1988; for Congressional elections, participation has dropped from 58.5 percent to 44.7 percent for presidential years and from 45.4 percent to 33.4 percent for off years (Ornstein, Mann, and Malbin 1990, 46). Foreign policy, formerly a consensual issue in which "partisanship stops at the water's edge," is now highly contentious (Spanier and Uslaner 1989, chaps. 4–5). As confidence in political structures has waned, people increasingly distinguish between favored leaders (such as their own members of Congress) and the institution. This same disjunction applies elsewhere. People do not feel very warm to the insurance industry, yet they still favor their own agents. Similar results hold for lawyers, bankers, and physicians (Herman Group 1987).[23] In divorcing the institution from its members, we strain traditional concepts of loyalty.

---

23. Physicians as a group are more highly regarded than the other professions.

Specialization and seniority, the two workplace norms, stabilized labor-management relations (Sabel 1982, 60). When key industries, especially automobile manufacturers, faced increased competition from Japan, many adapted by applying Japanese-style management that abjured specialization. The breakdown in labor-management comity in the mid-1960s and early 1970s led many companies to look to new forms of organization (Katz 1985, 42–44). Grievances increased by more than 40 percent from 1960 to 1973. Union demands in contract negotiations with General Motors increased 3.5-fold from 1958 to 1973. Workers engaged in strikes and production slowdowns. Rates of absenteeism multiplied. Unions no longer secured victories in collective bargaining. They failed to organize new workers. Management increasingly succeeded in decertifying existing unions. Unfair labor practice complaints soared. The social contract between workers and companies that traded job security and automatic pay increases for labor peace ended in the late 1960s (Edsall 1984, 141–54; Goldfield 1986; Dionne 1987). Management sought to find ways to change the work environment, making it less contentious. Teamwork, or "Ad-Hocracies" in Toffler's (1970, 131) terminology, was the solution.

Workers joining teams would be hired according to merit rather than seniority. Experimentation in the automobile industry began in the early 1970s. This new form of organization dates back to the 1950s, when it was largely confined to nonunion plants in the automobile and other industries. The pace picked up dramatically in the 1960s and 1970s (Katz 1985, 74, 88). The first union at an automobile plant to accept a complete restructuring along Japanese lines did so under duress in 1981. Almost half of the work force was laid off at the Ford plant in Michigan. Unlike the Congress, in which legislators struggled to undo expectations of specialization and seniority, automobile workers felt that management's actions constituted severe violations of norms (Kaboolian 1989, 16, 20–21, and 1990, 523, 556–59).

Not surprisingly, people do not hold car dealers, either individually or collectively, in high regard. Aside from the unseemly portrait of automobile dealers, especially purveyors of used vehicles, there is a rational basis for differentials in trust. People have ongoing relationships with their attorneys, bankers, physicians, and insurance agents. Most do not have regular interactions with car dealers. These merchants, like those in bazaars abroad, have few incentives to treat consumers well. The customer is not likely to return (cf. Hardin 1982, 214). More critically the customer expects to be cheated and is more willing to cast aside a bad deal in search of a better one.

Throughout the work force, and not just in the automobile industry, tasks became more complex. In 1969-70, 64 percent of respondents to the Quality of Employment survey said that it was "very true" that "I have enough information to get the job done." By 1977, only 51.8 percent did. The demand for teamwork also grew. In 1969-70, 61.7 percent strongly agreed that "my responsibilities are clearly defined." Just 48 percent did so in 1977 (Quinn and Staines 1979, 218).

Seniority was also undermined in the 1960s. Title VII of the Civil Rights Act of 1964 took aim at historical patterns of job discrimination against minorities and women. While the act appeared to protect seniority systems, the courts (including the Supreme Court) in the 1970s restricted seniority rights because they were discriminatory; in the recessions of the 1970s, a disproportionate number of workers who were laid off were women and minorities (Flanagan, Smith, and Ehrenberg 1984, 316).

The six norms atrophied at a similar pace to the four values. Since the norms derive from the values, this is precisely as it should be. Most of the societal values and norms began to wane in the late 1960s or early 1970s, slightly before the more rapid deterioration of Congressional maxims. What is the linkage between the two arenas in which comity has declined?

Can We Trust Trust?

The most important value underlying "self-interest rightly understood" is trust in other people. It has dramatically, if not monotonically, declined from 1960 to 1988 (fig. 4.1). Why should we care? The waning of enlightened individualism has consequences. It drives a wide range of changes in American society and politics, from the waning of the other values to one behavioral manifestation of reciprocity (individual charitable giving) to high agricultural price supports and the budget deficit and the capacity of Congress to make major policy innovations (see chap. 6). It moves most of the behavioral indicators of Congressional norms. Can trust in people outdo other contenders that also seem reasonable? In most cases I examine, it performs at least as well as other variables. Communitarianism matters. Its decline should concern us.

The four values decline over time. We know this from figure 4.1. We can get a bit more specific by looking at the correlations among the values and how each tracks with a simple counter for time (table 4.2). Many of the variables are based on very small samples (as few as six or seven cases), so strong caveats apply. There is a general picture that emerges, especially from the variables with larger samples. The four tenets all decline over time (except one indicator for science) and the correlations are quite large. The other three values (including both indicators for science) closely track the decline in trust in others. The measures for egalitarianism, science, and religion display a mixed pattern of intercorrelations, not surprising given the small sample sizes and the noisiness of the indicators. Recognizing this and not wanting to make too much of small correlations from small samples, it is pleasing to note that all correlations are positive.

There are two very plausible societal alternatives to communitarian sentiment as driving forces in the national malaise. The most commonly cited source of national gloom is distrust of government, not of people (Lipset and Schneider 1987). People's attitudes toward their government seem a more proximate cause of the ill will and stalemate in Congress than does some remote sense of enlightened self-interest among the people.

Distrust in government has increased over time, and the correlation is almost as impressive, despite the much smaller sample size, as that for trust in people. Yet the two measures of trust do not mirror one another: Their simple correlation is only $-.535$. Both types of trust were very high in the early 1960s, and both fell in the mid-1970s. Distrust in government fell during the Reagan years, only to bounce back up toward the end of the administration and to stay low into Bush's presidency.[24] There was a blip upward in trust in people in 1984, but for most of the Reagan years, enlightened self-interest remained at or below the levels of the late 1970s. Distrust in government is not as strongly related to the other values as trust in people.

Another likely contender to explain the decline of legislative norms and the policy rut in which we find ourselves is the growth

---

24. The government measure is coded as distrust rather than trust. The data for 1958 to 1984 were taken from Lipset and Schneider (1987, 17). The 1986 and 1988 figures were provided by Jennifer Bagette of *American Enterprise*. The distrust in government measure is not adjusted for "don't knows" or other nonrespondents.

TABLE 4.2. Correlations of Values with Each Other, Time, Distrust in Government, and Public Mood

	Time	Trust in People	Job Guarantee	Trust in Religion	Trust in Science	Trust in Medicine	Distrust of Government
Trust in people	-.833 (19)	—					
Job guarantee	-.849 (13)	.815 (10)	—				
Trust in religion	-.627 (11)	.714 (11)	.343 (6)	—			
Trust in science	-.009 (11)	.576 (11)	.833 (6)	.605 (11)	—		
Trust in medicine	-.867 (18)	.719 (11)	.214 (8)	.316 (9)	.032 (9)	—	
Distrust of government	.788 (11)	-.552 (10)	-.719 (10)	.379 (7)	-.102 (7)	-.345 (7)	—
Public mood	-.535 (34)	.405 (19)	.676 (13)	-.295 (11)	.037 (11)	.298 (18)	-.895 (11)

Note: Entries in parentheses are numbers of cases.

of conservatism in America. Might communitarianism be nothing but old-fashioned liberalism? In the 1960s we trusted each other and the government. We also voted (narrowly) for John F. Kennedy and by a wide margin for Lyndon B. Johnson, whose Great Society marked the greatest surge in domestic legislation in American history. If Congressional liberals led the charges against the old systems of norms, they found much support among their fellow partisans in the electorate.

Stimson (1991) has proposed a sophisticated measure of the public mood (liberalism). It too decreases, but not nearly as convincingly as either trust in people or confidence in government. It has weak relations with all the other values except, not surprisingly, the job guarantees. While liberalism is strongly related to distrust in government ($r = -.859$), it has at best a moderate (.405) correlation with trust in people. As distrust in government fell during the Reagan years only to rebound again, so liberalism plummeted before picking up steam toward the middle of the Reagan regime. Communitarianism and liberalism have much in common, but "self-interest rightly understood" is not simply a particular ideology.

While both public mood and trust in government trend downward over time, they are also cyclical. When inflation and unemployment are high, people lose faith in government. When inflation is high, people are more likely to be conservative. There is only a very weak relationship between trust in others and unemployment and none at all with inflation.[25] The declines in trust in government and liberalism lead one to be optimistic about the rebirth of comity. What goes down will come up. Liberalism among the public is already resurgent (Stimson 1991). On the other hand, there is no evidence of a rebound in trust in others.

What does trust move? If it is central to the reciprocity norm, it ought to affect charitable contributions. It does (see table 4.3). Charitable contributions increase when inflation is low, when people are more liberal, and—critically—when communitarian sentiments are strong. The 1981 change in tax laws did boost contributions,

---

25. These results are based on generalized least squares regressions that also include a control counter variable for time. The coefficients in the distrust of government model are significant at $p < .05$ (unemployment) and $p < .001$ (inflation), despite the small sample size. For policy mood ($N = 34$), inflation is significant at $p < .01$. For trust, unemployment is significant only at $p < .10$.

TABLE 4.3. The Determinants of Individual Charitable Contributions

Variable	Coefficient	Standard Error	t
Constant	.010	.017	5.613***
Trust in people	.00005	.000	2.175**
Public mood	.00003	.000	2.400**
Inflation (CPI)	−.0001	.000	−2.974***
1981 dummy	.0001	.000	1.564*

$N=16$, $R^2=.894$, SEE$=.0004$, rho$=.262$,
*$p<.10$ **$p<.05$ ***$p<.01$.

though the impact is not very powerful. The dummy variable for the 1981 change is significant only at $p<.10$. The most powerful determinant of individual contributions is the rate of inflation. Public mood and trust in people are both significant at $p<.05$, but the coefficient for trust is almost twice as large as that for liberalism. Distrust of government is even more strongly related to charitable contributions ($r=-.94$), but the much smaller number of cases (ten) makes comparisons hazardous. All three measures of the public malaise seem to drive charity, but there remains a clear and perhaps even central role for communitarian values.

How do communitarian values in society affect Congress? Shifts in the behavioral indicators of Congressional norms vary directly with the key indicators of "self-interest rightly understood" for the country—trust in people and charitable contributions by individuals. Charity might seem far removed from the day-to-day workings of Congress, yet it taps a central element of reciprocity. Charitable contributions are more than just donations to the less fortunate; they represent a bond between members of society. The statistical results clearly reflect commonalities in the two time series that are tied to shifts in public attitudes. Changes in Congressional norms mostly do not reflect changes in the policy preferences of legislators themselves. Something beyond the confines of Capitol Hill—a sense of communitarianism in the nation—drives Congressional behavior. More impressively, a societal account fares far better than one based on the "new members, new values" argument. The former thesis holds that norms derive from values, while the latter maintains that norms follow policy preferences.

The linkages in tables 4.4 and 4.5 are based on very small samples (nine cases except for the Senate regressions on charity, which have eight cases) from the 86th to the 99th Congress, because the data on

TABLE 4.4. Regressions of Behavioral Indicators of Congressional Norms on Congressional Ideology and Trust in People

Indicator	Trust		Ideology			
	b	t	b	t	R^2	SEE
Amending activity: 12 terms house	−.099*	−2.805	.0002	.449	.652	.573
Amending activity: 3–4 terms house	−.126*	−2.371	.0002	.329	.384	1.015
Nonmember amendments: house	−2.004**	−5.324	.003	.529	.744	7.199
Nonmember amendments adopted: house	−2.286**	−4.289	−.007	−.945	.750	8.901
Nonmember amendments adopted: senate	−.284	−1.300	.013	3.493	.768	3.747
Amending activity: senate	−.192*	−2.876	.0004	.588	.690	.968
Amending activity: senate freshmen	−.164	−1.112	.002	.971	.338	2.351
Nonmember amendments: senate	−1.849**	−3.995	.020	3.196	.886	6.929
Senate generalists	−1.150*	−2.893	.009	1.811	.802	5.762
Percentage generalists: senate freshmen	−1.414	−1.289	.016	.858	.469	18.589

*$p<.05$ **$p<.01$.

TABLE 4.5. Regressions of Behavioral Indicators of Congressional Norms on Congressional Ideology and Charitable Contributions

Indicator	Charity[a]				Ideology			
	b	t	R^2	SSE	b	t	R^2	SSE
Amending activity: 1–2 terms house	−.745***	−9.243	.901	.317	−.001*	−2.615	.901	.317
Amending activity: 3–4 terms house	−.840***	−10.055	.906	.392	−.001*	−2.947	.906	.392
Nonmember amendments: house	−10.850***	−22.405	.980	2.022	−.097**	−6.003	.980	2.022
Nonmember amendments adopted: house	−9.098**	−5.509	.847	5.164	−.098+	−1.987	.847	5.164
Nonmember amendments: senate	−10.609***	−8.674	.951	3.129	.021	5.178	.951	3.129
Amending activity: senate	−1.144**	−4.458	.798	.855	.0003	.456	.798	.855
Amending activity: senate freshmen	−1.268+	−1.601	.464	2.206	.001	.623	.464	2.206
Nonmember amendments adopted: senate	−2.639*	−3.447	.859	3.009	.010	4.035	.859	3.009
Senate generalists	−9.084***	−10.119	.951	3.129	.006	1.978	.951	3.129
Percentage generalists: senate freshmen	−9.099+	−2.058	.544	14.415	.009	.613	.544	14.415

[a]Coefficients are divided by 1,000. +$p<.10$ *$p<.05$ **$p<.01$ ***$p<.001$.

norms are not available for all years and because the trust, charity, and ideology measures had to be aggregated by Congress rather than by year. Despite these caveats, the results are robust.[26] The behavioral indicators and the measures of trust and charitable contributions are familiar. To test the "new members, new values" thesis more systematically, I computed a measure of "ideology" from *Congressional Quarterly's* Conservative Coalition indicators on the assumption that the old norms favored the interests of the right. For each Congress—and each chamber—I multiplied the mean Conservative Coalition support score by the frequency of the coalition's appearance. Higher scores indicate that the coalition of Republicans and Southern Democrats appeared often and won often.

Societal values have a much greater impact than ideology. Trust is statistically significant (at $p<.05$ or better) in seven of the ten regressions. In the three equations focusing most directly on the reciprocity norm (nonmember amendments proposed in the House and the Senate and nonmember amendments adopted in the House), the relationships are very strong (statistically significant at $p<.01$), despite the small samples. Two of the three indicators that do not make the grade—percent of generalists among Senate freshmen and Senate freshmen amending activity—are less clearly connected to the reciprocity norm. No coefficient for ideology is significant. Two have large t-values that signify significant relationships—nonmember amendments offered and adopted in the Senate—yet the relationships are in the wrong direction. Senate violation of committee reciprocity increased when the Conservative Coalition was strong. Changing values in the society directly affect Congressional behavior.[27]

The impacts are even stronger for charitable contributions: In each of the ten equations, charity has a significant impact. The rela-

---

26. In small samples, regression estimates can be very sensitive to extreme values on individual cases. For each of the ten behavioral indicators of Congressional norms, I "jackknifed" the regressions—deleting one observation at a time. Only 6 percent of all regressions that were statistically significant at the .10 level or better (5 percent of all regressions, whether significant or not) failed to achieve significance in the "jackknife." Only .8 percent (one) of the regressions that was significant at $p<.05$ or better failed to reach significance at least at $p<.10$. When cases were deleted, strong relationships got stronger and weak ones became weaker.

27. Even the rough measure of egalitarianism is related to the norms of behavior. The correlations range from a low of $-.31$ (adoption of nonmember amendments in the Senate) to $-.88$ (offering of nonmember amendments in the Senate). The average correlation, which was the same for the House and Senate, was $-.67$.

tionships are strongest for those indicators most directly related to the reciprocity norm and weakest where the linkage to reciprocity is weakest (freshmen amending activity and freshmen generalists in the Senate). If the linkages with charity were spurious, they should not be so patterned. Six of the equations find very powerful connections: nonmember amendments offered in both chambers and adopted in the Senate, overall amending activity for first- or second-term representatives and for third- or fourth-term representatives, and Senate generalist share. Overall amending activity in the Senate and nonmember amendments in the House are also strongly related to charitable contributions. Ideology is now significant in four equations: nonmember amendments offered and adopted in the House and amending activity by first- or second-term and third- or fourth-term House members. Members' preferences do affect norms but to a far lesser extent than their more fundamental values. Each time ideology is significant, it still is dwarfed by charitable contributions.[28]

Congressional norms ironically relate more strongly to the level of liberalism in the public than to ideology. Yet, the correlations are negative (averaging $-.67$). As with ideology, the norms *withered* when conservatism triumphed. The public mood also moves the behavioral indicators of legislative norms but fares no better than trust in people.[29] Trust in government has erratic effects. Congress might be a cozy environment, but it is far from insulated from its constituents. When values are in flux, legislators quite readily look toward the people who elect them for cues. As constituents cry out for more vigilant protection, representatives of all stripes will respond. In some cases, liberals might be somewhat more willing to break the rules established by a conservative regime, but the COS seems even less bound by strictures to be nice than the Democratic

---

28. Perhaps looking at chamber conservatism is not the best strategy, since individual members are not the ones who must maintain the norms. The greatest beneficiaries were the committee leaders, who sustained their power through reciprocity, specialization, hard work, and apprenticeship. To test this thesis, I replaced the measure of ideology with Sinclair's (1989a) indicator of the representativeness of Senate committee leaders. The results were even weaker.

29. When I substitute the public mood for ideology in the regressions, liberalism is significant in three equations when trust is not, trust is significant in three when liberalism is not, both are significant in two equations, and there are two regressions in which neither is significant. The job guarantee measure also tracks most of the behavioral indicators of legislative norms, but not quite so strongly. There are too few cases to generalize from the religion, medicine, and science measures.

Study Group of the late 1950s was. Once people begin to defect (from norms) in a collective action problem, others, regardless of their preferences, will follow. Trust, not legislators' ideology, sustains cooperation.

The relationship is not always quite as simple as a linear model might suggest. The behavioral indicators of Congressional norms do not all demonstrate ever-increasing trends. Some measures, including the total number of amendments offered in the Senate (fig. 2.1), peak in the mid-1970s and decrease after that. The Congressional agenda has become less crowded in an era of resource constraints (Davidson 1986), so it is not surprising that amending activity has leveled off. Even so, the relationships with trust and charity are quite strong. The biggest changes for both measures of communitarianism occurred from 1960 through the late 1970s. The statistical results show that communitarian values track the behavioral indicators of some Congressional norms very strongly during this period. Both then fluctuate, sometimes seemingly aimlessly, after that. Trust in people, charitable contributions, and amending activity all reached new equilibria in the late 1970s—and never returned to their previous levels.

Other measures such as nonmember amendments offered and adopted in both chambers, more central to the reciprocity norm, did not fall much; House nonmember amendments adopted continued to rise throughout the time period covered. These indicators vary even more strongly with trust in people (and with charity). They pick up the lesser shifts after the 1970s in communitarian values. The overall relationships are not perfect, but they are strong enough to suggest something systematic is going on. If Congress seems to be an even less pleasant place than it was in the late 1970s, this is largely attributable to a decline in civility, which is less easily measured.

The linkages between Congress and society do not stop at behavioral norms. The waning of values has policy effects as well: The budget deficit, the level of agriculture price supports, and the more general ability of Congress to enact nonincremental policies all reflect changing American values—more so than they do cyclical factors such as trust in government or the public mood and more so than they reflect Congressional norms (chap. 6). The next story, however, is why values and norms have declined.

Chapter 5

The Decline of Comity in the Nation

> It was the best of times, it was the worst of times, it was the age of wisdom, it was the age of foolishness, it was the epoch of belief, it was the season of Light, it was the season of Darkness, it was the spring of Hope, it was the winter of Despair, we had everything before us, we had nothing before us, we were all going direct to Heaven, we were all going direct the other way.
> —Charles Dickens, *A Tale of Two Cities*

Values and norms come under attack in periods of economic and political turbulence. Americans were buffeted in the 1970s by economic shocks, most notably the oil embargos of 1973–74 and 1979. Economic problems from that decade onward are only part of the story. Traditional coalitions in the electorate and among policy-makers split apart, putting the United States in the trough of a realignment cycle. Despite economic tough times, there was no shock large enough to reshape national politics. For more than two decades, neither party has been able to establish electoral hegemony. Americans are unwilling to make choices about fundamental values or even the parties that govern them.

Value change began during good times as the boom years of the 1960s opened up politics to hitherto excluded groups with agendas that divided the public along new lines, a traditional harbinger of realignments (Sundquist 1973). The harder times that followed led to increased demands for protection against the demise of exceptionalism and a declining communitarianism, much as in previous realignments. The social and economic turbulence paralleled earlier conflicts, but with far less severity.

From the 1960s until 1981 the story was largely one of how boom and bust cycles affected people's values. Afterwards, politics becomes central: Ronald Reagan attempted to engineer a realignment that would produce a new order in American politics and values. Reagan governed as if he had already achieved such political dominance. The electorate, buffeted by the 1982 recession, did not respond immediately, so the president tried to induce a realignment through the issue of tax reform. The attempt largely failed, traditional values continued to atrophy, and the parties were locked in an ever more stinging conflict. The nastiness of the 1970s was now overlaid with sharp partisan divisions, and regular order seemed even further away.

Uncivil Wars

Social and especially economic turbulence are central to realignments and the waning of norms and values. The present conflicts are far less severe than the antebellum battles that ultimately tore the country apart. Individualism, under the banner of states' rights, and egalitarianism, through the abolitionist movement, challenged each other for supremacy. The nation lurched between the depression of 1837-43 and the rapid economic growth and consumer culture that followed (Morison 1965, 574; Wiebe 1984, 323). Public morals collapsed, as male brawls, free-for-alls, cockfighting, carousing, public drunkenness, and prostitution abounded (Nichols 1962, 20).[1] Political campaigns were so passionate that "only bloodletting, occasional or wholesale, could relieve the tension" (Wiebe 1984, 328-29). A messianic revival arose in revolt, demanding prohibition, laws against Sabbath desecration, restrictions on immigration, and the end of slavery.

The two major parties were split over these cultural issues; state organizations readily adopted platforms that differed from national party policies, and even local parties were free to repudiate the programs (Gienapp 1982, 48). Parties in Congress preferred to concentrate on distributive benefits rather than the more divisive issues facing the nation; because there never were enough benefits to satisfy all demands, "[i]nevitably those who lost called into question the legitimacy of bestowing special privileges on some and depriving others" (McCormick 1986, 207).

---

1. By one estimate, 10,000 women in New York City—two percent of the population—were prostitutes (Lockwood 1990).

The Decline of Comity in the Nation

Perhaps more so than at any other time in American history, the economy went through boom and bust cycles of great magnitude during the realignment of the 1890s. Some areas prospered, while others languished. Drought and crop failure wrecked the farm economy in 1890. Litigation over negligence by railroads and industries skyrocketed. Violence, stemming from labor conflict, racial and ethnic hatred, and simple vigilantism, became commonplace (Keller 1977, 372, 574, 401, 486-87). Bands of unemployed men roamed the West, seizing railroad trains, looting food, and marching on foot to the East. "General" Jacob Coxey led his "industrial army" on such a rampage on Washington in 1894. Labor-management relations had grown increasingly violent since the end of the Civil War; in 1894, almost 750,000 workers struck while employers strove to cut wages in a period of economic turmoil. The violent strike of Pullman workers was among the most famous in American history (Josephson 1938, 560-82; Morison 1965, 768).

The wide economic swings raised hopes and quickly dashed them. As Morgan (1969, 390) argued:

> No economy had ever produced so much material wealth for so many people, but every increase in well-being prompted cries for more security, social balance, and luxuries that denoted success.

In 1890, according to Morison (1965, 789), "American politics lost their equilibrium."

The Populist movement mixed egalitarianism with revivalist religion and intense dislike of immigrants. The Women's Christian Temperance Union convinced most states to adopt Prohibition. With its allies, it pressed for the removal of the alien doctrines of immigrants in the public schools and the substitution of a Christian curriculum. Most states enacted blue laws requiring stores to close on Sunday; Congress and almost every state enacted antilottery laws. The mix of religion and egalitarianism, so prominent in the antebellum period, was highlighted in the Social Gospel movement (Wiebe 1980, 57, 139; Keller 1977, 508). These new tensions split the parties along regional lines, with several third parties emerging to exploit public disgust with the old order. Individualism defeated egalitarianism when the Republicans became the dominant party following the realignment.

The Great Depression overshadowed any economic troubles the United States had ever experienced, yet the prerealignment years of the 1920s were also wracked by social and religious conflicts, with nativism and religious revivalism reacting to the close association of Catholic and Jewish immigrants with urban Democratic machines and the nomination of Catholic Al Smith as the Democrats' presidential nominee in 1928. Economics was fundamental to this realignment. The conflict between individualism and egalitarianism was joined when President Herbert Hoover sent federal troops to roust "Bonus Marchers" seeking additional veterans' benefits from the Capitol. The New Deal would reconcile individualism (capitalism) with egalitarianism (a more equitable distribution of resources) through the welfare state.

In all three realignments, traditional economic issues that had divided the major parties tore them apart. Conflicts among fundamental values led to a passionate politics that made compromise impossible and wrecked havoc with policy-making. People distrusted both political leaders and each other. Good economic times made possible the emergence of new issues, yet prosperity raised expectations to a level beyond which political leaders can deliver. Economic collapse diminishes living standards. Elevated expectations lead people to reassess their values.

Baby Boomers

The current era has not faced economic crises of the magnitudes of the 1890s or 1930s. Compared to the 1960s, boom-and-bust cycles in the economy have become more frequent. Expectations had skyrocketed. The post–World War II boom made many Americans believe that the good times would just roll on and on. Government now played a central role in ensuring prosperity. Increased state intervention in the economy, legitimized by the New Deal, exploded during the Great Society. The state was to be the "permanent receiver" (Lowi 1979), the guarantor against failure. People not only expected government to come to their rescue, they demanded that it do so—in extremely shrill voices. Groups began questioning the legitimacy of each others' demands. They insisted on largesse for themselves, but denied it to others. A new form of American exceptionalism arose. The greater the economic dislocations, the more shrill the demands. Dodd (1981, 400–405) has linked all these forces to a more contentious Congress. I take his analysis as a point of departure and expand on it.

The end of World War II brought a great economic boom. Real family income set new records every year. By 1973, postwar real income had doubled. By the mid-1960s income growth significantly outpaced inflation, while unemployment remained low. Inflation-adjusted family income rose by 30 percent during the Eisenhower administration and by another third in the Kennedy-Johnson years (Levy 1987, 3–55). The 1960s were a decade of rising expectations, a confirmation of the fundamental American belief that unlimited resources could resolve all problems. People could focus on issues other than getting by. Affluence brought not only high levels of trust and optimism for the future but also greater personal happiness, less social alienation, declining class tensions, more religious tolerance, and a very restrained partisanship (Lane 1965). In good times people could afford to "rightly understand" self-interest. In bad times they were less generous.

The prosperity of the post–World War II era made it possible for people's attention to shift to other problems, including the defining issue of the 1950s and 1960s, civil rights (Barone 1990, 386). The civil rights movement met with "massive resistance," even with—or perhaps especially with—the Supreme Court on its side. Civil rights workers, even when committed to nonviolence, became embroiled in physical confrontations others started. The politics of civil rights leaders was necessarily confrontational.[2]

In the late 1960s, blacks demanded more than a share of an increasing economy. They sought power as well. Political control, unlike economic resources, was not so fungible. The tolerance of leaders expressing nonviolence gave way to militants who shunned reciprocity and were willing to resort to violence to achieve their ends. The civil rights movement formed the model for others who used confrontation as a strategy of first rather than last resort. Traditional institutions did not work well in the early civil rights battles.

---

2. Note the lyrics in Judy Collins's folk song about the civil rights movement: "It isn't nice to block the doorways. It isn't nice to go to jail. There are nicer ways to do it. But the nice ways always fail."

Congress stalled major civil rights legislation until the 1960s. So protestors not only took to the streets but also to the courts, bypassing the legislature altogether.

While civil rights groups were pushed into conflict, their successors actively sought it out. Blacks, antiwar activists, and young people and later women, gays, and environmentalists became radicalized. A common theme among these diverse activist groups was the opening up of the political system by mobilizing people who had not previously participated (Bellah et al. 1986, 213). Groups emerging on the right, from supporters of George Wallace in 1968 to the religious right, had been similarly marginal to politics.

People lost faith in each other and in their government. Vietnam and Watergate combined to tumble confidence in the 1970s. The rhetoric of the various protest movements was antiinstitutional (cf. Barone 1990, 386), yet it was explicitly communitarian. The civil rights movement spread the word of equality among all peoples. The counterculture emphasized love and peace. Divisions in the civil rights community led to the urban riots of the mid-1960s. The counterculture was always adversarial despite its language (Barone 1990, 421). Young antiwar protestors promoted peace while chanting, "Don't *trust* anyone over 30."

The civil rights movement began during an era of great trust—in both institutions and other people. The struggle took on a moral tone stressing core American values. While it might have challenged traditional institutions, it placed a heavy emphasis in faith in people. Its communitarian foundation withered when racial violence spread northward and especially as black-white tensions escalated in the 1980s and 1990s. They became increasingly distrustful of each other. Now most Americans see civil rights not as a moral crusade but as the demands of a particular interest group, according to Cornel West (quoted in Applebome 1991, A1). Similarly, the Vietnam experience tore the communitarian foundation apart by replacing a trusting environment with a cultural war pitting old values and life styles against newer ones (Barone 1990, 392). Neither side accepted the legitimacy of the other's claims.

Baby Busters

Even while prosperity fostered new groups, the economy weakened. The war in Vietnam produced a short-term gain in growth and employment rates, but the deficits to finance both guns and butter would lead to sharply higher inflation in the 1970s. Food prices skyrocketed in 1972, and the first energy shock came the next year. Real income began falling, and plunging productivity could not resuscitate the economy. The oil shocks led to spiraling inflation. Blue-collar jobs fled to countries with cheaper labor forces. In a postindustrial era, service and high technology employment supplanted traditional manufacturing jobs (Bell 1973, 14-17). The news on the economy was not all bad. The South and West benefited at the expense of the Northeast and Midwest (Levy 1987, 60-67, 108).

The dislocations led to a new set of cleavages and different expectations. Political conflict now stressed postmaterialist issues such as the environment and equality and not only economic concerns (Inglehart 1971). The growth era led to its own dialectic. The boom fanned expectations so great that no system could possibly meet them. When this prophecy proved true, Americans who had become accustomed to continued growth demanded that the government that presided over the boom protect them against the bust (cf. Inglehart 1990, 271).

Left-right and partisan coalitions that typified American politics and notably resource issues crumbled. Not only were there more interests than in the past, but old allies had become adversaries. The New Deal realignment that had put the Democratic party into power and the economic boom that kept it there was hit by a quadruple whammy. The civil rights movement mobilized blacks but sent many Southern whites into the Republican party (Petrocik 1987). Old issues either faded in public appeal (labor concerns) or were marked by new cleavages (energy). Issues such as the environment, abortion, and school prayer cut across old fault lines; environmental activists also challenged the idea that resources were unlimited. The changing economy not only facilitated new political conflicts but also weakened the clout of old-line actors such as unions.

Regional disparities, which had narrowed from 1929 to 1979, widened in the 1980s ([U.S.] Department of Commerce 1987). The inflation generated by energy price spikes reverberated throughout the economy. The economic revival of the 1980s, brought about in part by the decline of oil prices that began in 1981, temporarily arrested the problems, but the pattern of growth was not uniform. By 1982, unemployment had reached a post-Depression high. The remainder of the decade was marked by wide swings in the economy and the stock market. Unpaid credit loans grew from $300 billion in 1980 to $795 billion a decade later; corporate debt rose from 34 percent to 46 percent of capital stock. Personal bankruptcies set a record in 1990 (Brenner 1990).

Isn't That Special?

The politics of the 1960s changed expectations in another way. The Great Society expanded entitlement programs from the 1930s and converted existing grants to entitlements. By 1985, 47 percent of all U.S. households received some form of direct benefits from the federal government (Pear 1985a). Such payments increased from 5 to 12 percent of the gross national product from the end of World War II to 1984, jumping from 21 percent of all government spending in 1947 to a third by 1984. Only one-fifth were subject to means tests (Levy 1987, 152, 166). The greatest period of expansion occurred during the 1970s (Weaver 1987).

What had been government largesse turned into rights. As the economy reeled upward and downward, with different effects in American regions, demands for protection against risk multiplied. As one group makes such a claim, others will be sure to follow. The role of government as guarantor of the economy, no matter how badly managed any particular sector is, is strained in an era of limits. The public purse seems to be the only way out because the size of the stakes is too large for any private guarantor to back. The government was called to bail out New York City, Chrysler, and the Continental Illinois bank and later the entire savings and loan industry and the nation's farmers. When the stock market crashed in 1987, the Federal Reserve Bank stepped in to insure credit for member banks (Silk 1990). Less prominent but equally willing to drink at the government trough were the uranium and nuclear industries, which respectively sought government expenditures of $1 billion and $9 billion (Davis 1987; Peterson 1988). Public policy-making became a tug of war among groups that demanded government support to protect them against the boom-and-bust cycles that typified the post-exceptionalism era.

Claims for exceptionalism turn into nonnegotiable demands, or rights (Lowi 1986, 216). Such rights also imply an absolution from incurring one's fair share of costs. Each group that is special (in time, everyone) will be entitled to benefits without regard to costs. In a period of scarcity, the assertion of specialness is a recipe for political stalemate and harsh words for anyone who attempts to challenge one's rights. The claims for rights can be translated into arguments that one's own position is sacred, leading proponents to argue that contrary views must be censored (Vobejda 1986). Protagonists attack the give-and-take that is the cornerstone of reciprocity.

No one is willing to assume any costs or risks. Raising taxes has become political suicide, and people demand that the government eliminate virtually all hazards, real (terrorism on airlines, dangerous drugs) or threatened (apples treated with the pesticide Alar or Chilean grapes that might not have been tainted with cyanide after all) (Dionne 1989). Even the wealthy who sell expensive artworks now demand minimum price guarantees from auction houses such as Christie's and Sotheby's (Reif 1990). Many claimants obtain benefits because they have widespread public support (environmentalists or farmers), because they have only weak opposition, or because there is no alternative (the savings and loan industry). There are few incentives to restrain demands for some collective good. With cries of an imminent fiscal apocalypse, each claimant had better get its share now.

The part of the story common to the 1970s through the 1990s is one of economic turbulence and social transformations leading to a more confrontational style of politics. Courtesy went by the wayside. Traditional institutions bore much of the brunt of criticism. Why work hard when you can get what you want by shrieking loudly? If your faith in the future has been shaken, there are few incentives to sacrifice for some collective goal. Seniority was overtaken by the emergence of young people as a political force. The new era of fluid coalitions made specialization a luxury few groups could afford. By joining one's own issue with another's, one could either garner additional support or, more likely in an era of attack politics, drag an opponent's issue down to defeat. By the end of the 1970s politics was in flux. The next decade sought to restore some regular order to our politics.

The Reagan Revival and American Values

America's ability to solve its problems was no longer taken for granted. Even President Carter admitted the nation faced overwhelming obstacles in what became known as his "malaise" speech of July,

1979. He blaimed everyone, from petroleum exporters to big business to the American people, for the "crisis of confidence" that was "threatening to destroy the social and political fabric of America."[3] The gloom of the 1970s, especially the latter part of the decade when American hostages were held captive in Iran and inflation failed to fall when unemployment rose, gave way to Ronald Reagan's unbridled optimism. Republicans not only won the White House but took control of the Senate for the first time since 1952 and made substantial gains in the House. Younger voters became more Republican (Norpoth 1985). The new president sought to convert his mandate into something far more enduring, a new era of Republican politics. The chaos of the 1970s would yield to regular order with a majority party and a dominant ideology.

The Reagan revival centered around a renewal of American exceptionalism. The president proudly proclaimed, "America is back!" Reagan believed that he could engineer not just a revival in American values but also a whole new political alignment that would make Republicans the majority party. His message included a revival of individualism at the expense of egalitarianism and of the need to restore religious values while keeping the faith in science (particularly through the Strategic Defense Initiative in military technology). The Democrats' strategy was based on universalism, whereas Reagan's message was majoritarian.

Ronald Reagan and Majoritarianism

As a firm believer in the American tradition of social engineering, Reagan could pursue the strategy of creating a new political order. The "teflon president" then sought something new in American politics: a man-made "polyester realignment." His vehicle was first the conservative agenda and later the highly atypical "triggering mechanism" of tax reform. The president attempted to govern the country and to implement his agenda as if he had majorities in both houses of Congress, as if he were a prime minister in a Westminster majoritarian system.

Reagan secured extraordinary Republican unity in adopting the

---

3. Carter never actually used the word "malaise" in his speech. See Uslaner (1989, 79).

administration's 1981 budget cuts and tax reductions. Republican members of the House also relished the idea of becoming—for the first time for virtually all of them—the majority party; the GOP had already taken the Senate. The COS's guerilla tactics led to heightened partisan rancor, as did the Democrats' attempts to restore order in Congress through restrictive rules for considering legislation (Bach and Smith 1988). Legislators had been calling each other names in the 1970s. While such incivility continued across party lines, the shouting became much more patterned in both chambers. This was reflected in greater party unity, initially just in the House but later also in the Senate (Sinclair 1989b).

Reagan's policies challenged the fundamental preconceptions of universalism. The budget cuts and tax reductions disrupted the consensus of between ten and fifty years on such issue areas as education, social welfare, the environment, and government regulation of business. Budgetary and tax policies led to a sharp redistribution of income from the lower-income groups to those at the higher end of the economic spectrum and dramatic shifts away from enforcement in the areas of civil rights, environmental and consumer protection, and economic regulation. The reductions of spending were particularly sharp for programs benefiting lower-income groups (see the essays in Palmer and Sawhill 1982; Eads and Fix 1984).

The administration did not seek broad consensus but narrow coalitions with just enough supporters to gain passage of its agenda. The Gramm-Latta budget reduction resolution passed by the slim margin of 217 to 210. Much vote trading occurred, among some recalcitrant Republicans but most prominently among Southern Democrats (Sinclair and Behr 1981; Lambro 1986). Reagan did not disrupt interest group politics but only changed the constellation of constituencies that are favored by government (Lowi 1984, 39). The president's strategy was radical. Even Republican presidents since Hoover had admitted the necessity of governmental social programs (Weatherford and McDonnell 1990, 130–31).

The reconciliation process employed in the 1981 budget was specifically designed to disrupt traditional bipartisan logrolling coalitions. Gilmour (1990, 94, cf. 123–24) maintained that the new budgetary enviroment had made Congress "a majoritarian body, to a degree unprecedented in modern times." Reagan's support for a constitutional amendment giving the president an item veto is another tool of universalism busting (King 1986, 16–17). The president also took direct aim at water projects throughout his administration. The Reagan White House maintained virtually no contact with interest group representatives with Democratic leanings (Peterson 1986, 617–18). Social service organizations and groups promoting liberal social or regulatory policies report difficulties in achieving cooperation with federal agencies in the Reagan White House; the administration has been particularly impressive in introducing partisan and ideological considerations into the bastions of universalism, the "iron triangles" (Peterson and Walker 1986, 167–70).

The idea of governing as if the administration had majority control of both houses of Congress had significant appeal to Republicans in the Congress. Gingrich argued early in Reagan's first term that the president had the opportunity to "create a *de facto* parliamentary system of government here" (quoted in Farney 1981). Party cleavages became more pronounced on many issues, including economic management, social welfare, civil rights, and the environment (Sinclair 1985). Economic management and social welfare divide the parties according to their core constituencies. Any attempt to govern according to majoritarian principles will magnify these cleavages. Attitudes among the population on civil rights have become more polarized along partisan lines over the past several decades (Carmines and Stimson 1989), but environmental issues remained consensual. In both cases the Reagan administration proposed radical departures from past policies (Pear 1985a; Portney 1984).

Majoritarianism Outside Congress

Partisan conflict was not restricted to the Congress. It permeated the bureaucracy, the courts, and the mass public in this decade. The White House sought to exert control over the administrative agencies that implement the policies and often devise regulations. The administration removed many career civil servants from the upper echelons of the bureaucracy and replaced them with political appointees who were carefully recruited and systematically checked by the White House for ideological loyalty. This "strategy for infiltrating the bureaucracy ... went way beyond anything Nixon had attempted" (Moe 1985, 261). By September, 1983, political appointees constituted over 10 percent of federal executives for the first time (Goldenberg 1984, 394).

The Office of Management and Budget (OMB) under David Stockman became a central clearinghouse for all regulations promulgated by any administrative agency; between 1981 and mid-1983, the OMB had revised 6,700 regulations and had vetoed 1 out of every 9 that it reviewed (Rauch 1985). By 1986 the administration was seeking a Supreme Court ruling that would deny independent regulatory agencies the power to enforce regulations (Kamen 1986).

The Reagan administration attempted to politicize not only the bureaucracy but also the judiciary—the first sustained attack on that branch since Franklin D. Roosevelt's attempt to pack the Supreme Court five decades earlier. The courts were a prime target for the administration because they were a major line of defense against the social agenda of the New Right (abortion, prayer in school, women's rights) and for the legacies of the Great Society era (civil rights, criminal justice, and government regulation of business). Reagan appointed more than half of the nation's 743 federal judges by 1988. The administration was diligent in insisting that nominees be strong conservatives (Press 1986). Administration officials, including the president and the attorney general, attacked Supreme Court rulings and even particular justices (*New York Times* 1986b; Shenon 1985; Pear 1986).

The new regime took a decidedly majoritarian stand toward labor unions. The administration broke an air traffic controllers' strike in 1981 and refused to intervene as major companies ranging from airlines to beef processors to newspaper publishers to the Greyhound Bus company replaced striking workers with replacements. The working class was a key target of the Reagan realignment. As long as workers were tied to unions, however, their Democratic leanings would be reinforced at the workplace. Workers freed from the chains of union politics would be up for grabs politically.

Reagan's chief accomplishment was gaining virtually complete control over the nation's agenda to a degree unprecedented since Franklin Roosevelt. The president appeared to dominate the debate on virtually every issue (Merry and Mayer 1986). The politics of majoritarianism is revealed in public attitudes toward the Reagan administration as well. Citizens' opinions of Reagan have been more polarized than toward any other president, or any other presidential candidate (including George McGovern), in the Survey Research Center/Center for Political Studies time series from 1952 to 1984 (Wattenberg 1986b).

A New Regime?

There were some signs that a realignment might be possible. Trust in government increased during Reagan's first term. In 1983 there was a spurt upward in confidence in science and religion. Support for science remained strong in 1984, while faith in medicine caught up (table 4.2). There was a surge in trust in other people the same year. The Republican share of party identifiers—including leaners—increased from the low 30s in the 1970s to almost 40 percent by 1984 (Stanley and Niemi 1992, 158). Both values and partisanship were moving in the right direction.

Despite the good fit between Reagan and the American public, a realignment was not imminent (Wattenberg 1986a). Republicans were split between their "Main Street" members, who had long dominated the party, and the newly active Christian Right, which sought to take over many local party organizations (Fialka 1986). The Democrats were also divided. Despite high cohesion on Congressional roll calls, the party had internal conflicts over such issues as foreign policy, health, education, crime, taxation, gun control, civil rights, trade, and energy (Dewar 1991). The GOP lost twenty-six House seats in 1982 amidst high unemployment; even the president's forty-nine-state landslide in 1984 gave the party just fourteen new House seats. The administration's second term began much as the first did, with proposals for massive budget cuts through the elimination of programs that were part of the traditional universalistic coalition (*New York Times* 1986a). Congress demured.

Tax Reform and Realignment

By the beginning of Reagan's second term there were few specific issues on which the majority of Americans agreed with the president (Hume 1986). To provoke a realignment, Reagan needed to sponsor a cause that would overwhelm all other issues and target precisely the group that had the power to make the Republicans the majority party. Such an issue also must be symptomatic of the old, discredited, crumbling normative order.

Tax reform had a strong appeal as a potentially realigning issue. The current income tax system was the product of years of Democratic party control of the Congress. Tax policy was largely made in Congress and was a mishmash of special interest provisions. Few knew about most of them, and almost no one understood the entire system. Americans viewed the federal income tax, the most progressive levy, as the least equitable, even when arrayed against decidedly regressive measures such as state sales taxes or local property taxes (Birnbaum and Murray 1987, 9). When both Reagan and Mondale had promised tax reform in the 1984 election, the issue appeared to grab people's attention—60 percent of respondents to an April, 1985, survey believed that tax reform should be the government's first priority, with only 34 percent citing the deficit (Cohen 1985, 1348). Because the tax code was so complicated, a successful attempt to change policy would be a major legislative accomplishment for Reagan. It would shift momentum on controlling the agenda back to the White House.

Tax reform could link the politics of ideas to the critical interest of the 1980s. Ideas define political movements and are central to the establishment of a regime of norms. The nation had seemingly forsaken "self-interest rightly understood" with nothing firm to take its place. Many Americans interpreted the individualistic philosophy of the Reagan administration as a license to pursue pure self-interest. By the end of the first term and the beginning of the second term, there was no longer a central idea.

Central to tax reform was a reduction in individual rates with no loss in revenue. The people who felt the tax system to be most unfair, the middle and lower-middle classes, would have their rates lowered. The 1984 election was partially a referendum on whether taxes needed to be raised to reduce the deficit. Lowering the rates and simplifying the code would constitute a frontal attack on "the system of particularistic policies essential to the politics of interest group liberalism" (King 1986, 21). As Merry and Shribman (1985, 1) argue:

> Most Republicans view the [president's tax reform] plan . . . as a lever for nudging themselves back into their long-lost position of

the country's majority party. They see it as a powerful metamorphosis from country-club conservatives to a new coalition reaching a broader spectrum of Americans—workers, Catholics, new immigrants and entrepreneurs as well as old-style Republicans.

The budget and tax cuts of the first Reagan term had failed to bring about a Republican majority. Some majoritarian strategies, notably on the environment, had backfired. By 1985 almost half of Americans believed that their own families would be hurt by the further budget cuts sought by the president (Oreskes 1985a).

Taxation appeared ideally suited to the idea of a "polyester realignment." Like the president's attempt to build a new majority party without a major political upheaval, tax simplification was an exercise in social engineering. As Birnbaum and Murray (1987, 288) stated, "Tax reform was a uniquely American idea—that somehow the nation could start over and rebuild its entire tax system." The idea of tax reform was not new. Representative Jack Kemp (R—N.Y.), Senator Bill Bradley (D—N.J.), and Representative Richard Gephardt (D—Mo.) had long favored bills that would repeal most income tax deductions while lowering rates for individuals and (for Kemp only) corporations (Fessler 1984a).

Less than a month after Reagan's reelection, Treasury Secretary Donald T. Regan announced what would be the adminstration's first tax reform proposal. The plan would replace the existing individual tax rates ranging between 11 and 50 percent with three rates of 15, 25, and 35 percent. The personal exemption would be increased from $1,090 to $2,000. Deductions would be streamlined, but mortgages on principal residences would be retained. Corporate taxation would be at a flat 33 percent rate rather than a progressive levy ranging up to 46 percent. Many corporations had escaped taxation or paid very low rates because of extensive deductions. Many of these would be repealed, notably the 10 percent credit for new investments and the accelerated depreciation for capital investments enacted in 1981. Capital gains, presently taxed at a lower rate, would be considered to be ordinary income (Fessler 1984b).

This first shot in the tax reform war was targeted to reward groups that were becoming increasingly Republican and to punish core Democratic constituencies. The heaviest burden would fall on Democratic high tax states, mostly in the Northeast and urban Midwest, where people would no longer be able to deduct state and local taxes from their federal returns and where tax exemptions for bonds would be repealed. The proposed repeal of the investment tax credit would hurt traditional smokestack industries hard ([U.S.] Department of the Treasury 1984, xiii) and benefit the new high technology industries. The former were based in Democratic territory, the latter in the target areas for Republican growth (Florida, Texas, Arizona, California, and Colorado).

The Democrats, bolstered by their continued control of the House and the constitutional requirement that revenue raising legislation begin in that chamber, had strategic advantages. Ways and Means Committee chair Dan Rostenkowski (D—Ill.) offered a plan with more progressive rates than the administration proposal; it also took away benefits for independent oil and gas producers, a key GOP target group. Some Republicans, angered that the president's bill was too tough on business, offered their own legislation with more progressive individual rates. A revised administration bill (Treasury II) increased rates on corporations and further cut individual rates, especially on lower income people; families making less than $12,000 would be cut from tax rolls (Fessler 1985).

The Ways and Means Committee reported the Democratic bill in December, 1985, with unanimous support from panel Democrats and the support of five of the thirteen Republicans, yet the House defeated the rule for the bill. To keep the issue alive, Reagan forged a deal with Speaker O'Neill in which the president would pressure Republicans to support the rule, let the House pass Rostenkowski's bill (which it did on December 17 by voice vote), and hope for the best in the GOP-controlled Senate. When the legislation got to the Senate, Senators responded to the pleas of constituency groups by reinstituting tax breaks for oil, gas, timber, private pensions, tax-exempt bonds, and foreign levies for an overall revenue loss of $29 billion (Fessler 1986a and 1986b).

By May, 1986, Senate Finance Committee Chair Bob Packwood (R—Oreg.) had forged an alliance with Bradley and produced a clean bill eliminating most major special interest provisions while retaining the deductibility of state and local taxes and oil tax shelters (Shanahan 1986). The full Senate approved the bill by a ninety-seven to three vote on June 24 after including a large number of transition rules that would waive increased rates for specific firms for varying periods of time. Reagan won his fight against greater progressivity in individual rates, while the Democrats prevailed in keeping most middle-income deductions.

The Limits of Reform by Design

Legislators convinced themselves that the public demanded tax reform, despite no strong evidence to support that claim. Birnbaum and Murray (1987, 285), the major chroniclers of the legislation, noted:

> ... beneath the apparent public indifference ... boiled a potential gusher of discontent that could prove to be a fearsome force. Few members of Congress cherished the thought of ending up on the wrong side of the popular President's battle against the special interests. They may not have wanted reform, but they were not about to be seen standing in its way either. As a result, tax reform acquired an extraordinary momentum once it got going.

The prospect of lower rates for individuals clearly was appealing to legislators. Most of the losers believed that any attempt to mount a lobbying campaign against a popular measure would be fruitless (Russakoff and Swardson 1986).

Political gains were elusive. The administration had to admit that Democrats shared the credit in enacting the legislation (Broder 1986). Some losers, such as realtors, threatened to reopen the issue in the next Congress. The public was not nearly as excited as legislators believed. A national survey of 5,000 families by the Conference Board indicated that approximately the same percentage expected to pay higher taxes (44) as lower (40). About the same share believed that the new system will be less fair (33) than more fair (36) compared to the existing tax code. The less affluent were more likely to expect to pay higher taxes and to see the new system as less fair. Younger voters, supposedly the target of the realignment, anticipated higher rather than lower rates by a two to one margin (Conference Board 1986).

Half of Americans preferred the present tax system, while only 38 percent backed the pending legislation (Gibson with Hildreth 1986,

15). After the legislation had passed, it proved even less popular. In 1988, 58 percent said that their taxes were higher and just 22 percent said lower under the new system; a year later an additional 5 percent said they paid more (Crenshaw 1989). There was no political bounty for the Republicans because there was no bounty for the taxpayers. Reductions of 9 percent or more appeared quite appealing to legislators. The benefits from such cuts were later found to be largely illusory, amounting to between $2.50 and $8.00 per week for all but 1 percent of taxpayers (Russakoff 1986).

Perceptions that the new system was less fair than the old killed tax reform as a realigning issue. Tax reform fits none of the major conditions for such a major political transformation. A realigning issue must be salient to the electorate (Sundquist 1973, 29-30). Even in the midst of the tax reform debate, 63 percent of the respondents to a national survey said that they did not know enough about the issue to form an opinion (Broder 1986b, A8). An almost identical share indicated that a Congressional candidate's stand on the bill would not affect their voting decision (Dionne 1986).

Only easy issues can transform politics; these are questions to which people respond on a gut level. Voters need little additional information, nor must they have a well-developed ideology that encompasses a wide range of issues (Carmines and Stimson 1989, 11-12). Reagan's original proposal would have drastically simplified the tax system, but revenue raising has always been a complex, hard issue (Manley 1970). By the time the various proposals had wound their way through the Congress, even accountants were confused. Almost certainly no single individual understood the complex set of transition rules. In realignments politicians rarely lead the charge toward a new political order. Instead, they struggle to catch up with changes in mass behavior that emerge, like norms, without institutional prodding. Politicians may try to stir things up, but they cannot force a new alignment on an unready population.

The Reagan victory in 1980 ratified an ideological shift that had begun in the American electorate in the early 1970s (Stimson 1991, 42). Even though the COS was not formed in the House until 1983, Gingrich and his allies began their kamikaze tactics in 1979 (Rohde 1991, 129). Senate Republicans began to pursue a strategy of disruption at the same time (Beth 1990, 25). The minority in both chambers was responding to a perceived ideological shift in the electorate. The attempted realignment was designed to cement the link between ideology and voting behavior.

The elite aspect of the decline of comity in Congress paralleled the decline of comity in the nation and depended on it. The harsh tactics within the halls of Congress were more than simply an ideological assault on liberalism. They marked a change in tactics that followed the waning trust in other people among their constituents. This elite-mass nexus is reflected in partisanship in voting on special rules in the House from the 84th to the 100th Congress (1955-90). Rohde (1991, 102) finds that party-line voting greatly increased on these obscure procedural votes since 1979. What drives this spike in partisanship?

Ideology matters, but only modestly. The more conservative the public's mood, the greater the partisan differences on special rules, but the correlation is just $-.29$ with liberal opinions. Distrust in government is also slightly related to partisan conflict ($r=.31$ for ten cases). Trust in other people, including estimates for all Congresses according to a technique discussed in chapter 6, is strongly related to battles between Democrats and Republicans ($r=-.69$). I provide a more fully specified model in table 5.1.

If party conflicts on special rules were driven mostly by elite battles, then we would expect institutional factors such as the share of House Democrats, unified versus divided government, and the overall level of partisan conflict to shape the battles. To a considerable extent, they do. The percentage of all House votes that pit a majority

TABLE 5.1. Regression of Mean Partisanship on Special Rules in the House of Representatives, 1955-1990

Variable	Coefficient	Standard Error	t
Constant	122.200	24.465	4.996**
Percent unity votes	.795	.114	6.977***
House democratic percentage	−65.976	33.638	−1.961*
Estimated trust in people	−1.595	0.178	−8.957***
Single party control	7.666	2.743	2.795**

Note: $N=17$, $R^2=.874$, SEE$=5.338$, and rho$=-.506$.
***$p<.0001$ **$p<.01$ *$p<.05$

of Democrats against a majority of Republicans—party unity votes (Ornstein et al. 1990, 198)—is strongly related to partisanship on special rules. There is a weaker relationship with the Democratic share of the House: As Republicans become more numerous, they become bolder in waging party battles on the floor. Unified party control of the legislative and executive branches heightens partisanship, perhaps surprisingly. The strongest impact is for trust in other people. If we take the regression coefficients and multiply them by the range of the predictors, we find that going from divided to unified party control increases partisanship on special rules by 7.7 percent. When the share of House Democrats increases from .533 to .678, the mean partisanship difference goes up by 23.9 percent. When trust in others falls from 57.7 percent to 38.2 percent, party cohesion on special rules increases by 31.1 percent, the greatest impact of any variable. Looking only at the impact of the variables from the 84th to the 100th Congresses, changes in interpersonal trust have more than twice the force of the major institutional factor, the share of party unity votes.

The pitched partisan battles of the 1970s through the 1990s represented more than struggles over ideological hegemony. Even the most inside of all votes—those over obscure procedural tactics invisible to most constituents—reflected the waning values in the larger society. Even when Reagan's attempt at a realignment faltered and the public moved toward greater liberalism, communitarian ideals continued to flounder. The top-down realignment failed only in part because the public did not accept conservative ideals. More critical was the electorate's refusal to sort out its fundamental values. The elites helped shape what the fight was about—the increasing partisan nature of the rancor in Congress—but the public set the stage for the altercation.

Stuck in Neutral

The economic roller coaster of the 1970s and 1980s shook people's faith in America's core values. Individualism fell into disfavor as we demanded that someone or some institution ensure our success. Egalitarianism fell into disfavor when people wanted special treatment, not an equal chance to succeed or fail. Religious values were shaken when people looked to Washington, not to God, for salvation. Faith in science atrophied when it became clear that we expected more of social and technological engineering than it could provide.

The social and economic turbulence led to the decline of comity in the nation in two ways. First, when values come into conflict, tension alone will produce louder voices. The second dynamic stems from the specific conflicts over ideals. The clash between individualism and egalitarianism was a frontal assault on universalism. Americans turned away from enlightened self-interest and toward more egoistic concerns. Strong support for egalitarianism gave way to harsh debates over quotas. Racial tensions increased, and each side became ever more militant. Selfish individualism led to claims that one's own demands were special and others' were illegitimate. Unlike individualism rightly understood, such a perspective could not dwell comfortably with egalitarianism. Nor could science and religion coexist when the mainstream faiths came under assault from less tolerant fundamentalist beliefs.

These value conflicts weakened norms. Reciprocity and courtesy gave way to nonnegotiable demands. When people see government as the ultimate protector, hard work loses some of its luster. Militancy leads people to go outside traditional institutions, from legislatures to the electoral system to churches. In the labor force, workers see challenges to standards such as seniority and specialization as attacks on long-standing traditions by unlikely allies, management and minority groups. With these threats coming on top of increasing economic uncertainty and management efforts to decertify unions, organized labor became increasingly strident.

The strain on resources in the 1970s, the uneven distribution of the bounty of the 1980s, and the economic uncertainty of the early 1970s all contributed to the decline of comity, yet the story involves more than economic scarcity. The boom years of the 1950s and especially the 1960s raised expectations and brought new groups into politics. Many of these interests were never committed to a civil politics. The civil rights movement and the war in Vietnam led to more confrontational politics; the war and Watergate eroded confidence in both government and other people. The economic troubles of 1982 and the rise in partisanship exacerbated the conflicts, but they did not produce them. Economics matters, but it is not everything. Recall that trust in people barely increases or decreases with the state of the economy. Perceptions of the future, not of the present, have eroded communitarianism in America. We do not anticipate an ever-increasing bounty, so we demand more for ourselves and less for others. We are quicker to impeach others' motives and thus less willing to trust our fate to them.

When values conflict, there is no regular order. Clashes in American politics and the electoral systems that encompass them have historically been cyclical. Values collide, norms wane, tempers fray, and comity withers. Ultimately one side wins, and after a period of majoritarianism under which the new regime is established, people accept the new order and get along with each other once again. Ironically, the nation has undergone far more severe shock therapy in previous realignments than it has since the 1970s. The recessions of 1973–74, 1979, 1982, and 1991 hardly compared with the economic crises before the end of party systems in the antebellum years, the 1890s, and the 1920s. The social conflicts of the earlier periods far exceeded the current nastiness. There are few violent mass protests and much less random violence. Because incivility is tempered, it is more difficult to resolve. A high fever shakes a virus out of one's body; passionate politics wrenches the mania out of politics. The tempered discourtesy is like a low-grade fever that hangs on and defies a cure. The attempt to induce a realignment in the mid-1980s exacerbated conflicts.[4] The cross-cutting cleavages that shaped the 1970s have been overlaid by sharp partisan divisions. Support for the core values fell once more in the late 1980s, and social conflict has not let up. The loss of social cohesion had powerful effects on policy-making.

---

4. Ironically, the debate over tax reform was not as nasty as many other policy issues. The exceptions were largely intramural Republican affairs: criticism of the White House by COS members over the Reagan-O'Neill deal and a sharp exchange over transition rules between Senators Alan Simpson (R—Wyo.) and Ted Stevens (R—Ark.).

Chapter 6

Policy-Making in an Era of Resource Constraints

> We Americans have mostly believed in happy endings. . . . But now . . . our optimism has been wounded by the growing pessimism of public powerlessness, by the growing suspicion that government, the chosen instrument of our collective will, has been paralyzed by indifference, ineptness and the pervasive influence of special interests, as well as by a public debt that saps our confidence.
> —Mark Shields

Comity, more particularly the communitarian values it encompasses, helps overcome the collective action problems inherent in policy-making. Legislators want to make deals with each other, but each has incentives to defect to a more profitable, more narrowly based coalition. Trust holds them together. In good times legislators can accommodate more demands, so defection is not quite so tempting. Yet trust is in greater supply as well. When the future looks grim, legislators face more demands for protection but have fewer resources. Communitarian values ebb, so there are many reasons for collective action to collapse.

Confidence in others is hardly a sufficient condition for resolving collective action dilemmas. Communitarian values do not dictate any particular solution to policy problems. If the public mood does not support legislative initiatives, government will not be activist, as in the 1950s. Communitarian values need not be liberal. Both trust in people and conservativism spiked upward in 1980, providing the push for the adoption of the Reagan agenda of budget and tax cuts. When "self-interest rightly understood" is widely shared, the citizenry and its elected representatives will be more likely to take initiatives to solve pressing problems. There is a liberal tilt to communitarianism:

Trust in people and public mood are positively correlated (see table 4.2). The greatest spurt in legislative activity occurred in the 1960s, when both trust in people and liberalism were at their zenith. They are not identical, as the modest correlation (.405) shows.

When "self-interest rightly understood" gives way to a more egoistic individualism, the result is likely to be either stalemate or bad policy. Stalemate is easy to characterize, but what is bad policy? It is decision making based on nonnegotiable demands, without the benefit of deliberation. Loud voices make compromise difficult. Energy and the budget have been characterized by deadlock for two decades. Agriculture and the environment did not implode on themselves, but their politics became increasingly bitter. The legislative outcomes reflect these tensions. Agriculture price supports grew exponentially in the 1970s and especially the 1980s, often out of all proportion to demonstrated needs of farmers. The environment is a classical consensual issue but has become so polarized that the political stakes seem clearer than the ecological ones.

Congress has rarely been known for its policy initiatives. There have been periods when legislation seems to spew forth like a river freed from a burst dam (TRB 1966; Price 1972). These are not normal times. They require something resembling a mandate for a president and his party's oversized Congressional majority. The Congress has enacted some far-reaching nonincremental policy changes, ranging from civil rights to environmental protection to trucking and airline deregulation to reform of Social Security, immigration, and taxation. Much of this legislation was passed in the "new Congress." However, each measure was backed by either a national consensus or an absence of opposition (Uslaner 1989, 203–8).

Many other issues that have crowded the Congressional agenda since the 1970s have been far more contentious with no ready solutions. School prayer, gun control, abortion, drug control, energy, agriculture, comprehensive medical care, foreign policy, trade, and other impending resource crises such as water and even garbage crowd the Congressional agenda. The budget encompassed many of the conflictual issues, so it is hardly surprising that it was the most conspicuous aspect of legislative gridlock. Congress has never wanted for things to consider. Since the New Deal legitimized extensive government intervention in the economy, the legislature has been abuzz with new things for the government to do. The Congress is most likely to undertake major initiatives when communitarian values are high. The public mood and the partisan composition of the legislature matter too, but not quite so much as enlightened self-interest. Stalemate—on energy and the budget deficit—and bad policy—on agriculture and the environment—are more likely when confidence in others is low.

Good Policy, Bad Policy, and Stalemate

Good policy stems from deliberation and ideas. A problem and its solution are joined by an analytical argument, not just electoral threats. Parents clearly understand the distinction between reasoning (or trying to reason) with a child and giving in to tantrums. Legislative decision making is only slightly different. Good policy requires "public spiritedness" (Kelman 1987, 10). Legislators must adhere to a set of norms that encourage reciprocity, for without give-and-take, the benefits of exchanging ideas and the room for compromise are lost.

Denying the legitimacy of opposing viewpoints leads to a politics based on nonnegotiable demands and threats. When legislators respond to such threats, policy-making loses its moral force, its claim to be based on general principles. Policy advocates need not seek consensus, nor must they be altruists. They ought to present their views forcefully, but if they maintain that opposing perspectives are illegitimate, they risk the same charge about their own.[1] A civil environment depends on reciprocity, which depends on bargaining, compromising, and coalition formation (Eulau 1977, 22).

Civility need not depend on some concept of the public interest but only some tilt toward generality, toward a breadth of view. This might mean nothing more than reasonableness. It certainly excludes the sort of self-centeredness encompassed by nonnegotiable demands and threats. Breadth of view means going beyond mere interests to justifiable interests, to the merging of ideas and advantage. Good policy must be based on some ethical justification, so that those who do not benefit directly can nevertheless understand and empathize

---

1. This characterization of deliberation is an amalgam of Kelman (1987, 10, 22, 34, 208, 212); Bessette (1983, 3, 5); Nagel (1987, 232); and Fisher and Ury (1983, 93).

with the decision. These outsiders must trust the decision in the same way that they have faith in those who chose the policy.

When good will is missing, the result will likely be stalemate or bad policy. When legislators are split into two camps, one will have a majority and will usually be able to prevail. More commonly, legislators will have diverse preferences among a wider range of alternatives. No policy proposal can command a majority against all others. Diverse interests can form a "destructive coalition of minorities" to defeat any alternative on the table (Oppenheimer 1973; Uslaner 1989, chap. 2). Stalemate ensues.

If an issue area attracts only a narrow range of interests or one bloc is advantaged over others, stalemate is unlikely and bad policy more probable. Narrow interests often do not attract substantial opposition. When they stand alone, it is easier to assert their right to special treatment. Once that claim is accepted, entreaties spiral out of all proportion to either actual need or to the group's political clout. The steeper the demands, ironically, the more likely they are to be met. Risk-averse politicians find it difficult to reject ultimatums.

Oil as a Sticky Wicket

Energy since the 1970s and the budget politics of the 1980s and 1990s have led to stalemate. Agriculture and the environment in recent years are examples of what I call bad policy. While these four policy areas might not be typical of all issues from the 1970s through 1990s, all are central to the national political agenda. The story of their pathologies ties in directly with a more polarized environment.

Energy was the issue of the 1970s, and it marked the beginning of the contemporary era of nasty politics.[2] Motorists in gas lines during the 1973–74 and 1979–80 embargoes came armed with pistols to punish those who refused to wait their proper turn. The Congress was used to finding new energy sources so that consumers would pay less; from time to time, the legislature would regulate prices at the behest of producers to prevent profits from falling through the floor. In the 1970s the legislature had a rude welcome to the age of resource constraints. Supplies fell, prices skyrocketed. After years of

---

2. The following discussion is based on Uslaner (1989).

treating each fuel as a specific policy area, Congress now found coal, oil, natural gas, electricity, and nuclear power confronting each other with conflicting demands. All of a sudden Presidents Nixon, Ford, and Carter insisted on national energy policies. The Congress did not know how to handle this hot potato, so highly salient to so many interests. Not surprisingly, it dropped it.

Congress proclaimed an energy policy in 1977, but not until a destructive coalition of minorities had emasculated Carter's proposed legislation. Three years later the legislature enacted a massive synthetic fuels bill that resembled more a pork barrel bill than a national energy strategy. That program fell apart a few years later when fuel from rocks and slate once more proved far too expensive to be practical and far too dirty to replace even coal.

When natural gas prices soared in the early 1980s, Reagan proposed deregulation of that fuel, while a bipartisan group in Congress sought to reinstitute expired ceilings. Both sides lost by margins of two to one. The traditional producer-consumer division became exquisitely complex on the gas issue. Interstate pipelines were villains to both, as well as to intrastate pipelines; major and independent producers were badly divided. The major players could not even agree who had power and who did not. I asked a sample of the central groups with whom they worked; 60 percent of interest group respondents gave answers that were not reciprocated (cf. Salisbury et al. 1987). This is the perfect recipe for a destructive coalition of minorities.

Energy issues in the 1970s and early 1980s were highly salient to legislators' constituents. Although the many questions involved in gas deregulation were invisible to the public, the costs of decontrol were not. Sacrifices were central to the conflict. The losers would bear costs, and they lobbied vigorously not to have to pay them. There was no simple majority for any proposal, and none of the parties was willing to compromise, much less give in, on any of the issues. Many issues in the 1970s and 1980s were so ensnared. Resource scarcity issues came to the fore and threatened to impose costs on people. There was no willingness to bear the costs, nor was there even a viable coalition that could impose them on others. No proposal could get anywhere near majority support in the country or in the Congress, where 83 committees and subcommittees in the House alone handled some aspect of energy policy. The wide range of cross-cutting perceptions of the problem and the solutions gave virtually every actor (and many committees and subcommittees) effective veto power.

Energy is just the most prominent of resource constraint issues. A water crisis is looming, especially in the West. Americans have been accustomed to cheap and unlimited water, just as they have with energy. Parts of the West already ration water; California faced a severe crisis in 1991, threatening cuts of up to 75 percent to farmers (Reinhold 1991). By the late 1990s half of U.S. municipalities will run out of landfill space. Richer states now ship their excess refuse to poorer ones, but there is increasingly no room at their sites. There was 80 percent more garbage in 1988 than in 1960, with an additional 20 percent forecast by 2000; costs to some communities are expected to increase by more than 500 percent (Kurtz 1987; Shabecoff 1987b and 1988).

The water and garbage crises remain localized. Congress has shied away from tackling them. There is little reason to believe that it would perform much better on these resource scarcity issues than it did on energy. Indeed, Congressional performance on the savings and loan crisis, now expected to cost at least $500 billion, offers little cause for optimism that legislators can untangle a web of cross-cutting cleavages. Oil and water used to mix very well in the pork barrel. Western legislators sought to dam the torpedoes and anything else that moved; Easterners sought sewer grants so that suburbia could grow with the flow. Garbage was out of sight and out of mind once the trucks hauled it away twice a week. The imposition of real costs changed all of this. Energy, traditionally a sign of American abundance, was the first crack in the fault line of the politics of prosperity. The nastiness of energy conflicts spilled over to other issues, indeed to American politics. The energy crises were not the *cause* of the decline of trust; they certainly were its smoking guns.

Let's Get Fiscal

The budget deficit is the energy crisis writ large. The deficit sharply increased each year during the 1970s; the tax cuts and high levels of military spending in the 1980s took the deficiency to new heights. By 1988 it had reached $155.1 billion. Economists warned that the nation's economic health depended on reducing the deficit. The stock market crash in 1987 was said to be a warning signal much like a mild coronary, yet Congress could not cut the deficit. Energy was important for many groups, but a sideshow for others. The budget was central to everybody. The economic stakes, of course, were far greater. With so many actors with such diverse preferences, it is hardly surprising that there was no backbone to cut pet projects for some.

The 1974 budget reforms neither rationalized decision making nor cut the deficit. Congress has been less willing to pass the thirteen annual appropriations bills needed to keep the government functioning (Ellwood 1985). Like energy, the budget has been a scarcity issue in recent years. Members have had little room to expand spending as deficits have soared. There have been demands for dramatic cutbacks, and this has set legislators against each other. In 1986, 32 percent of respondents to an NBC News-*Wall Street Journal* poll said that the budget deficit was the most important issue in that fall's Congressional election campaign, yet substantial majorities opposed tax increases and cuts in any programs except defense (Shribman and Hume 1986). The deficit encompasses so many issues that no majority coalition can possibly form. The budget was an atypical resource constraint issue. Its costs were hidden, in part because of the magnitude of the problem and because "it is a crisis that can't be seen and whose ill effects are hard to isolate" (Mufson and Yang 1990, A17).

Budget politics in the post-1981 Reagan years was an elaborate minuet in which the president and Congress each proposed economic packages unacceptable to the other. Democrats and Republicans danced each year, tripping occasionally when the government shut down. President George Bush and the Democratic leaders in Congress strongly attacked each other in the fall of 1990. Public confidence in both declined. Shamed by pictures of tourists—some from as far away as China—stranded outside the national zoo and other monuments, the president and Congress agreed on a five-year plan that would cut the budget deficit by $500 billion, with immediate savings of $40 billion.

The package was a mixture of the taxes Bush had abjured since his 1988 campaign and the spending cuts resisted by Democrats. Savings would come from expenditures on defense ($9.8 billion), Medicare ($64 billion), and Medicaid ($2.8 billion), as well as higher Medicare taxes ($14 billion), housing programs ($3.9 billion), agriculture ($14.3 billion), $.10 a gallon increases in energy taxes ($50.4 billion), a $.02 a gallon tax on home heating oil ($13.2 billion), increased levies on tobacco and liquor ($18.5 billion), and limiting itemized deductions for wealthier taxpayers ($18.5 billion) (Cranford 1990, 3198–99).

The plan had something to offend everyone. The public objected, often by overwhelming margins, to most of the provisions (table 6.1). Only sin taxes and levies aimed at higher income taxpayers, amounting to about a tenth of the total deficit reduction, had considerable support. The cuts in Medicare, energy taxes, and even a minor item such as a higher levy on airplane tickets drew top-heavy opposition. Even military spending came close to a draw. By a plurality, Americans thought the plan was unfair (47 percent to 44 percent); but by

TABLE 6.1. Public Attitudes toward Key Provisions of 1990 Budget Accord and Deficit Reduction Plan's Fairness

Provision	Favor	Oppose
Alcohol tax increase	77	20
Tax on luxury items	76	21
Cigarette tax increase	71	25
Eliminate deductions for returns over $100,000	54	42
Cut military spending	49	46
Cut aid to farmers	34	63[a]
Airplane ticket tax increase	30	63
Gasoline tax increase	26	72
Higher costs for Medicare recipients	15	83

Effects on	Fair	Unfair
Everyone	44	47
Wealthy	75	18
People like yourself	35	61
Middle class	32	63
Younger Americans	25	61
Poor	16	80
Elderly	13	83

Source: Yankelovich, Clancy, Shulman 1990a, 8–11, for all items other than aid to farmers, which comes from Times-Mirror Corporation (1990), p. 109.

[a]Opposition includes 50 percent favoring more spending on agriculture and 13 percent wanting expenditures to remain at the same level.

61 to 35 percent they felt it was unfair to people like themselves. Only the wealthy were seen to benefit.

The package was a perfect target for a destructive coalition of minorities. The opposition was an unlikely coalition of right and left. Liberals objected to cuts in Medicare and feared that the "sin" and energy taxes would put an unfair burden on lower-income people. Conservatives rebelled against any new taxes. Capitol Hill became an armed camp of lobbyists. The elderly raised their voices against Medicare and Medicaid cuts; farm groups warned of the decline of American agriculture; beer companies feared that their lower-income clientele would soak up more of the sin tab than the Dom Perignon crowd; oil producers warned that energy taxes would also hit the poor and middle class particularly hard.

The Congress listened and a destructive coalition formed on the House floor on October 5. Liberals and conservatives—including Gingrich, the assistant minority leader—ganged up against the middle; the plan lost, 179 to 254 (Hager 1990b). The most electorally secure legislators voted for the agreement; those with close races ahead bolted in large numbers.[3] When the president and Congressional leaders called on legislators to impose costs, even if modest ones, on their constituents, a collective action problem arose. There were 115 detailed arguments opposed to the agreement and 59 in favor of it in the House debate.[4] Each claim was classified as either collective or individualistic, insofar as the reasoning reflected self-interest or some modicum of communitarian sentiment (table 6.2). Supporting statements were overwhelmingly collective (fifty-five of fifty-nine). Legislators favoring the accord stressed a sense of responsibility (seventeen), a need to restore faith in the system (eleven), better fiscal policy (eleven), and the health of the economy (nine). A handful of members stressed either specific programs or district support. All but fifteen of the opposing arguments were individualistic. Members opposed tax increases (twenty), Medicare cuts (eighteen), provisions that would hurt the lower or middle classes (thirteen), gas taxes (ten), and provisions that would affect the elderly or disabled (twelve).

3. Elving et al. (1990, 3443) report that 46 percent of safe Democrats and 42 percent of safe Republicans voted for the agreement, compared to 16 and 27 percent of Democrats and Republicans classified as nonsafe. These numbers translate to a phi coefficient of .18 and $Q = .52$.

4. Nalini Verma performed the content analysis under my guidance.

TABLE 6.2. Collective Action and the House Budget Debate

Statements in Support of Bipartisan Budget Agreement

Collective		Individualistic	
Congressional responsibility	17	Protects Social Security	1
Promotes faith in system	11	Protects low income programs	1
Better fiscal policy	11	Gives more to transportation	1
Good for economy	9	District favors plan	1
Spending cuts worthwhile	3		
Need to compromise	2		
Deficit threatens Desert Shield operation	2		
Total	55	Total	4

Statements in Opposition to Bipartisan Budget Agreement

Collective		Individualistic	
Fairness	5	Oppose tax increases	20
Harms economy	3	Medicare cuts	18
Does not address deficit	3	Hurts lower/middle classes	13
Spending does not decrease	2	Gas taxes	10
Accord is "un-American"	2	Unfair to elderly/disabled	12
		Benefits wealthy	9
		Defense cuts	6
		Unemployment checks delayed	3
		Agriculture cuts	3
		Education cuts	3
		Might lead to furloughs	1
		Hurts wine industry	1
		Unfair to Arkansas	1
Total	15	Total	100

Classifying arguments as collective or individualistic does not cast judgment on the moral positions of the claimants. Even if we reclassify class arguments, the balance would not be affected. The refusal of major interests to seek a solution to the budget deficit doomed the bipartisan accord.[5] The defeat emboldened Democratic leaders in Congress, who pressed for a "more fair" budget agreement. By late in the month, the president and Congress had agreed to a less comprehensive package that shifted the burden away from Medicare and toward the wealthy. Both sides read the polls: Americans were very pessimistic in October, 1990, and not very pleased with the performance of their leaders. Only 1 percent believed that the state of the economy was very good, and just 29 percent said it was fairly good; 42 percent replied fairly bad, and 25 percent very bad. Two percent thought the economy was getting better; 69 percent felt it was deteriorating. Nineteen percent of Americans believed the country was "on the right track," compared to 79 percent who said the United States was "on the wrong track."

Confidence in Congress sank to 30 percent; 61 percent were negative. Bush's popularity fell from 61 percent in early October to 53 percent late in the month. By 54 to 38 percent the electorate disapproved of the president's handling of the deficit. Its view of Congress was even more negative: 71 percent unfavorable to 21 percent positive. Just 12 percent of Americans believed the budget impasse was based on real differences between Bush and Congress on the issues; 75 percent felt both sides were simply jockeying for political advantage (Yankelovich, Clancy, Shulman 1990a; CBS News press 1990b and 1990c; Morin and Taylor 1990; NBC News 1990f). With confidence in institutions and leaders plummeting and an election just a few weeks away—and incumbent legislators were stuck in Washington rather than back home campaigning—both sides had strong incentives to appear communitarian.

But not too communitarian. The president and Congress ostensibly made deep cuts in the budget ($42.5 billion in fiscal 1991, almost $500 billion over five years) while imposing limited costs on most constituents. The Medicare cuts, reduced from $60 billion to $43 billion, would hurt doctors and hospitals more than the politically powerful elderly. Cuts in veterans' benefits were minimized (*New*

---

5. Legislators from both parties whose reelection was not secure were most likely to vote against the pact (Jacobson 1992b).

York Times, 1990). The hike in gasoline taxes was halved. The slashed agriculture budget was a divide and conquer game, pitting some farmers who would gain against others who would lose (see below). Even the fairness issue, which so energized Congressional Democrats seeking to "soak the rich," proved to be much rhetoric, as wealthy taxpayers were likely to get off fairly lightly (Wool 1990).

The new bipartisan accord accomplished far less than its advocates could admit. The Congressional Budget Office admitted that the fiscal 1991 deficit would jump substantially from fiscal 1990 levels even with the accord—and without any costs of a recession or a potential war with Iraq. The 1992 deficit would likely be almost $100 billion more than that for 1990, assuming an extraordinary 3.8 percent growth rate, lower oil prices, and the lowest interest rates since 1977 (Morgan and Pincus 1990). Since the budgeteers eliminated the automatic cuts that led to their collective embarrassment, future deficits were likely to explode (Hager 1990c).

Neither party trusted the other to commit to a binding agreement. The soaring deficits reflect a less trusting environment more than institutional forces. Divided control does not drive the deficit up,[6] nor does the party of the president, the relative shares of House seats, or the liberalism of the mass public. Faith in other people matters. To increase the number of cases I devised an estimate of trust that permits an examination of budget deficits from 1957–88 (see table 6.A in the appendix to this chapter).[7] Controlling for the previous

---

6. McCubbins (1991) found that one form of divided control—when Republicans held the White House and control of Congress was divided between a Republican Senate and a Democratic House—strongly affected the real deficit from 1929 to 1988. His two other measures of divided control—Democratic president and Republican Congress, Republican president and Democratic Congress—were not significant predictors of the deficit. I estimated the model below with McCubbins's Republican president/split Congress variable added to the model in table 6.3; it was significant at $p < .001$; all other variables except the share of Senate Democrats remained highly significant. I do not include McCubbins's variable in my model because I see no theoretical justification for treating divided control of Congress differently from split authority in the legislative and executive branches—especially as the deficit is now ballooning under ordinary divided control.

7. I estimated trust from the generalized least squares regression analysis in table 6.A in the appendix to this chapter. The results were very satisfactory ($R^2 = .898$). Where the actual values of trust were available, I employed those; see Franklin (1990). The estimated values were substituted when data were missing. Since the charitable contributions series ends in 1984, there is no estimate for 1985 (or 1986, when lagged). Employing this instrumental variable technique increases the number of cases from nineteen to thirty-two for the deficit, from sixteen to seventeen for agriculture price

values of the deficit, every one percent decrease in trust in others is associated with an increased deficit of $2.9 billion the next year. The impact of trust in others is lagged rather than immediate (table 6.3). In contrast, 1 percent more distrusting government costs $1.4 billion the next year.[8]

Inflation drives down the deficit, as does the number of Democrats in the Senate. High inflation indicates a stimulated economy, with correspondingly swollen tax revenues and lower deficits. The high deficit years largely corresponded with GOP control of the Senate. Communitarian values matter, while the public's ideology does not.[9] The lag in the effects of trust in people reflects normal budgetary politics: This year's deficit reflects decisions made last year—and sometimes even longer ago. The deficit is less an ideological fight than a struggle over collective action, although the strong impact of Senate Democrats suggests that elite opinions matter.

TABLE 6.3. Determinants of Budget Deficits in the United States, 1957–1989

Variable	Coefficient	Standard Error	t
Constant	−284.381	55.524	−5.122**
Lagged deficit	.728	.065	11.143**
Estimated trust (lagged)	2.917	.813	3.588**
Inflation	2.702	1.053	2.565*
Senate Democrats	194.432	52.993	3.669**

$N=32$, $R^2=.940$, SEE$=20.510$, and rho$=-.370$.
*$p<.01$ **$p<.001$.
Note: 1986, when there is no estimate of lagged trust, is omitted.

---

supports, and from fourteen to seventeen for major laws adopted. The regressions all yield highly significant results for trust for the smaller samples. Most critically, extending the last analysis by three Congresses permits an examination of part of the Eisenhower administration, which has a different dynamic.

8. Higher deficits are coded as negative numbers. All figures are in real 1982 dollars. The correlation of public mood with the deficit ($N=34$) is .212. Trust in people and distrust of government are lagged by one year. The simple correlations with the deficit are .627 for trust in people ($N=19$) and −.407 for distrust of government ($N=11$). The estimate of the impact for distrust of government comes from a regression with the same other predictors as trust in people. Despite the small sample, the coefficient for distrust of government is significant at $p<.025$, while that for trust in people is significant at $p<.001$. The coefficient for inflation is significant at $p<.001$ and that for Senate Democrats at $p<.01$. The lagged deficit is significant at $p<.001$. Had not trust in others rebounded in 1984, the relationship would have been much stronger.

9. The correlation between the real budget deficit and the public mood is .212 ($N=34$).

How're You Going to Keep Them Down and Out on the Farm After They've Seen D.C.?

The 1980s were the decade of sky-high deficits and farm failures. They were also the decade of movies about the agriculture crisis featuring Sissy Spacek, Jessica Lange, and Sally Fields and of exploding farm subsidies to prevent foreclosures because of natural (drought) and human (mismanagement) disasters. The U.S. government spent $133.5 billion in farm subsidies in the 1980s. Some members of Congress felt that sheep growers were pulling the wool over their unsuspecting colleagues' eyes by collecting $100 million in subsidies a year (Hershey 1990).

Even as the farm economy rebounded from its troubles and the Congress and the White House sought to limit subsidies, payments remained high by historic levels and sometimes even increased (Robbins 1987; Schneider 1990a). Farmers have received federal assistance since 1933. Subsidies were designed to protect farmers against wide spreads of profits and losses (Schneider 1990b). When the first supports were enacted, the United States still had a large rural population: about a quarter of Americans lived on farms (Joint Economic Committee 1987, 123). Until 1940 a majority of members of the House came from districts with farm populations of 20 percent or more. In the rest of the country the "yeoman myth" idolizing the farmer was strong (Hofstadter 1955a, chap. 1).

The farm bloc has faced many internal squabbles but could count on the support of urban and suburban legislators and organized labor in Congress until the late 1950s, when just 12 percent of all House seats had a significant agricultural base. Agriculture was the third largest item in the federal budget. The farm bloc was battered in the late 1950s, but the urban-rural coalition was reestablished in 1964 when the bloc agreed to support food stamps (Ferejohn 1986).

Agricultural expenditures had been rather modest before the mid-1970s. The 1960s and early 1970s were boom years for farmers. In 1960 farm income was only 60 percent of urban earnings; by 1973 it had surged to 150 percent of the national average (Robbins 1990). Exports surged in the 1970s through sales to the Soviet Union and to third world nations with expanding economies. In return for export limitations on soybeans, subsidies increased in the 1970s (Rapp 1987b).

Price supports were modest until the 1970s. The economic disruptions of that decade changed the politics of abundance to one of scarcity. Unlike energy, food supplies were not limited. They were increasingly plentiful throughout the United States and the world. The bounty put pressure on small farmers who could not easily compete with high-tech agribusiness at home. Greater harvests throughout the world meant increasing competition for U.S. producers. Exports plunged from an all-time high of $44 billion in 1981 to $26 billion in 1986. American farmers lost substantial market shares in wheat, feed grains, and soybeans (Schneider 1986). Farm debt soared to over $200 billion in 1982–84.

Farm foreclosures became common, the grist for movies such as *Places in the Heart*. In 1986 one-third of Iowa farmers faced foreclosure; other states had smaller numbers, but an estimated 5 percent of all farmers were unable to finance their spring planting. Over 400 farms went out of business every day. The United States, which had not had an unfavorable balance of farm trade since 1971, reported a record agricultural deficit in 1985 (Sinclair 1986). The Farm Credit System, which is responsible for a third of farmer-financed lending, required a federal bailout of $6 billion in 1987 to prevent collapse (Sinclair 1987; Schneider 1987).

Subsidies exploded in the mid-1970s and the 1980s as the farming community was shrinking. By 1988 only 2 percent of Americans were farmers. Just forty-six Congressional districts were farm-oriented. In such districts at least one-third of counties derive 20 percent or more of their total income from agriculture (Nelson 1990, 3). By 1989, 82 percent of growers of crops such as wheat, corn, and rice received subsidies; these payments now represent almost 32 percent of these farmers' family incomes compared to 8.1 percent in 1980 (Cloud 1990a). Payments to corn, wheat, and rice growers grew from 7 percent of the crops' values in 1980 to 57 percent in 1986; subsidies represented 40 percent of net cash income for farmers in 1986 compared to 6 percent six years earlier (Rapp 1987a, 304). Despite the cinematic portrayal of the family farmer facing foreclosure, which created much public sympathy for the plight of the tillers of the soil, these payments were highly skewed. Only 1 percent of the farmers, those with sales over $500,000 a year, received 13 percent of all subsidies (Robbins 1987). Almost four-fifths of all payments go to just one-fifth of the farmers, mostly large producers with incomes much greater than the average nonfarmer (Runge 1988, 138; Nelson 1990, 5).

Federal subsidies did little to quell the stirrings on the hustings. Politics, as well as life, got nastier. Even as the national crime rate was declining, arson, suicides, and other offenses increased in the farm belt and the similarly depressed oil patch (Associated Press 1986; Reinhold 1986a and 1986b; Robbins 1986b). Suicide rates of rural adolescents were fifteen times the national average; clinical depression among Nebraska farm families doubled between 1981 and 1986, while Oklahoma reported a 143 percent rise in farmers seeking treatment for alcoholism in 1987 (Gugliotta 1990). Troubles in the farm belt were also linked to support for candidates backed by right-wing extremist Lyndon LaRouche in an Illinois primary election in 1986 (Malcolm 1986).

Agriculture receives more federal support relative to its contribution to the economy than any other sector of the American economy (Nelson 1990, 2). What sustained the agriculture coalition, which on its face should be unstable? The idealization of the farmer played no small role, but so did the nature of the program. The scope of conflict was restricted. Agriculture interests were not united, but the nay-sayers were effectively outvoted by a reasonably cohesive group of benefit seekers. Even the dairy interests eventually sought government assistance, ranging from price supports to import limitations to marketing orders restricting competition (Derthick and Quirk 1985, 229). Most critically, there were few dissenting voices outside the agriculture community. The costs of the program were not apparent either (Hansen 1987, 9).

The wellspring of goodwill the Americans have for farmers complicates any attempt to upset agricultural price supports. By margins of more than four to one, Americans support federal assistance to farmers. Five of six in 1986 believed that half or more of American farmers faced "serious economic problems." Americans also have idealistic views of rural life: Half say that they would like to live on a farm. Most Americans see farmers as more moral and honest than others (Robbins 1986a; Clymer 1986). This idealization of the small farmer permits the agriculture bloc to raise the stakes continually. So does farmers' political volatility. They are more likely than most other voting blocs to shift their partisan allegiances and to reward politicians who support their goals (King 1983). Farmers also vote more frequently than most other groups (Wolfinger and Rosenstone 1980, 32–33).

Both inside and outside observers have noted the farm bloc's strategy of demanding exceptionally high payoffs. Cloud (1990b, 1468) stated that legislators from farm states "are desperately trying to control their own weaknesses for increasing agriculture spending." Representative E. "Kika" de la Garza (D—Tex.), who chairs the House Agriculture Committee, admitted, "We have promised policies we do not have money for" (Cloud 1990b, 1468). In 1986 government subsidies for rice exceeded the value of the crop (Rapp 1987a, 304). The Department of Agriculture spent $566 million to export food at a loss and $3.3 billion to induce farmers to leave their land idle. James Brovard (1990), a conservative critic of farm policy, estimates that taxpayers and consumers subsidize farmers by $40 billion a year, including all direct and indirect subsidies.

Farm policy, unlike energy and the budget, did not result in stalemate. Instead, the farm bloc responded to an ever-worsening economy with ever more strident demands, and legislators did not resist pressures for high levels of price supports. Even as farm income rebounded in the late 1980s, support levels did not revert to their earlier levels before the 1982 surge. Farm policy did not simply respond to need but to political pressure and thus was anything but communitarian.

Subsidies ought to rise when farm income falls, especially relative to the rest of the society. Farm income, an indicator of need, is measured as the ratio of farm income to average income. Divided control, the share of Democrats in the House and Senate, and the president's party do not affect the level of price supports, yet trust in others does, controlling for the previous year's price support level and inflation (table 6.4).[10] The impact is strongest for farm income parity, lagged one year, and trust in others: A .10 drop in relative

---

10. The institutional variables have moderate correlations with price supports, but the impacts vanish once controls for farm income parity, trust in others, and public mood are employed. The simple correlation of distrust of government and price supports is $-.20$, while that for the public mood is .10. The effect of trust in people is contemporaneous (not lagged). The statistical significance of the variables ranges from $p < .001$ for lagged supports to $p < .0025$ for estimated trust to $p < .025$ for lagged income parity to $p < .05$ for inflation. Richard Pazdalski of the Department of Agriculture provided the data on price supports and Katherine H. Reichelderfer of Economics Research Service the data on relative farm income.

income leads to a rise in subsidies of $921 million, while a similar drop in trust increases price supports by $716 million. The coefficient for trust in people is more stable, as the *t*-ratios indicate. Price supports do respond to economic need, but they also depend on interpersonal confidence.

Decreasing trust did not kill price supports. If anything, the more strident demands led to greater constituency benefits even in the face of budgetary strain. Not until the late 1980s did the reverse dynamics of the loss of trust hit the farm bloc. Subsidies decreased when the farm crisis began to ease but also when critics of spiraling payments became more vocal. Representative Dick Armey (R—Tex.), a COS member, has joined with Representative Charles E. Schumer (D—N.Y.), a leading liberal, to form a coalition of the right and the left to limit price supports. They tried to form an alliance with environmentalists against the farm bloc in 1990 but did not prevail. Public support for subsidies fell by 8 percent from 1987 to 1990, and agricultural assistance now ranks above only aid to minorities (Times-Mirror Corporation 1990, 109). Debate in Congress has shifted from how price supports help the consumer as well as the farmer to whether the agricultural sector is special.

The farm bloc ultimately was one of the few well-organized interests to lose badly in the 1990 budget agreement. Farm programs are slated to lose $13.6 billion over five years. The budget makers hit farming interests by giving benefits to some (wheat, oat, canola, and barley farmers) at the expense of the rest (Ingersoll 1990b). Inequities in price supports have led to grass roots splits in the farm bloc (Ingersoll 1990a). Because farmers began with such strong public support, they were able to maintain high price supports while other groups fared far worse. The cuts of the 1990 budget deal still leave

TABLE 6.4. Determinants of Agriculture Price Supports 1971–1988

Variable	Coefficient	Standard Error	t
Constant	46194.600	8831.440	5.231***
Lagged price supports	.609	.081	7.530***
Estimated trust	−715.970	178.361	−4.014**
Lagged income parity	−9218.570	3532.330	−2.610*
Inflation	−384.794	209.567	−1.836+

Note: 1985, when there is no estimate of trust, is omitted. $N=17$, $R^2=.916$, SEE = 3126.83, and rho = −.306.

***$p<.001$ **$p<.0025$ *$p<.025$ +$p<.05$

farmers with far greater subsidies than they had two decades ago; with budget deficits ready to seek new heights, there will be less pressure to single out agriculture for further cuts and more pressure in a presidential election year to reward farmers. The hue and cry against means testing for Social Security might ultimately save agribusiness from the left-right coalition that would restrict subsidies to the wealthy.

Clean Air, Dirty Politics

In contrast to agriculture, environmental policy has been, by most accounts, much more successful. The Clean Air Act Amendments of 1970 set standards that scientists did not know how to implement and that bureaucrats could not readily regulate (Jones 1975, chaps. 7–8), yet according to Vogel (1986, 156), "the United States has made measurable progress in reducing emissions and ground concentration levels of both particulates and sulfur oxides" so that "by 1980 almost all air pollution control regions had met the [Environmental Protection Agency's (EPA's)] primary standards for these two hazardous pollutants."

Automobile emissions have also dropped dramatically since 1970. Between 1977 and 1980 alone there was a 64 percent decline in ambient lead concentrations in a ninety-two-city survey. The number of days with unhealthy air pollution levels dropped by more than 50 percent (and even more for hazardous days) between 1974 and 1981. Water pollution control was not so successful. While two-thirds of the states reported "generally improving" water quality to EPA in 1982, Vogel (1986, 156–59) argues that ameliorations in rivers and streams have been offset by deteriorating lakes and reservoirs.

Americans are supportive of spending more on the environment. By margins as large as 65 percent to 22 percent they agree that "protecting the environment is so important that cost is no object" (May 1988). Devotion to this cause is so widespread that 46 percent claim to contribute money to environmental groups regularly or occasionally (as opposed to 43 percent responding rarely or never).[11] By

---

11. Clearly there is a collective action problem here, yet these responses might not be quite as untrustworthy as they seem: Only 8 percent claimed that they took part in meetings of environmental groups regularly; 12 percent said occasionally, 21 percent rarely, and 47 percent said never. The poll results reported in this paragraph were taken from press releases from NBC News (1990b and 1990c) for NBC-*Wall Street Journal* polls and from CBS News (1989b) for CBS-*New York Times* polls.

a margin of 84 percent to 11 percent, Americans say that pollution is a serious problem. No wonder that environmental regulation consumed almost 2 percent of U.S. gross national product in the mid-1970s through early 1980s (Vogel 1986, 169). Despite considerable evidence of progress, most Americans remain unconvinced that much has been done. Two-thirds believe that the environment is worse than in 1970; only 16 percent say that it has improved. Three-quarters believe air pollution has deteriorated, only 6 percent that it has gotten better. The figures for water quality are similar: 80 percent versus 8 percent. We are, in Wildavsky's (1979) words on medical care, doing better but feeling worse. Why?

Much of the explanation lies in the confrontational nature of environmental politics (Vogel 1986). There are conflicts among producers, citizen groups, and government in the United States and among business firms. Some environmentalists fight ranchers over federally subsidized grazing lands (Royte 1990) while others, as noted above, have taken an active role in agricultural policy. Groups that do not get their way in normal legislative-executive decision making take their cases first to the electorate and then to the courts.

Business initially resisted comprehensive environmental legislation. The environmental movement struck back in kind. It was, after all, Environmental Action with its "Dirty Dozen" campaign in 1970, not the New Christian Right, that engineered the use of campaign scorecards in election campaigns. Business interests, especially utilities and the automobile industry, not only command low public esteem but also have little credibility with the Congress since they have fought environmental legislation vociferously only to meet the standards anyway (Hager 1990a, 145-46).

In the Reagan era, business sought the effective dismantling of the EPA. Environmental organizations similarly "believe that they thrive on conflict and cannot successfully raise funds from their constituent groups without portraying the other side as an implacable foe" (Stanfield 1986a, 2765). Politics on this highly consensual area is also marked by loud voices and little real discourse. Does the greenhouse effect threaten the earth or is it much ado about little? Most people have little idea, in part because the issues are so technologically complex but also because neither side in the debate really talks to the other. Eighty percent of Americans agreed in 1990 that "there are so many contradictory things said about the environment that it is sometimes confusing to know what to do" (Yankelovich, Clancy, Shulman 1990b).

Environmental politics increasingly moves beyond the routine channels of the legislature and even the courts. Activists who found normal politics unsatisfying have placed many referenda on California state ballots. Groceries must indicate which of their products might have adverse impacts on health. Environmentalists attempted a more wide-ranging ban on all pesticides found to cause cancer in laboratory animals as part of an omnibus "Big Green" proposition that would also protect redwoods, prohibit offshore oil drilling, and tax oil companies to pay for future oil spills. Scientists disputed each other's claims, charging the other side with "hysteria" (Mathews 1990, A5). The confused California electorate, perhaps the nation's most environmentally conscious, rejected the referendum. The highly popular Endangered Species Act has come under fire by timber interests in Oregon and landowners in California who fear major job losses to protect the spotted owl and the gnatcatcher; in a recession, the environmentalists no longer have the upper hand (Davis 1992). More radical activists forsake the political process entirely. Earth First often pursues violent tactics to protect older trees, especially redwoods, against loggers (Gabriel 1990).

Must we fight so dirty? Even when our policy instruments achieve reasonably lofty goals, we cannot seem to escape from the incessant name-calling and threats that typify stalemate and bad policy. The president and Congress finally reached agreement on an extension and expansion of the Clean Air Act in 1990, but not before the conference committee endured a shouting match between House and Senate members (Weisskopf 1990).

We can get away with such high volume politics when there is consensus on proposed solutions and when the costs of programs are effectively hidden from public view. Even then, as the case of agriculture shows, we can adopt policies with outcomes (large expenditures that do not benefit the target groups) that public opinion would not support. The environment is an example of an issue area where the substantive outcomes appear desirable but the process corrupt. The process has the potential to disrupt progress on substance, as the California "Big Green" campaign demonstrates. Each side cries "wolf." Business does so because it is outnumbered by a very supportive public. Environmentalists do so because strong-arm tactics often work. Earth First has made saving the redwoods a public issue and has dragged more mainstream organizations such as the Sierra Club into the fray (Gabriel 1990, 62). Traditional environmental lobbies have been pulled in two ways. Some have emphasized bargaining with business interests and focused their attention on gaining clout in Washington. They are scorned by the more aggressive actors who disdain compromise and have dragged some formerly quiet organizations with them (Arrandale 1992). The organizations that shun confrontational tactics lost clout when business interests became more assertive in their opposition to environmental regulations during the Reagan and Bush years (Schneider 1992). The hushed voices were buffeted from both the left and the right.

The lesson of "Big Green" is that contentiousness can backfire, perhaps ultimately threatening the broad basis of public support on a wider range of environmental issues. Bad politics destroys consensus. It also leads to demands that, like "Big Green," might not be so worthy—or at least not obviously so. If the best drives out the good, what does the bad drive out?

Trust and the Policy Agenda

Civility also affects the larger picture. Four policy areas are interesting, but it is unclear how representative they are. Mayhew (1991), seeking to determine whether divided control limits effective governance, has tabulated the major policy innovations enacted from 1946 to 1990. He demonstrates that unified party control does not make a difference, but two other factors do make a significant difference in Congress's capacity to enact "important laws": More initiatives are enacted in the first two years of a president's term and during the "activist mood" from 1961 to 1976 (Mayhew 1991, 177).

Mayhew's measure, a count of nonincremental initiatives adopted, does not distinguish the importance of bills considered. It also makes no ideological distinctions among laws. Yet, as an aggregate measure, it is well-suited for an examination of communitarianism. If Congress enacts legislation in bursts, what accounts for such cycles? Is the partisan balance and the party of the president the central factor, or is there something more?

From the 89th to the 93rd Congress (the mid-1960s to the mid-1970s), Congress enacted between sixteen and twenty-two major laws.

From the 96th to the 99th Congress (1979–86), it passed between seven and nine such bills. As with the budget deficit and agricultural price supports, neither the party of the president nor the Democrats' share of House seats predicts policy innovations. The aggregate numbers suggest that the 1960s through the mid-1970s did represent an activist mood. But what is an activist mood? It is neither the public commitment to liberalism nor confidence in government.[12]

The condition for an activist mood is communitarianism, trust in people. When trust is high, people recognize their obligations to other members of the society and are more willing to support the enactment of policies that meet others' needs. I aggregate faith in others to the level of the Congress (see table 6.5). Trust does not have uniform effects for the entire period as it did for the deficit and for price supports. In the 1950s trust was high and stable (from 53 to 58 percent), yet neither the Eisenhower administration nor the Democratic Congress (after 1955) pursued an activist program. The 84th and 86th Congresses enacted fewer major laws than any other from 1947 onward. I thus constructed two measures of estimated trust, one for the 84th through 86th Congresses and the other for the 87th through 100th Congresses.[13] The impact of trust in the later period, when trust began high and sunk sharply, was 1.6 times as

TABLE 6.5. Determinants of the Adoption of Major Laws, 84th–100th Congresses, 1955–1988

Variable	Coefficient	Standard Error	t
Constant	−24.608	6.699	−3.674**
Estimated trust 84th–86th	.567	.123	4.588***
Estimated trust 87th–100th	.836	.148	5.652***
Unified party control	−3.479	1.644	−2.116**
Start of administration	2.401	1.671	1.437*

Note: $N=17$, $R^2=.767$, $SEE=2.978$, and $rho=-.150$.
***$p<.10$ **$p<.05$ *$p<.0005$

---

12. From the 86th Congress (1959–60) to the 101st (1989–90), the correlation between liberalism (aggregated to the Congress) and policy innovations is .055; the relationship between distrust of government and policy innovation is −.244. The relationships with a dummy variable for Republican presidents and the Democrats' share of House seats are −.151 and .264, respectively.

13. For estimated trust for the 84th through 86th Congresses, I employed the aggregated values for those three Congresses, setting the remaining cases at zero. For the measure for the 87th through 100th Congresses, I employed the aggregated measures for those Congresses and set the 84th through 86th at zero.

great as during the three Eisenhower Congresses. Each 10 percent increase in trust led to half a law in the earlier period but to almost a full one (.836) in the later period. These results are highly significant (each $p < .0005$).

The dynamic changed after the 1950s. Neither trust in government nor the public's mood accounts for variations in the number of important laws enacted. Nor do internal variables such as Conservative Coalition strength in the House or Senate or the percentage of House or Senate Democrats. Trust seems to account for much of the activist mood, but its effects are not uniform across time. In the Eisenhower years, there were fewer demands for major policy innovations than during either the Democratic *or* Republican administrations of the 1960s and 1970s.

The first two years of an administration produce 2.4 additional laws, while unified party control yields almost 3.5 fewer innovations. While divided government might not matter for the entire period of Mayhew's analysis, it was important—in an almost perverse way— from the Eisenhower administration onward: Congress was more productive during the first Nixon administration than it was in the Kennedy and Carter years.

When we think of bursts of policy innovation, we are drawn to the 89th Congress (1965–66), which enacted the widest range of social welfare legislation in American history following one of the greatest landslides in American politics. The 89th Congress enacted Medicare, the Voting Rights Act, open housing, child nutrition programs, expanded aid to education, antipollution standards, the Teacher Corps, Food for Peace, truth in packaging, $7.8 billion in housing assistance, Appalachian development, and automobile safety legislation (*Congressional Quarterly* 1969, 3–5). After Lyndon B. Johnson's presidency, the next Congress in which there was unified party control was Jimmy Carter's 95th (1977–78). Its first session was marked by "an unusually uncompromising mood" (*Congressional Quarterly* 1978, 11). The House and the Senate of the second session were "unmanageable institutions" driven by "a public mood that seldom showed a consensus on major issues because of narrow self-interests" (*Congressional Quarterly* 1979, 3).

The 89th Congress, by Mayhew's tally, enacted twenty-one major laws, compared to only ten for the 95th. Trust in the early 1960s hovered around 50 percent or higher; in the mid-1970s it had dropped by five percentage points. Is communitarianism the answer, or did the record of the 89th Congress reflect the huge Democratic majorities in Congress? Democratic strength in the House could not make the difference, because Carter faced just three fewer Democrats than did Johnson. There were seven more Democrats in the 89th Senate; given the greater opportunities for obstructionism in that chamber, this is a likely source for the differences. Yet Senate Democrats were more loyal to Carter than they were to Johnson (table 6.6). The mean Presidential Support Score for Senate Democrats was six points higher in 1977 than it was in 1965 (the first sessions of the two Congresses) and nine points higher in 1978 than in 1966. Republicans were about as supportive in each Congress in both the House and the Senate, while House Democrats backed Johnson more strongly in 1965 than Carter in 1977 (but not in 1966 compared to 1978).

If we multiply the average support scores by the number of senators from each party in each chamber, we can derive a measure of the president's base support. Johnson had a higher base in the House in both Congresses, though not by much in the second session. He had expected working majorities. In the Senate, where Carter faced fewer Democrats, he nevertheless had a stronger base—by four votes in each session. The extraordinary record of the 89th Congress cannot simply be attributable to the Democrats' overwhelming majorities. The 91st (1969–70) and 93rd (1973–74) Congresses were, by Mayhew's count, as productive as the 89th with substantially reduced Democratic majorities and an often hostile Republican president (Nixon). Interpersonal trust remained relatively high (approaching 50 percent) throughout the period; when it began to decline, so did the number of major laws passed.

Carter did not have Johnson's mandate; neither did either Nixon in his first term or the Congressional Democrats. Mandates depend on something more than numbers. They require a national mood that makes collective action possible. The strong party ties that produce mandates following realignments and when party systems are renewed (as in 1964) reflect coherent value systems, including enlightened self-interest, that sustain collective action. The weakened partisanship that crested in the mid- to late- 1970s mirrored the waning of values and norms that form the basis for collective action.

TABLE 6.6. Presidential Support in the Johnson and Carter Administrations

	Mean Presidential Support Scores				Presidential Base			
	House		Senate		House		Senate	
Year	Democrats	Republicans	Democrats	Republicans	Total	Democrats	Total	Democrats
1965	74	41	64	48	276	218	59	44
1966	63	37	57	43	238	186	53	39
1977	63	42	70	52	244	184	63	43
1978	60	36	66	41	227	176	57	41

Sources: *Congressional Quarterly* 1966, 991, and 1979 24-C.

Note: Entries in columns 2–5 are mean presidential support scores for representatives and senators. Entries in columns 7 and 9 are the products of mean support scores for each chamber multiplied by the number of Democrats in each chamber. Entries in columns 6 and 8 are the sums of this measure for Democrats and a similar measure for Republicans.

Policy and Civility

Did we always behave so poorly? Certainly the 1950s and 1960s had their share of bad, indeed awful, confrontations. The filibusters over civil rights, when Southerners read the telephone book into the *Congressional Record* twenty-four hours a day, were hardly clarion calls to reason. McCarthyism spoiled our national temper in the early 1950s. The 1950s and 1960s were periods of neglect of the environment. The Army Corps of Engineers strove to exclude environmental concerns (as well as concerned citizens) from its studies on dam construction (Maass 1951, 51–52). Senator Thomas Kuchel (R—Calif.) worried about air pollution in 1955, but he could only convince his colleagues to enact a $5 million annual appropriation for research. As late as 1960, Eisenhower still maintained that water pollution was an issue for the states alone (Sundquist 1968, 331, 347).

The United States moved to a more activist, comprehensive environmental program with the 1970 Clean Air Act. While most business interests opposed the law, the conflict did not demonstrate any of the bitterness of the environmental battles that would ensue. Many of the partisan battles that took place centered around jockeying for political credit between Nixon and his party, on the one hand, and the Congressional Democrats on the other. Each was trying to convey a message of "greener-than-thou" (Jones 1975, chap. 7). The Clean Air Act called for more pollution reduction than technology could provide (Jones 1975, chap. 8). Erstwhile opponents became energized to fight the new regulations (Vogel 1986), but this could not be the whole story, for it does not explain the level of hostility that marked not just energy but so many other issue areas.

Energy never was a consensual issue. Coal miners long fought with mine owners. Private and public utilities battled with each other. Oil and gas interests initially sought price controls to protect them from wide swings in prices (just as farmers did). Producers later argued that the regulations artificially held down their profits, just as consumers vociferously defended the price caps. Traditional politics on energy were left-right and often quite vocal. However, there was little overlap among the arenas of the various fuels. Nor did energy become a highly salient issue for most Americans until the first embargo of 1973. Before then, energy was abundant rather than scarce. There were periodic warnings of impending shortages, but like Godot, they never seemed to come (Uslaner 1989, chaps. 1, 5).

If the American bounty only encompassed one sector of the economy, it was agriculture. Farm price supports began during the New Deal to ensure that the bounty would continue. Throughout the 1950s and 1960s the level of agricultural supports divided both parties and commodities. The resulting compromise, which all seemed to accept, gave farmers modest levels of price supports, providing enough income to protect farmers from wide price swings in the market but not enough to make them rich (*Congressional Quarterly* 1965, 665). Budget deficits were also modest from 1953 to 1964. The average deficit was $4.4 billion (in actual dollars); the median was just $3.5 billion. Three times (1956, 1957, and 1960) the federal government actually ran a surplus. By 1988 the deficit had reached $155.1 billion. The ratio of deficits to expenditures averaged .06 from 1953 to 1964; in 1988 it was 0.13.[14]

The boom years of the 1960s raised expectations and brought new actors into the political fray. Confrontation worked. When resources became less abundant, this tactic became more widespread, even legitimate. The give-and-take that makes for compromise gave way to nonnegotiable demands. Nor was there the traditional alternative route to policy innovation following realignments—majoritarian government (Brady 1988; Sundquist 1973). Our policy predicament reflects our atrophied values.

---

14. These figures were either taken directly from or computed from *Congressional Quarterly* (1965 and 1990).

Appendix

TABLE 6.A. Regression for Estimated Trust Instrument

Variable	Coefficient	Standard Error	t
Constant	−31.771	28.191	−1.127
Charitable contributions	432.338	164.974	2.621**
Inflation	.496	.304	1.637*
Unemployment	−2.333	.736	−3.169***
Public mood	−.064	.241	−.269
Senate Democrats	14.032	20.938	.670
House Democrats	29.096	32.731	.889
Republican president	4.788	2.728	1.755*

Note: $N=16$, $R^2=.898$, $SEE=2.318$, and $rho=-.360$.
***$p<.10$ **$p<.025$ *$p<.01$

Chapter 7

A New Order in the New World?

> The fault, Dear Brutus, is not in our stars, but in ourselves.
> —William Shakespeare, *Julius Caesar*

We should not weep for the good old days. In many ways we are far better off today. Our less communitarian society is more tolerant than it was in the 1950s and 1960s. We are spared the witch-hunts of McCarthyism and the state-supported violence against minorities (particularly those who demonstrated for civil rights). We are wealthier than we were then, even if we are not collectively as well off as we were a few years ago.

We have lost—or at least misplaced—our faith that the future will be even better. We have tired of government and of ourselves. We have no national terror such as McCarthyism, but we have a multitude of lesser kamikaze movements that feed off each other's tactics in a way the anti-Communist fervor never did. Few movements mimicked McCarthy's tactics; many legislators who agreed with him ideologically disapproved of his tactics and shunned him (Rovere 1959, 135). The South's massive resistance to civil rights later in the decade demonstrated that even a trusting environment can be exclusionary, yet confidence in others outside the South gave the civil rights movement the support it needed to push through major legislation once the public mood had shifted in the next decade.

Even if we are better off now in many ways, we are far worse off in others. The fever pitch of our arguments crowds out real deliberation. The stratospheric budget deficits push out serious consideration of new policies at all, so that so much of our debate relies on how much we can no longer afford. If the market prevails, it is not because we have chosen the market in a strong debate between left and right. We do not choose much at all; we have insured our political and economic systems against choice. We can take solace that we are not alone—comity has declined elsewhere—but we should not be too sanguine. Structural reform does not seem to be the answer, and a realignment is not in sight.

I'm All Right, Jack?

Some see public spiritedness alive and well in American politics. Steven Kelman and Ronald Inglehart are among the optimists. Kelman looks back and finds that Congress has done much good; Inglehart looks forward, sees self-interest waning, and believes that the best is yet to be. Have I missed something?

Kelman (1987, 250-51) argues that the social welfare programs and health, safety, and environmental regulations of the 1960s and 1970s cannot reflect self-interest. Nor do the politics of deregulation in the late 1970s and the 1980s, the massive rollbacks in government spending in the 1980s, or tax reform in 1986. He is correct on the social legislation of the 1960s and early 1970s, as well as environmental and other regulations, yet the 1960s was a decade of greater trust and communitarianism in American politics. Kelman (1987, 295) admits as much. The 1970 Clean Air Act was enacted with far less acrimony than its 1990 extension. Yet business was not simply caught napping in 1970 and only later woke up to the legislation's consequences. Outside of a few issues such as civil rights, politics was less high-pitched than it is today. If campaigns were not more educational, they certainly were more civil and thus had the potential for discourse. There is now less respect for others, be they fellow legislators or opposition candidates. The benefits of holding one's fire are sharply reduced.

Inglehart finds striking increases in postmaterialist values throughout the Western and non-Western world in the 1970s and 1980s. These ideals call for giving people more say in governmental decisions, protecting freedom of speech, extending workplace democracy, making cities and countrysides more beautiful, and moving toward a society that is friendlier and less impersonal and where ideas count more than money (Inglehart 1990, 74-75). If things go well, he imagines, that "we could go on to heights still undreamed of, reaching a nobility a little lower than the angels" (Inglehart 1990, 433).

The United States is more postmaterialist than most European nations surveyed (Inglehart 1990, 93).[1] Espousing communitarian values is not the same thing as behaving cooperatively or even treating others civilly. The peace movement of the 1960s, after all, initiated the slogan, "Don't trust anyone over 30." Environmentalists initiated the use of scorecards in political campaigning and are now about as vociferous and nasty as other interests in American politics.

Like those advocating political correctness, today's citizens, groups, and legislators all take themselves too seriously. Each issue becomes a fight to the death. Republicans in the House do not seek to win a share of the pie, to cooperate with Democrats on some issues where there is a common bond. Today's enemy will be tomorrow's enemy. Recall H. R. Gross, the Iowa Republican who roundly attacked pork barrel spending. Yet he was widely admired and liked by his House colleagues. Gross did not take himself very seriously. He often made himself the butt of his barbs. In contrast, his contemporary successor as defender of the budget, Robert Walker, has gone out of his way to alienate other members, especially Democrats (Merry 1991). Republican House leader Michel, asked to supply anecdotes about the 1990 budget debate, replied, "Nothing is funny any more" (Kenworthy 1990, A25).

Ups and Downs of the Realignment Cycle

Realignment theory should make us hopeful. If our current malaise is part of a realignment cycle, we will ultimately work our way out of it, as we have many times before. A new regime of values and norms will emerge, policy-making will become more coherent (Brady 1988), and people will be nice to each other once the initial majoritarian phase of the new party system has passed. Even if our consensus has waned, it will come back. This optimistic scenario runs aground on timing. If a party system lasts a generation, we should be at the tail end of our second post–New Deal alignment, yet no new durable coalitions have emerged since the 1930s and none is in sight. We seem stuck at the trough of a cycle; realignments might no longer be reasonable expectations in American politics (Carmines and Stimson 1989; Shafer 1991b).

---

1. Only the Netherlands, West Germany, and Denmark rank higher. Great Britain is effectively tied with the United States.

Complex issues such as tax reform will not grab the attention or the zeal of a large number of people; "Easy" issues will. Consider two questions with realigning potential: race and abortion. Carmines and Stimson (1989) argue that the Democratic and Republican parties have become increasingly polarized on race since the 1960s; by the late 1980s, Republican leaders and followers were considerably more conservative on race than Democrats. The Republicans correspondingly gained strength among white voters, especially in the South. In the 1950s and 1960s the parties were not so polarized on race; the Republicans, the party of egalitarianism in the Civil War era, were sometimes positioned to the left of the Democrats. Even conservatives such as Senate Minority Leader Dirksen joined with Democrats to enact civil rights legislation.

In the past two and a half decades, not only has the old Northern consensus fallen apart, but racial divisions have reemerged. Whites believe that race relations have gotten better from 1986 to 1991 by a two to one margin; blacks say that they have gotten worse by identical figures. Half of whites, but just one quarter of blacks, believe that civil rights laws have led to discrimination against people who are not minorities (NBC News 1991b and 1991c).[2] Racial politics have gotten quite bitter, with the emergence of white supremacist candidates such as David Duke and calls for a separate black party (see also chap. 4). If the civil rights movement presaged the era of confrontational politics, it now typifies it.

The civil rights movement initially emphasized core American values, according to Cornel West; it is no longer perceived as a moral crusade but as the demands of a particular interest group (quoted in Applebome 1991, A1). Support for civil rights is part of the American tradition of egalitarianism. In the 1980s a backlash against egalitarianism emerged, pitting equality against individual initiative. Racial epithets dominated social and political discourse: 40 percent of New Yorkers said people they knew regularly used racial slurs (WCBS-TV and *New York Times* 1991).

Yet racial politics did not produce a realignment (Carmines and Stimson 1989). The gains of the 1960s and 1970s were not totally

---

2. In 1989 both whites and blacks were less likely to say that the quality of life for blacks had improved over the past decade than either was in 1981 (for whites the figures were 69 and 77 percent, for blacks 47 and 60 percent). See Morin and Balz (1989).

ephemeral: There was sufficient agreement in 1991 to enact a civil rights bill restoring the rights of blacks and women to sue firms for discrimination without demonstrating bias in specific instances. For many blacks and whites, interpersonal relations have improved: Two-thirds of whites in 1989—compared to just over half in 1981—claim to have a close black friend, while 80 percent of blacks—up 10 percent since 1981—have a close white friend (Morin and Balz 1989). Collectively, things are not quite so rosy: 44 percent of blacks in 1989, compared with just a third eight years earlier, believe there is more anti-black feeling in the country.

More critically, racial politics does not touch people in their daily lives directly enough to cause massive political turmoil. Almost two-thirds of Americans in June, 1991, had not heard of the civil rights bill that ultimately was enacted into law. Even as Americans clearly saw the Democrats to the left and the Republicans on the right on civil rights, whites were almost equally divided in 1991 on which party best represented their views on this issue (NBC News 1991c).[3] Like on the environment, we are doing better but feeling worse, so on civil rights individual relations show improvement, but collectively we are worse off. The record on civil rights is mixed. It is hardly surprising that it is not the stuff of realignments. Yet, progress no longer seems inevitable.

It is unclear what would constitute progress on abortion, but it is clear that a realignment on this issue is also not in sight. Few issues are so contentious in contemporary American politics, yet abortion does not raise the core values of individualism and egalitarianism but the secondary ones of science and religion. Much of the opposition to abortion is religious, with Catholic and fundamentalist Protestant leaders at the forefront of the pro life movement. Pro choice and pro life forces on abortion have pitted scientific and religious claims against each other on the question of when life begins. Democratic and Republican elites are widely split on the issue, but rank-and-file party identifiers show far less cohesion. While Democrats are somewhat more likely to favor the unrestricted right to abortion than either Republicans or independents, virtually identical shares of each back complete bans.

Most Americans favor most abortion rights, but large majorities

---

3. On the favored party, 37 percent of whites chose the Democrats and 42 percent the Republicans.

back limited restrictions such as notification of parents when teenagers seek to terminate pregnancies while a smaller majority believes that abortion is wrong. A third of Americans say that they would never vote for a candidate who opposes abortion rights, but almost a quarter could not support pro choice candidates (CBS News 1989a; Yankelovich, Clancy, Schulman 1989a and 1991). The divisive politics crosses party lines; even as party platforms become increasingly polarized, many officeholders refuse to be dragged along (Rovner 1991). As the Supreme Court moves ever closer to reversing *Roe v. Wade*, its 1973 decision overturning restrictive abortion laws, predictions of imminent realignment abound. The electorate is too divided—along many different fault lines and within individuals—to send a clear message.[4]

The conflicts over civil rights and abortion, as well as energy and the environment (chap. 6), point to a highly polarized agenda that is unlikely to lead to a realignment. On civil rights and the environment, policy is not stalemated, but an implosion seems likely. Forces on each side grow ever more strident, taking voters along with them. What once worked no longer does, and what works now might not in the future. As long as no new party system is in sight, increased polarization can only lead to stalemate. Both the left of the Democratic party and the right of the Republicans—especially the COS—prefer confrontation. So do the external groups pushing the parties apart.

The Democrats and Republicans are now more polarized on the core values of individualism and egalitarianism (Wildavsky 1989). As increasing tensions have developed between science and religion on such issues as abortion and the teaching of evolution, the social consensus necessary for collective action wanes. Compromises on issues such as civil rights and the environment become more elusive than they were in the 1960s and 1970s. The Republicans are increasingly out of step with voters on government intervention in the economy (Jacobson 1990), but the Democrats have forsaken other traditional values, ranging from patriotism to the family (Galston and Kamarck 1989).

If social issues will not lead to a new political order, neither will

---
4. The conflicts over abortion are cross-cutting and do not overlap with most other salient issues.

economic ones. The role of government as "permanent receiver" prevents both economic and political collapse. With no economic interest permitted to fail, politicians no longer have to make choices (Lowi 1979). Realignments historically have depended on economic difficulties, which in turn lead to new issue coalitions and new policy choices by political leaders. If politicians respond to most demands for protection against economic swings, they prevent the economic fallout that is essential for the political shake-up of a realignment. Leaders of all stripes support this new protectionism, so fewer choices are made in politics. In an era when huge budget deficits crowd out even decisions on key issues, parties differ more on their promises than on their actions. Politicians' first priorities, whatever their philosophies, is protection of constituent interests.

Americans are the victims of their own success through a dialectic that no one foresaw. Establishing the state as permanent receiver effectively has prevented economic collapses of the magnitude of the Great Depression. No one wants such a catastrophe. If the economy were ever-expanding, or merely following traditional business cycles, government protection would sustain the optimism in the future that is essential for collective action. However, the long-term stagnation of the economy, the ever-increasing budget and trade deficits, and the growing inequalities in resources have drained Americans' faith in the future. We have prevented collapse, but we have not guaranteed long-term prosperity. The New Deal game plan put out a massive conflagration; it was never intended to handle brush fires.

In the period of stagnation, not only has confidence in government declined, but so have citizens' beliefs that public officials were listening to them and that ordinary people could do anything about government (Conway 1991, 47). The Gulf War led to a renewed optimism about the future, reversing a decade-long decline. Could a new world order emerge, or maybe even a resurgence of the traditional values? The increased faith in institutions turned out to be quite selective. Only those institutions that were directly involved in the conflict prospered: the president, the Congress, the media, and especially the military. Overall confidence in the future fell substantially just five weeks after the victory; by the next year, two-thirds of Americans saw the country as being on "the wrong track" and a majority felt that 1991 was either "below average" or "one of the [nation's] worst years" (Toner 1991; Broder and Morin 1991; *Newsweek* 1991; NBC News 1991a and 1992; Dionne and Morin 1991). We remain stuck at the trough of the cycle.

We Are Not Alone

We might take heart that our burden is shared. Internationally, disruptions are on the rise in the Canadian House of Commons, the normally staid Japanese Diet, and the West German and Taiwanese parliaments (Canadian Press 1986; Haberman 1988b; Schmemann 1990; Kristof 1989). Much of the worldwide evidence is less systematic than the American case, so it is difficult to generalize. The similarities seem greatest among the English-speaking democracies, and especially Great Britain, where the evidence is more detailed.

Norm-busting conservative governments came to power in the United States, Great Britain, and Canada. Each has targeted the labor movement and adopted tax policies that were touted as populist but actually replaced more progressive levies.[5] Beer (1982, 119) said of Britain, "it is no exaggeration to speak of the decline of the civic culture as a 'collapse.' The change in attitudes toward politics and government since the 1950s has been wide and deep." Prime Minister Margaret Thatcher's majoritarianism has been even more thoroughgoing than Reagan's. Like Reagan, she attempted to forge a realignment through public policy, in her case the sale of council houses to lower-income citizens; like Reagan, she failed (Crewe 1991).

In the House of Commons standing orders to punish members for violations of comity were employed nineteen times between 1945 and 1979, but fifteen times between 1979 and 1983 and eight times from June, 1983, to February, 1985 (Judge 1985, 370). The usually courteous British have fallen prey to bad manners. The owner of a firm hired by companies to encourage better service and more polite-

---

5. The Japanese Diet was similarly disputed in a debate over a more regressive tax structure (Burgess 1987). For a comparison, albeit not a balanced one, of the United States and Great Britain, see Krieger (1986). A better treatment of Prime Minister Margaret Thatcher's norm-busting is Hall (1986, 126–32). On the rancor over Britain's poll tax, see Raines (1988). On Canada, see Gibbons (1988). A report on the Canadian Broadcasting Corporation's *Sunday Morning* (June 21, 1987) compared the government's breaking of a postal strike to similar action by the U.S. government on the air traffic controllers' strike and to movements toward deregulation and privatization in both the United States and the United Kingdom.

ness acknowledges that Britons feel shocked that her efforts are needed: "People say, 'Oh God, it's so American'" (White 1990). Even more striking is the rise in violence at soccer matches that has led to Britain's banishment from most international competition. The antinuclear movement Greenpeace has engaged in confrontational demonstrations against NATO nuclear bases. Over the past decade, animal rights advocates have succeeded in cutting experimentation on live animals by half through break-ins at laboratories, violent demonstrations, and even death threats.[6]

Interpersonal confidence trends in Great Britain closely follow those in the United States for the three years where comparable data are available: 1960, 1981, and 1986 (Inglehart 1990, 438). This is not surprising. Even though Britain (and to varying degrees the other Anglo-American democracies) has traditionally been more majoritarian—and class-based—than the United States, it shares a strong commitment to individual rights and civil liberties. The Anglo-American economies are also closely interconnected. If British manners have fallen further and faster than American deportment, perhaps they started higher (Tocqueville 1945, vol. 2, chap. 14). British politics have always been more polarized along class lines. In recent years economic difficulties and polarization have been more pronounced in Britain than in the United States. The failure of realignment politics in the United Kingdom, where economic issues have been more front and center, should make us wary that a reshaping of American politics is in sight.

Rebuilding Institutions?

Can we dig ourselves out of our dilemma through tinkering? I think not. There is an irony in reform politics: Reforms are most likely but not very effective when they are most needed. One might expect a large scale shake-up in rules when a new regime is ushered into power, but this is not the case. Following a realignment, there is a large shift in Congressional membership. At least for a short period the legislature will be distinctively majoritarian in its norms.[7] The dominant

---

6. From a report on National Public Radio's Weekend Edition, April 27, 1991.
7. Stewart (1989, chap. 5) finds a distinct lull in attempts to reform the Congressional budget process during the realignment of the 1890s, while the other years covered in his study (1865–1921) were marked by extensive efforts to change the fiscal system.

party will generally have an oversized majority with a clear program. Rules of procedure will not suffice to block the party from implementing its platform. Reforms are not needed—and generally do not occur during realignment periods (Fink and Humes 1989).

Structural change is most likely to occur at the trough, when it is most needed. This should make us optimistic now. The reforms that occur at the trough often do not seem to work very well. Because the logjam over issues will spill over to structures at the trough, the range of feasible reforms is usually rather limited. The major reforms of the nineteenth century all occurred before realignments. Minority parties, invigorated by the issues that were to form the basis of the new partisan order, blocked legislation through dilatory tactics. The majority parties, each with reduced contingents, adopted reforms that hindered minority obstruction (Dion 1990, 9–11).

The major twentieth century reforms also took place when party systems were either aging or in midlife. In 1910–11 a majority of House members got sufficiently frustrated with the speaker's arbitrary use of power. They rebelled against Joseph Cannon; the new regime enshrined property rights over committee assignments, so the makers of the revolution were unambiguously better off until the committee system expanded so much that power was effectively dissipated. The Legislative Reorganization Act of 1946 reduced the number of committees and realigned jurisdictions but gave rise to a large number of subcommittees. The new jurisdictions written into law were mostly codifications of changes that had already occurred (King 1991). In 1975, when the most recent wide-ranging reforms were enacted, House Democrats had the sort of overwhelming majorities that ordinarily follow major presidential landslides. Yet the absence of a realignment found the party marked by internal divisions and without a clear-cut program. Structural reform was needed and the numbers were sufficient to achieve it. Congress became more decentralized, if not more deliberative and amenable to greater cooperation in the 1970s. Neither the new budget process nor Gramm-Rudman-Hollings reduced the deficit or gave Congress (or anybody else) any real control of a comprehensive economic plan.

What set these reforms apart from other, less successful, efforts was the ambiguity of the policy effects of such structural tinkering.[8]

---

8. In the 1970s the large Democratic majority in the Congress shared a vague commitment to party government, though little cohesion over specifics (Uslaner 1978).

Reforms do not fail simply because of collective action problems. More likely such efforts collapse because they threaten so many interests. Reforms are strategic responses to altered environments (Dodd 1986). In the highly polarized and partisan environment of the contemporary Congress, any reforms that might actually accomplish something reflect legislators' policy preferences (or, in Riker's [1980, 445] words, "congealed tastes"). If implemented, they will do little more than codify what Democratic Congressional majorities have been doing since the Reagan years: Restrict the Republican minority's ability to obstruct. Writing this case law into rules will hardly make the Republicans less hostile to the Democratic leadership. With controversial issues such as energy, abortion, agriculture, gun control, and others resisting the party discipline on economic questions, it is hard to see how one could put together a majoritarian coalition for any reform.

Whither Comity?

I am skeptical of tinkering because I do not think it will work. You can lead a legislator to the Rules Committee, but you cannot make him or her wink. Congress is stymied because it cannot produce the votes for controversial bills, not because its rules block collective action. Congress and the president enacted more major laws in the bad old days before reform than today, despite powerful committees (especially Rules) vetoing much progressive legislation (cf. Mayhew 1991). The House and Senate of the 1960s pushed aside the Rules Committee, first increasing its membership to ensure greater leadership control and then largely ignoring its gatekeeper role during the Great Society. A less powerful committee system might have produced more legislation in the 1950s, but the prevailing public mood was unlikely to have produced a legislative machine.

I am pessimistic because I don't see any reforms that could make daily life in Congress more tolerable or improve its legislative record. Nor is there a realignment on the way or any immediate hope for a restoration of a value consensus. The conclusion will be unsatisfying

---

Yet the Bolling Committee reforms of the same period failed dramatically, largely because they had clear policy consequences (Davidson and Oleszek 1977). Senate committee reforms of the same period streamlined some overburdensome procedures but did not realign jurisdictions (Parris 1979). On the direct relationship between interests and procedures on a reform that failed, see Uslaner (1989, chap. 6).

to many, if not most. It is like reading a murder mystery with the conclusion left out, yet we know whodunit (as in *Murder on the Orient Express*, we all did). Simply knowing that there is a problem does not mean that we have the answer—or even that there is an answer. The return to single-party control of the legislative and executive branches will not provide the answer as long as the public continues to send conflicting signals to decision makers on how to solve our national problems.

When Americans look to Congress, they are appalled at how poorly it seems to work. Major issues get caught up in all sorts of wrangling, both partisan and bipartisan. The stumbling over policy and ethical problems such as the House bank scandal make Congress look like the out-of-touch elite that talk show hosts love to disparage. Members of Congress have contributed to their own poor image by ethical lapses but more critically by tearing down the institution as they run for it (Fenno 1975). Ultimately, their protestations were bound to prove unconvincing.[9] President Bush fed the frenzy by supporting a constitutional amendment to limit Congressional terms.

Yet it does little good to blame Congress alone for its inability to resolve the nation's pressing issues. Nor does it help to carp at our legislators for carping at each other. Congress is first and foremost an institution of interest representation. If the cause of the decline of comity in Congress is a waning of values in the larger society, then neither structural reform nor exhortation can restore the folkways of the 1950s and 1960s.

If we toss the rascals out either through the ballot box or term limits, we will only get a different set of scoundrels. Term limits might lead to a less professional legislature, more dependent on special interests for information and money for campaigns and less knowledgeable about the nation's problems (Jacobson 1992a, 247). The focus on membership turnover shifts the blame from the public to the institution. People don't want to admit that members of Congress are stymied because there is so much dissensus and rancor in the larger society. They focus on the sideshows—the ethical problems of legislators and the need for structural reforms—as the explanation

---

9. Born (1991) demonstrates that the disjunction between the approval of Congress and support for one's own member of the House is overstretched. People who disapprove of Congressional performance are less likely to have positive evaluations of their own member.

for all of the legislature's difficulties. They shift blame away from themselves and toward "unrepresentative" institutions. Americans hope vainly that a new Congress that is less out of touch with the public will impose solutions on an electorate that has no tolerance for pain.

Extensive membership change can do the job; it has in the past. Simply replacing one group of legislators with another won't provide a new direction. A realignment would. Yet, there is no reshuffling of partisan loyalties in sight. One hopeful sign might have been the independent candidacy of H. Ross Perot for president; third-party movements have traditionally heralded realignments (Burnham 1970). The Perot candidacy offered no distinctive message other than throwing the insiders out and replacing them with televised town meetings at which pressing issues would be resolved much as winners on "The Gong Show" were declared. A realignment can tolerate—and seems to require—loud voices. Shouting is not enough. The public must be polarized into two opposing camps so that the din is about something. Our current Tower of Babel offers little hope for a straight fight. If new politicians won't do the job, the public ire will shift more squarely to institutional failure. When a reformed Congress still produces stalemate, we shall blame the members again. Anyone but ourselves.

References

Adams, Henry. 1918. *The Education of Henry Adams*. Boston: Houghton Mifflin.
Adler, Jeffrey. 1990. "Taking Offense." *Newsweek*, December 24, 48–54.
Alexander, DeAlva Stanwood. 1916. *History and Procedure of the House of Representatives*. Boston: Houghton Mifflin.
Almond, Gabriel A. 1991. "Rational Choice Theory and the Social Sciences." In Kristen Renwick Monroe, ed., *The Economic Approach to Politics*, 35–52. New York: Harper Collins.
Almond, Gabriel, and Sidney Verba. 1968. *Five-Nation Study*. Ann Arbor: Inter-University Consortium for Political Research.
Alston, Chuck. 1989. "Smear Tactics Overshadow Election of New Speaker." *Congressional Quarterly Weekly Report*, June 10, 1373–75.
Applebome, Peter. 1991. "Rights-Bill Backers Issue Call to More Transcendent Battle." *New York Times*, April 3, A1, A18.
Arrandale, Tom. 1992. "The Mid-Life Crisis of the Environmental Lobby." *Governing*, April, 32–36.
Arrow, Kenneth J. 1951. *Social Choice and Individual Values*. New York: John Wiley.
Asher, Herbert B. 1973. "The Learning of Legislative Norms." *American Political Science Review* 67 (June):499–513.
Associated Press. 1985. "G.O.P. 'Declares War' over Indiana Recount." *New York Times*, April 26, B20.
———. 1986. "Crime Rate Is Put at a 13-Year Low." *New York Times*, October 9, A23.
———. 1987. "4 Top Judges in Illinois Join to Scold Colleagues." *New York Times*, September 14, B14.
———. 1989. "I Am Speaking of a New Engagement in the Lives of Others." *Washington Post*, January 21, A10.
———. 1991a. "Only One Family in Four Is 'Traditional.'" *New York Times*, January 30, A19.
———. 1991b. "'Veggie Bill' Passes Colorado House." *Washington Post*, April 4, D4.
Austin, James H. 1977. *Chase, Chance, and Creativity*. New York: Columbia University Press.
Axelrod, Robert. 1984. *The Evolution of Cooperation*. New York: Basic.
———. 1986. "An Evolutionary Approach to Norms." *American Political Science Review* 80 (December): 1095–1111.
Bach, Stanley, and Steven S. Smith. 1988. *Managing Uncertainty in the House of Representatives*. Washington: Brookings.

Baker, Ross. 1980. *Friend and Foe in the U.S. Senate*. New York: Free Press.
Barone, Michael. 1990. *Our Country: The Shaping of America from Roosevelt to Reagan*. New York: Free Press.
Barone, Michael, Grant Ujifusa, and Douglas Matthews. 1980. *The Almanac of American Politics 1980*. New York: E. P. Dutton.
Barry, Brian M. 1970. *Sociologists, Economists, and Democracy*. London: Collier-Macmillan.
Barry, John M. 1990. "Games Congressmen Play." *New York Times Magazine*, May 13, 78–87.
Bates, Robert H. 1988. "Contra Contractarianism: Some Reflections on the New Institutionalism." *Politics and Society* 16 (June–September): 387–401.
Becker, Lawrence C. 1990. *Reciprocity*. Chicago: University of Chicago Press.
Beer, Samuel H. 1982. *Britain Against Itself*. New York: W. W. Norton.
Bell, Daniel. 1973. *The Coming of Post-Industrial Society*. New York: Basic Books.
———. 1991. "The Hegelian Secret: Civil Society and American Exceptionalism." In Byron E. Shafer, ed., *Is America Different? A New Look at American Exceptionalism*. Oxford: Oxford University Press.
Bellah, Robert N., Richard Madsen, William M. Sullivan, Ann Swidler, and Steven M. Tipton. 1986. *Habits of the Heart*. New York: Harper and Row.
Belsey, David A., Edwin Kuh, and Roy E. Welsch. 1980. *Regression Diagnostics*. New York: John Wiley.
Bendor, Jonathan, and Piotr Swistak. 1991. "The Evolutionary Stability of Cooperation." Stanford Business School. Mimeo.
Bercovitch, Sacvan. 1981. "The Rites of Assent: Rhetoric, Ritual, and the Ideology of American Consensus." In Sam B. Girgus, ed., *The American Self*, 5–42. Albuqurque: University of New Mexico Press.
Bessette, Joseph M. 1983. "Is Congress a Deliberative Body?" In Dennis Hale, ed., *The United States Congress*, 3–11. New Brunswick, NJ: Transaction.
Beth, Richard S. 1990. "Points of Order and the Conduct of Senate Business." Presented at the Annual Meeting of the American Political Science Association, San Francisco, August–September.
Bianco, William, and Robert Bates. 1990. "Cooperation by Design: Leadership, Structure, and Collective Dilemmas." *American Political Science Review* 84 (March): 133–47.
Birnbaum, Jeffrey H., and Alan S. Murray. 1987. *Showdown at Gucci Gulch*. New York: Random House.
Bishop, Katherine. 1990. "Militant Environmentalists Planning Summer Protests to Save Redwoods." *New York Times*, June 19, A18.
Blau, Peter M. 1955. *The Dynamics of Bureaucracy*. Chicago: University of Chicago Press.
———. 1964. *Exchange and Power in Social Life*. New York: John Wiley.
Bluestone, Harry, and Bennett Harrison. 1986. *The Great American Job Machine*. Washington: U.S. Congress, Joint Economic Committee.
Blustein, Paul. 1988. "U.S. Budget Increasingly Free of Pork-Barrel Spending." *Washington Post*, March 21, A1, A7.

Bogue, Alan G. 1989. *The Congressman's Civil War*. Cambridge: Cambridge University Press.
Bolling, Richard. 1965. *House Out of Order*. New York: E. P. Dutton.
Boren, David. 1991. "Major Repairs for Congress." *Washington Post*, August 6, A15.
Born, Richard. 1991. "Assessing the Impact of Institutional and Election Forces on Evaluations of Congressional Incumbents." *Journal of Politics*, August, 764-99.
Brady, David W. 1988. *Critical Elections and Congressional Policy Making*. Stanford: Stanford University Press.
Braungart, Richard C., and Margaret M. Braungart. 1988. "From Yippies to Yuppies: Twenty Years of Surveys of Freshman Attitudes." *Public Opinion*, September/October, 53-57.
Brenner, Joel Glenn. 1990. "Where Consumer Credit Is Due." *Washington Post*, October 21, A1, A22.
Broder, David S. 1986a. "The Politics of Change." *Washington Post Magazine*, February 2, 67, 148-51.
———. 1986b. "GOP Predicts Electoral Gain." *Washington Post*, August 19, A1, A8.
Broder, David S., and Richard Morin. 1991. "National Optimism Surges on War Success." *Washington Post*, February 28, A33.
Brovard, James. 1990. "Farm Subsidies: Milking Us Dry." *New York Times*, July 7, A27.
Brown, Wm. Holmes. 1979. *Jefferson's Manual and Rules of the House of the Representatives of the United States*. Washington: Government Printing Office.
Bruce, Robert V. 1987. *The Launching of Modern American Science 1846-1876*. New York: Alfred A. Knopf.
Bryce, James. 1915. *The American Commonwealth*. Vol. 1. Rev. ed. New York: Macmillan.
———. 1916. *The American Commonwealth*. Vol. 2. Rev. ed. New York: Macmillan.
Buchanan, John C. 1987. *How Superstition Won and Science Lost*. New Brunswick: Rutgers University Press.
Burgess, John. 1987. "Opposition's 'Ox Walk' Delays Nakasone Tax Bill." *Washington Post*, April 22, A21, A26.
Burnham, Walter Dean. 1970. *Critical Elections and the Mainsprings of American Politics*. New York: W. W. Norton.
Butterfield, Fox. 1990a. "Democrats Plan to Sue White House Official." *New York Times*, June 6, A18.
———. 1990b. "Disrupted Massachusetts Democrats File Suit." *New York Times*, June 14, A23.
Calmes, Jacqueline. 1986. "Sen. Zorinsky Considers a Return to the GOP." *Congressional Quarterly Weekly Report*, September 27, 2291.
———. 1987. "'Trivialized' Filibuster Is Still a Potent Tool." *Congressional Quarterly Weekly Report*, September 5, 2115-20.

Calvert, Randall. 1991. "Elements of a Theory of Society among Rational Actors." Presented at the 1991 Annual Meeting of the Public Choice Society, New Orleans, March.
Canadian Press. 1986. "Grow Up, MP Tells Colleagues." *Montreal Gazette*, June 5, 1.
Cannon, Clarence. 1935. *Cannon's Precedents of the House of Representatives*. Washington: Government Printing Office.
Canon, David T. 1989. "Political Amateurism in the United States Congress." In Lawrence C. Dodd and Bruce I. Oppenheimer, eds., *Congress Reconsidered*, 4th ed., Washington: Congressional Quarterly Press.
Carmines, Edward G., and James A. Stimson. 1989. *Issue Evolution*. Princeton, NJ: Princeton University Press.
CBS News. 1988. "Between the Conventions." August 6, press release.
———. 1989a. January 18, press release.
———. 1989b. April 19, press release.
———. 1990a. May 29, press release.
———. 1990b. October 8, press release.
———. 1990c. October 13, press release.
———. 1990d. "Election Eve: What *Are* the Voters Thinking?" November 3, press release.
Chevalier, Michel. 1961. *Society, Manners, and Politics in the United States*. Edited by John William Ward. Ithaca, NY: Cornell University Press. Originally published in 1839.
Christoff, Chris, and Dawson Bell. 1991. "It's Fight Day at the Legislature." *Detroit Free Press*, May 16, 1A, 8A.
Church, George J. 1986. "The Making of a Miracle." *Time*, August 25, 12–18.
Citrin, Jack. 1974. "Comment: The Political Relevance of Trust in Government." *American Political Science Review* 68 (September): 973–88.
Clark, Joseph S. 1964. *Congress: The Sapless Branch*. New York: Harper and Row.
Clines, Francis X. 1981. "Congress Now Suffers from Loss of Memory." *New York Times*, August 2, E4.
Clotfelter, Charles T. 1985. *Federal Tax Policy and Charitable Giving*. Chicago: University of Chicago Press.
Cloud, David. 1990a. "Logic Doesn't Always Apply to Multiyear Farm Bills." *Congressional Quarterly Weekly Report*, February 4, 576–82.
———. 1990b. "The Politics of '90 Farm Bill Revolve Around Budget." *Congressional Quarterly Weekly Report*, May 12, 1468–70.
Clubb, Jerome M., William H. Flanigan, and Nancy H. Zingale. 1980. *Partisan Realignment*. Beverly Hills, CA: Sage.
Clymer, Adam. 1981. "Poll Finds Nation Is Becoming Increasingly Republican." *New York Times*, May 3, 1, 62.
———. 1986. "Poll Finds Most Americans Cling to Ideals of Farm Life." *New York Times*, February 25, A22.
Cohen, Richard E. 1985. "Democrats, GOP Wary of Long-Term Political Fallout from Tax Reform." *National Journal*, June 8, 1346–49.

Collie, Melissa P. 1988. "Universalism and the Parties in the U.S. House of Representatives, 1921–80." *American Journal of Political Science* 32 (November): 865–83.

Commager, Henry Steele. 1950. *The American Mind.* New Haven, CT: Yale University Press.

Conference Board. 1986. "Information for the Press." Release #3487 (October 7).

Congressional Quarterly. 1965. *Congress and the Nation: 1945–1964.* Washington: Congressional Quarterly.

———. 1969. *Congress and the Nation: 1965–1968.* Washington: Congressional Quarterly.

———. 1971. *Congressional Quarterly Almanac 1970.* Washington: Congressional Quarterly.

———. 1976. *Congressional Quarterly's Guide to Congress.* 2d ed. Washington: Congressional Quarterly.

———. 1978. *Congressional Quarterly Almanac 1977.* Washington: Congressional Quarterly.

———. 1979. *Congressional Quarterly Almanac 1978.* Washington: Congressional Quarterly.

———. 1990. *Congressional Quarterly Almanac 1989.* Washington: Congressional Quarterly.

Congressional Quarterly Weekly Report. 1986. "No More Talk of the 'Other Body.'" November 11, 2985.

Congressional Record. 1985a. Daily ed. 99th Cong., 1st sess. April 23. H2650.

———. 1985b. Daily ed. 99th Cong., 1st sess. May 1. H2775.

———. 1986. Daily ed. 99th Cong., 2d sess. June 19. S7839.

———. 1988. Daily ed. 100th Cong., 2d sess. February 23. S1206.

———. 1989a. Daily ed. 101st Cong., 1st sess. March 3. S2111.

———. 1989b. Daily ed. 101st Cong., 1st sess. March 7. S2241.

Conway, M. Margaret. 1991. *Political Participation,* 2d ed. Washington: CQ Press, 47.

Cook, Timothy. 1989. *Making Laws and Making News: Media Strategies in the U.S. House of Representatives.* Washington: Brookings Institution.

Cooper, Joseph, and David W. Brady. 1973. "Organization Theory and Congressional Structure." Presented at the Annual Meeting of the American Political Science Association, New Orleans, September.

Cooper, Joseph, and William West. 1981. "The Congressional Career in the 1970s." In Lawrence C. Dodd and Bruce I. Oppenheimer, eds., *Congress Reconsidered,* 2d ed., 83–106. Washington: Congressional Quarterly Press.

Cox, Gary W., and Mathew D. McCubbins. 1989. *Parties and Committees in the U.S. House of Representatives.* University of California–San Diego. Mimeo.

Cranford, John R. 1990. "Budget Deal Claimed Real Savings: The Devil Lay in the Details." *Congressional Quarterly Weekly Report,* October 6, 3194–3202.

Crenshaw, Albert. 1989. "Poll: Most Find Tax Filing Is Overly Burdensome." *Washington Post,* April 5, F1, F6.

Crewe, Ivor. 1991. "Thatcher's Negative Legacy." *The Times* (London), January 4, 10.
Croly, Herbert. 1965. *The Promise of American Life*. Edited by Arthur Schlesinger, Jr. Cambridge, MA: Belknap.
Crossen, Cynthia. 1989. "Shock Troops: AIDS Activist Group Harasses and Provokes to Make Its Point." *Wall Street Journal*, December 7, A1, A9.
Davidson, Roger H. 1986. "The Legislative Work of Congress." Presented at the Annual Meeting of the American Political Science Association, Washington, August.
———. 1989. "Multiple Referral of Legislation in the U.S. Senate." *Legislative Studies Quarterly* 14 (August): 375–92.
———. 1990. "The Advent of the Modern Congress: The Legislative Reorganization Act of 1946." *Legislative Studies Quarterly* 15 (August): 357–73.
Davidson, Roger H., and Walter J. Oleszek. 1977. *Congress Against Itself*. Bloomington: Indiana University Press.
Davidson, Roger H., Walter J. Oleszek, and Thomas Kephart. 1988. "One Bill, Many Committees: Multiple Referrals in the U.S. House of Representatives." *Legislative Studies Quarterly* 13 (February): 3–28.
Davis, Joseph A. 1985. "Energy and Commerce Republicans Stay on 'Strike.'" *Congressional Quarterly Weekly Report*, March 9, 461.
———. 1987. "Senate Panel Moves to Rescue Uranium Industry." *Congressional Quarterly Weekly Report*, October 3, 2396–97.
Davis, Phillip A. 1992. "Economy, Politics Threaten Species Act Renewal." *Congressional Quarterly Weekly Report*, January 4, 16–18.
[U.S.] Department of Commerce, Bureau of Economic Analysis. 1987. *Commerce News*, August 20.
[U.S.] Department of the Treasury. 1984. *Tax Reform for Fairness, Simplicity, and Economic Growth*. Vol. 1, *Overview*. Washington: Office of the Secretary of the Treasury, November.
Derthick, Martha, and Paul J. Quirk. 1985. *The Politics of Deregulation*. Washington: Brookings Institution.
Deutsch, Claudia H. 1988. "Cheating: Alive and Flourishing." *New York Times Education Life*, April 10, 26–29.
Dewar, Helen. 1985. "Republicans Wage Verbal Civil War." *Washington Post*, November 19, A1, A5.
———. 1986. "Senate Civility Frays under Workload." *Washington Post*, August 11, A1, A4.
———. 1988. "Midnight Manhunt in the Senate." *Washington Post*, February 25, A1, A4.
———. 1990a. "Women Victims Back Anti-Crime Bill." *Washington Post*, June 21, A4.
———. 1990b. "Suspicions Simmer in the Senate." *Washington Post*, July 22, A16.
———. 1991. "Democrats on Hill Confront Old Adversary: Themselves." *Washington Post*, April 18, A1, A8.

Diesenhouse, Susan. 1990. "Women Victims Back Anti-Crime Bill." *Washington Post*, July 8, E4.
Diggins, John P. 1984. *The Lost Soul of American Politics*. New York: Basic.
Dion, Douglas. 1990. "Majority Rule, Minority Rights, and the Politics of Procedural Change." Presented at the Annual Meeting of the American Political Science Association, San Francisco, August–September.
Dionne, E. J., Jr. 1986. "'Star Wars' Fight Gives Republicans Way to Attack in 'Issueless' Election." *New York Times*, October 17, A18.
———. 1987. "In a Changed Economy, Labor Tries New Tactics." *New York Times*, October 26 A15.
———. 1989. "The Limits of Risk." *New York Times*, March 19, A1, A26.
———. 1990. "Vander Jagt Compares Foe to Saddam Hussein." *Washington Post*, November 2, A3.
Dionne, E. J., Jr., and Richard Morin. 1991. "Postwar Glow Has Faded, Poll Finds." *Washington Post*, April 12, A1, A4.
Dodd, Lawrence C. 1981. "Congress, the Constitution, and the Crisis of Legitimation." In Lawrence C. Dodd and Bruce I. Oppenheimer, eds., *Congress Reconsidered*, 2d ed., 390–420. Washington: CQ Press.
———. 1986. "Cycles of Legislative Change." In Herbert F. Weisberg, ed., *Political Science: The Science of Politics*. New York: Agathon.
Donald, David. 1967. *Charles Sumner and the Coming of the Civil War*. New York: Alfred A. Knopf.
Duke, Lynne. 1991. "Proliferating Boycotts Turn Buying Power into Political Clout." *Washington Post*, April 14, A1, A13.
Eads, George C., and Michael Fix. 1984. *Relief or Reform?* Washington: Urban Institute Press.
Economist. 1987. "Whatever Happened?" September 12, 11–12.
Edsall, Thomas Byrne. 1984. *The New Politics of Inequality*. New York: W. W. Norton.
Egan, Timothy. 1990. "Fighting for Control of America's Hinterlands." *New York Times*, November 11, E18.
Ehrenhalt, Alan. 1982. "In the Senate of the '80s, Team Spirit Has Given Way to the Rule of Individuals." *Congressional Quarterly Weekly Report*, September 4, 2175–82.
———. 1986. "Media Power Shifts Dominate O'Neill's House." *Congressional Quarterly Weekly Report*, September 13, 2131–38.
Elbaum, Bernard. 1989. "Why Apprenticeship Persisted in Britain but Not in the United States." *Journal of Economic History* 49 (June): 337–49.
Ellwood, John W. 1985. "The Great Exception: The Congressional Budget Process in an Age of Decentralization." In Lawrence C. Dodd and Bruce I. Oppenheimer, eds., *Congress Reconsidered*, 3d ed., 315–42. Washington: CQ Press.
Elving, Ronald D. 1988. "The War Between the States (Or Who's Really Getting the Most Money from Congress)." *Governing*, March, 19–23.
Elving, Ronald D., and CQ Politics Staff. 1990. "Fall Campaigns Put Incumbents

Between Budget, Hard Place." *Congressional Quarterly Weekly Report,* October 13, 3443-44.

Erikson, Robert S., and Kent L. Tedin. 1981. "The 1928-1936 Partisan Realignment: The Case for the Conversion Hypothesis." *American Political Science Review* 75: 951-62.

Erskine, Hazel Gaudet. 1964. "The Polls: Some Thoughts about Life and People." *Public Opinion Quarterly* 28 (Fall): 517-28.

Eulau, Heinz. 1977. *Technology and Civility.* Stanford: Hoover Institution Press.

Evans, Rowland, and Robert Novak. 1987. "The Kemp-Michel Row." *Washington Post,* April 1, A23.

Farhi, Paul. 1990. "FCC Bans All 'Indecent' Ads." *Washington Post,* July 13, A1, A12.

Farney, Dennis. 1981. "Republicans Reflect on What They've Wrought." *Wall Street Journal,* August 6, 22.

Fenno, Richard F., Jr. 1975. "If, as Ralph Nader Says, Congress Is 'the Broken Branch,' How Come We Love Our Congressmen So Much?" In Norman J. Ornstein, ed., *Congress in Change,* 277-86. New York: Praeger.

———. 1978. *Home Style.* Boston: Little, Brown.

———. 1989. "The Senate through the Looking Glass: The Debate over Television." *Legislative Studies Quarterly* 14 (August): 313-48.

Ferejohn, John A. 1986. "Logrolling in an Institutional Context." In Gerald C. Wright, Leroy N. Rieselbach, and Lawrence C. Dodd, eds., *Congress and Policy Change,* 223-53. New York: Agathon.

Fessler, Pamela. 1984a. "Wholesale Tax Reform Faces a Rough Congressional Road." *Congressional Quarterly Weekly Report,* October 27, 2787-93.

———. 1984b. "Treasury Tax Overhaul Excites Little Interest." *Congressional Quarterly Weekly Report,* December 1, 3016-19.

———. 1985. "Tax Reform Debate Opens with Reagan Plan." *Congressional Quarterly Weekly Report,* June 1, 1035-43.

———. 1986a. "New Threats to Tax Overhaul Come from Several Quarters." *Congressional Quarterly Weekly Report,* April 12, 795-96.

———. 1986b. "Finance Committee Suspends Markup of Tax Bill." *Congressional Quarterly Weekly Report,* April 19, 840-42.

Fialka, John J. 1986. "Conservative Evangelicals' Activism Shakes up Iowa's Traditionally Moderate Republican Party." *Wall Street Journal,* July 21, 42.

Fink, Evelyn C., and Brian D. Humes. 1989. "Risky Business: Electoral Realignment and Institutional Change in Congress." Presented at the Annual Meeting of the American Political Science Association, Washington, September.

Fiorina, Morris P. 1992. "An Era of Divided Government." In Bruce Cain, Gillian Peele, Christopher J. Barley, and eds., *Developments in American Politics* 324-54. London: Macmillan.

Fisher, Roger, and William Ury. 1981. *Getting to Yes: Negotiating Agreement Without Giving In.* New York: Penguin.

Flanagan, Robert J., Robert S. Smith, and Ronald G. Ehrenberg. 1984. *Labor Economics and Labor Relations.* Glenview, IL: Scott Foresman.

Foderaro, Lisa W. 1989. "Bickering Splits Westchester's Legislature." *New York Times*, October 24, B1, B6.
Foley, Michael. 1980. *The New Senate*. New Haven, CT: Yale University Press.
Frank, Barney. 1985. "A Rhetorical Quadriad for the Busy Politician." *Washington Post*, May 9, A19.
Frank, Robert H. 1988. *Passions within Reason*. New York: W. W. Norton.
Frankel, Glenn. 1989. "Cameras Come to Commons." *Washington Post*, November 22, D3.
Franklin, Charles. 1990. "Two Stage Auxiliary Instrumental Variable Estimator." In James A. Stimson, ed., *Political Analysis*, 1. Ann Arbor: University of Michigan Press.
Franklin, Mary Beth, and Linda Werfelman. 1988. "Rostenkowski Blames Senate for Hill's 'Do-Nothing' Notoriety." *Washington Post*, February 14, A21.
Freeman, J. Lieper. 1965. *The Political Process*. Rev. ed. New York: Random House.
Fudenberg, Drew, and Eric Maskin. 1986. "The Folk Theorem in Repeated Games with Discounting or with Incomplete Information." *Econometrica* 54:533-44.
Fuerbringer, Jonathan. 1986. "Temper, Temper, Temper." *New York Times*, February 11, A26.
Gabriel, Trip. 1990. "If a Tree Falls in the Forest, They Hear It." *New York Times Magazine*, November 11, 34, 58-64.
Gais, Thomas L., Mark A. Peterson, and Jack L. Walker. 1984. "Interest Groups, Iron Triangles, and Representative Institutions in American National Government." *British Journal of Political Science* 14 (April): 161-85.
Galloway, George B. 1962. *History of the House of Representatives*. New York: Thomas Y. Crowell.
Galston, William. 1991. *Liberal Virtues: Goods, Virtues, and Diversity in the Liberal State*. Cambridge: Cambridge University Press.
Galston, William, and Elaine Ciulla Kamarck. 1989. "The Politics of Evasion: Democrats and the Presidency." Washington: Progressive Policy Institute.
Gallup, George H. 1972. *The Gallup Poll: Public Opinion 1935-1971*. 3 vols. New York: Random House.
Gallup, George, Jr. 1985. "50 Years of Gallup Surveys on Religion." *Gallup Report*, May, 3-15.
Gallup Report. 1985. "Confidence in U.S. Supreme Court, Congress Up Sharply." July, 2-9.
———. 1987. "Importance of Religion: Majority of Americans Say Religion Is 'Very Important.'" April, 13.
Garand, James C., and Kathleen M. Clayton. 1986. "Socialization to Partisanship in the U.S. House: The Speaker's Task Force." *Legislative Studies Quarterly* 11 (August) 409-28.
Gibbons, Roger. 1988. "Conservatism in Canada: The Ideological Impact of the 1984 Election." In Barry Cooper, Allan Kornberg, and William Mishler, eds., *The Resurgence of Conservatism in Anglo-American Democracies*, 332-50. Durham, NC: Duke University Press.

Gibson, John R., with James M. Hildreth. 1986. "What Americans Want." *U.S. News and World Report*, September 8, 14–16.

Gienapp, William E. 1982. "'Politics Seem to Enter into Everything': Political Culture in the North, 1840–1860." In Stephen E. Maizlish and John J. Kushma, eds., *Essays on American Antebellum Politics, 1840–1860*, 15–69. College Station: Texas A&M Press.

Gilmour, John B. 1990. *Reconcilable Differences?* Berkeley: University of California Press.

Glazer, Sarah. 1991. "Whatever Happened to the Malpractice Insurance Crisis?" *Washington Post Health Magazine*, July 9, 10–13.

Goldenberg, Edie N. 1984. "The Permanent Governmnent in an Era of Retrenchment and Redirection." In John L. Palmer and Isabel V. Sawhill, eds., *The Reagan Record*, 381–404. Washington: Urban Institute Press.

Goldfield, Michael. 1986. "Labor in American Politics—Its Current Weaknesses." *Journal of Politics* 48 (February): 2–29.

Gouldner, Alvin W. 1960. "The Norm of Reciprocity: A Preliminary Statement." *American Sociological Review* 25 (April): 161–78.

Granat, Diane. 1984a. "Whatever Happened to the Watergate Babies?" *Congressional Quarterly Weekly Report*, March 3, 498–503.

———. 1984b. "The House's TV War: The Gloves Come Off." *Congressional Quarterly Weekly Report*, May 19, 1166–67.

Greenberger, Robert S. 1986. "Sen. Helms, No Stranger to Controversy, Draws Ire of Unexpected Critics: His Peers on Right." *Wall Street Journal*, August 13, 52.

Greenhouse, Linda. 1986. "Why Housing Act of 1986 Isn't." *New York Times*, August 25, A22.

Greer, William R. 1986. "In the 'Lite' Decade, Less Has Become More." *New York Times*, August 13, A1, C10.

Gugliotta, Guy. 1990. "Down on the Farm: The Other Depression in Rural America." *Washington Post*, November 11, A18.

Haberman, Clyde. 1988. "Wrestler Fails to Keep Hold on an Honorable Past." *New York Times*, January 2, 4.

Hager, George. 1990a. "For Industry and Opponents, A Showdown Is in the Air." *Congressional Quarterly Weekly Report*, January 20, 145–47.

———. 1990b. "Defiant House Rebukes Leaders; New Round of Fights Begins." *Congressional Quarterly Weekly Report*, October 6, 3183, 3186–88.

———. 1990c. "One Outcome of Budget Package: Higher Deficits on the Way." *Congressional Quarterly Weekly Report*, November 3, 3710–13.

Hall, Peter. 1986. *Governing the Economy*. New York: Oxford University Press.

Hall, Richard L., and C. Lawrence Evans. 1990. "The Power of Subcommittees." *Journal of Politics* 52 (May): 335–55.

Hamilton, Richard F., and James D. Wright. 1986. *The State of the Masses*. Hawthorne, NY: Aldine.

Hammond, Thomas, and Gary Miller. 1990. "Incentive Compatible Mechanisms Are Not Credible." Presented at the Annual Meeting of the American Political Science Association, San Francisco, August–September.

Hansen, John Mark. 1987. "The Ever-Decreasing Grandstand: Constraint and Change of an Agricultural Policy Network, 1949-1980." Presented at the Annual Meeting of the American Political Science Association, Chicago, September.
Hanson, Russell L. 1985. *The Democratic Imagination in America*. Princeton, NJ: Princeton University Press.
Hardeman, D. B., and Donald C. Bacon. 1987. *Rayburn: A Biography*. Austin: Texas Monthly Press.
Hardin, Russell. 1971. "Collective Action as an Agreeable in Prisoners' Dilemma." *Behavioral Science* 16 (September): 472-81.
———. 1982. *Collective Action*. Baltimore: Johns Hopkins University Press.
Harrington, Ty. 1989. "Extremism while Capturing Brand Loyalty Is No Vice." *Wall Street Journal*, September 9, A16.
Hart, Gary. 1989. "Stuart Symington's Senate." *Washington Post*, January 10, A23.
Hartz, Louis. 1955. *The Liberal Tradition in America*. New York: Harcourt, Brace, and World.
Haynes, George H. 1960. *The Senate of the United States*. 2 vols. New York: Russell and Russell. Originally published in 1938.
Heclo, Hugh. 1986. "General Welfare and Two American Political Traditions." *Political Science Quarterly* 101 (Summer): 179-96.
Herman Group. 1987. "National Opinion Poll for Independent Insurance Agents of America." Charlotte, NC.
Hershey, Robert D., Jr. 1990. "Many Interests at Stake as Farm Act Is Rewritten." *New York Times*, April 25, A20.
Hess, Stephen. 1986. *The Ultimate Insiders*. Washington: Brookings Institution.
Hetherington, Alastair, Kay Weaver, and Michael Ryle. 1990. *Cameras in the Commons*. London: The Hansard Society for Parliamentary Government.
Hibbing, John R., and Sue Thomas. 1990. "The Modern United States Senate: What Is Accorded Respect." *Journal of Politics* 52 (February): 126-45.
Hindle, Brooke. 1956. *The Pursuit of Science in Revolutionary America 1735-1789*. Chapel Hill: University of North Carolina Press.
Hochschild, Jennifer. 1981. *What's Fair?* Cambridge, MA: Harvard University Press.
Hofstadter, Richard. 1955a. *The Age of Reform*. New York: Random House.
———. 1955b. *Social Darwinism in American Thought*. Boston: Beacon.
———. 1963. *Anti-Intellectualism in American Life*. New York: Alfred A. Knopf.
———. 1970. *The Idea of a Party System*. Berkeley: University of California Press.
Hook, Janet. 1987. "Senators Look for Ways to Increase Efficiency." *Congressional Quarterly Weekly Report*, December 5, 3001-2.
———. 1988. "House-Senate Acrimony Bedevils Democrats." *Congressional Quarterly Weekly Report*, February 13, 296-98.
———. 1989. "Passion, Defiance, Tears: Jim Wright Bows Out." *Congressional Quarterly Weekly Report*, June 3, 1289-94.

Hume, Ellen. 1986. "Americans See Deficit as a Disease, but They Balk at Proposed Cures." *Wall Street Journal*, February 11, 1, 29.

Huntington, Samuel P. 1981. *American Politics: The Promise of Disharmony*. Cambridge, MA: Belknap Press of Harvard University Press.

Ignatius, David. 1989. "Trout Fishing in America, Circa 1989." *Washington Post*, September 10, C2.

Ingersoll, Bruce. 1990a. "Small Minnesota Town Is Divided by Rancor over Sugar Policies." *Wall Street Journal*, June 26, A1, A11.

———. 1990b. "Efforts Led by Foley and Dole Give Grain Farmers Ingredients to Make Dough With Agriculture Bill." *Wall Street Journal*, November 19, A16.

Inglehart, Ronald. 1971. *The Silent Revolution*. Princeton, NJ: Princeton University Press.

———. 1990. *Culture Shift in Advanced Industrial Society*. Princeton, NJ: Princeton University Press.

Jacobson, Gary C. 1985. "Parties and PACs in Congressional Elections." In Lawrence C. Dodd and Bruce I. Oppenheimer, eds., *Congress Reconsidered*, 3d ed., 131–58. Washington: Congressional Quarterly Press.

———. 1987. "The Marginals Never Vanished." *American Journal of Political Science* 31 (February): 126–41.

———. 1990. *The Electoral Origins of Divided Government*. Boulder, CO: Westview.

———. 1992a. *The Politics of Congressional Elections*, 3d ed. New York: HarperCollins.

———. 1992b. "Deficit Politics and the 1990 Elections." Presented at the Annual Meeting of the American Political Science Association, Chicago.

Jewell, Malcolm E., and David Breaux. 1988. "The Effect of Incumbency on State Legislative Elections." *Legislative Studies Quarterly*, November, 495–514.

Johnson, Dirk. 1990. "Population Decline in Rural America: A Product of Advances in Technology." *New York Times*, September 11, A20.

———. 1991. "Discovered, at Edge of Known Civilization, the Sub-Suburb." *New York Times*, April 28, E6.

Johnson, Haynes. 1990. "Durenberger: Symbol of Decline." *Washington Post*, June 15, A2.

Joint Economic Committee. 1987. *The 1987 Joint Economic Report*, 100th Congress, First Session. Washington: Government Printing Office.

Jones, Charles O. 1970. *The Minority Party in Congress*. Boston: Little, Brown.

———. 1975. *Clean Air: The Policies and Politics of Pollution Control*. Pittsburgh: University of Pittsburgh Press.

Josephson, Matthew. 1938. *The Politicos, 1865–1896*. New York: Harcourt, Brace, and Co.

Josephy, Alvin M., Jr. 1975. *On the Hill: A History of the American Congress*. New York: Touchstone.

Judge, David. 1985. "Disorder in the House of Commons." *Public Law*, Autumn, 368–76.

Kaboolian, Linda. 1989. "Changing Gears: Auto Workers View the Restructuring of Their Industry." John F. Kennedy School of Government, Harvard University. Mimeo.
———. 1990. *Shifting Gears: Auto Workers Assess the Transformation of Their Industry*. Ph.D. diss., University of Michigan.
Kamen, Al. 1986. "A Series of High Court Rebuffs for Reagan." *Washington Post*, July 7, A7.
Kassebaum, Nancy Landon. 1988. "The Senate Is Not in Order." *Washington Post*, January 27, A19.
Katz, Harry C. 1985. *Shifting Gears: Changing Labor Relations in the U.S. Automobile Industry*. Cambridge, MA: MIT Press.
Katz, Jeffrey L. 1991. "The Power of Talk." *Governing*, March, 38–42.
Katzenstein, Peter J. 1985. *Small States in World Markets*. Ithaca, NY: Cornell University Press.
Keller, Morton. 1977. *Affairs of State*. Cambridge, MA: Belknap.
Kelman, Steven. 1987. *Making Public Policy: A Hopeful View of American Government*. New York: Basic.
Kelves, Daniel J. 1978. *The Physicists: The History of a Scientific Community in America*. New York: Alfred A. Knopf.
Kenworthy, Tom. 1990. "On Hill, 'Nothing Is Funny Anymore.'" *Washington Post*, October 18, A25, A32.
Kernell, Samuel. 1986. *Going Public*. Washington: CQ Press.
Kerr, Peter. 1990. "Assembly Democrats Avert Revolt in Trenton." *New York Times*, December 4, B8.
Kettering Foundation. 1991. *Citizens and Politics: A View from Main Street America*. Dayton, OH: The Foundation.
Kiewiet, D. Roderick. 1983. *Macroeconomics and Micropolitics*. Chicago: University of Chicago Press.
Kilpatrick, James J. 1985. "Anarchy in the Senate." *Washington Post*, December 9, A15.
King, David C. 1991. "Congressional Committee Jurisdictions and the Consequences of Reform." Presented at the Annual Meeting of the Midwest Political Science Association, Chicago, April.
King, Ronald F. 1986. "The New Fiscal Revolution: Taxation Politics in the Reagan Years." Presented at the Annual Meeting of the American Politics Group of the Political Studies Association of the United Kingdom, Oxford, January.
King, Seth S. 1983. "Formidable Farm Bloc's Political Power Ebbs." *New York Times*, December 8, A1, B16.
Kingdon, John W. 1984. *Agendas, Alternatives, and Public Policies*. Boston: Little Brown.
Klein, Frederick C. 1989. "Fans Play 'Get the Guest.'" *Wall Street Journal*, January 13, A10.
Kornberg, Allan. 1964. "The Rules of the Game in the Canadian House of Commons." *Journal of Politics* 26 (May): 358–80.
Krehbiel, Keith. 1986. "Unanimous Consent Agreements: Going along in the Senate." *Journal of Politics* 48 (August): 541–64.

———. 1987. "Why Are Congressional Committees Powerful?" *American Political Science Review* 81 (September): 929–35.
Kreps, David M. 1990. "Corporate Culture and Economic Theory." In James E. Alt and Kenneth A. Shepsle, eds., *Perspectives on Positive Political Economy*, 90–143. New York: Cambridge University Press.
Krieger, Joel. 1986. *Reagan, Thatcher and the Politics of Decline*. New York: Oxford University Press.
Kristof, Nicholas. 1989. "Debut at the Polls Delights Opposition in Taiwan." *New York Times*, December 4, A3.
Kurtz, Howard. 1987. "Landfill Closings: Costly Crisis for the Northeast." *Washington Post*, December 14, A1, A21.
Lafollette, Marcel C. 1990. *Making Science Our Own: Public Images of Science 1910–1955*. Chicago: University of Chicago Press.
Lambro, Donald. 1986. "Stockman's Parting Shots." *Penthouse*, March, 64–66, 130, 132.
Lane, Robert E. 1965. "The Politics of Consensus in an Age of Affluence." *American Political Science Review* 59 (December): 874–95.
Langbein, Laura I., and Lee Sigelman. 1989. "Show Horses, Work Horses, and Dead Horses." *American Politics Quarterly* 17 (January): 80–95.
Larson, Deborah Welch. 1986. "Game Theory and the Psychology of Reciprocity." Columbia University. Mimeo.
Levy, Frank. 1987. *Dollars and Dreams: The Changing Economic Income Distribution*. New York: Russell Sage Foundation.
Lewin, Tamar. 1986. "Business and the Law: The Big Debate over Litigation." *New York Times*, May 13, D2.
Lewis, Paul. 1986. "As Protest Turns Ugly, Cherchez le Provacateur." *New York Times*, December 12, A4.
Lipset, Seymour Martin. 1967. *The First New Nation*. New York: Anchor.
———. 1990. "The Work Ethic—Then and Now." *The Public Interest*, Winter, 61–69.
Lipset, Seymour Martin, and William Schneider. 1987. *The Confidence Gap*. Rev. ed. Baltimore: Johns Hopkins University Press.
Lockwood, Charles. 1990. "Gangs, Crime, Smut, Violence." *New York Times*, September 20, A21.
Loomis, Burdett. 1988. *The New American Politician*. New York: Basic.
———. 1990. "Everett Dirksen and the Evolution of the Senate Minority Leadership." Presented at the Conference on Senate Leadership, Everett McKinley Dirksen Center, Washington, D.C., May.
Lowi, Theodore J. 1979. *The End of Liberalism*. Rev. ed. New York: W. W. Norton.
———. 1984. "Ronald Reagan: Revolutionary?" In Lester W. Salamon and Michael S. Lund, eds., *The Reagan Administration and the Governing of America*, 29–56. Washington: Urban Institute Press.
———. 1986. "The Welfare State: Ethical Foundations and Constitutional Remedies." *Political Science Quarterly* 101 (Summer): 197–220.
Lyall, Sarah. 1991. "Suffolk County Leadership Is in Turmoil over Budget." *New York Times*, January 15, B1, B4.

Lynn, Frank. 1990. "The Stakes Are Raised For Catholic Politicians." *New York Times*, June 17, E5.
Maass, Arthur. 1951. *Muddy Waters: The Army Corps of Engineers and the Nation's Rivers*. Cambridge, MA: Harvard University Press.
McCloskey, Herbert, and John Zaller. 1984. *The American Ethos: Public Attitudes toward Capitalism and Democracy*. Cambridge, MA: Harvard University Press.
McCormick, Richard L. 1986. *The Party Period and Public Policy*. Oxford: Oxford University Press.
McCubbins, Mathew D. 1991. "Government on Law-Away: Federal Spending and Deficits Under Divided Party Control." In Gary W. Cox and Samuel Kernell, eds., *The Politics of Divided Government*, 113-54. Boulder, CO: Westview.
McDowell, Charles. 1986. "Trust Me." *Washingtonian*, May, 134-50.
McGill, Douglas C. 1989. "Why They Smile at Red Lobster." *New York Times*, April 23, F1, F6.
McKelvey, Richard D. 1976. "Intransitivities in Multidimensional Voting Models with Some Implications for Agenda Control." *Journal of Economic Theory* 12: 472-82.
McLaughlin, Andrew C., and Albert Bushnell Hart, eds. 1914. *Cyclopedia of American Government*. New York: D. Appleton.
McLaughlin, Merill, with Jeffrey L. Sheler and Gordon Witkin. 1987. "A Nation of Liars?" *U.S. News and World Report*, February 23, 54-60.
Malcolm, Andrew H. 1986. "LaRouche Illinois Drive Focused on Rural Areas." *New York Times*, March 31, A12.
Manley, John F. 1970. *The Politics of Finance*. Boston: Little, Brown.
Mansbridge, Jane. 1980. *Beyond Adversary Democracy*. New York: Basic.
———. 1986. *Why We Lost the ERA*. Chicago: University of Chicago Press.
Margolick, David. 1991. "At the Bar." *New York Times*, June 14, B9.
Margolis, Howard. 1982. *Selfishness, Altruism, and Rationality*. Cambridge: Cambridge University Press.
Markle Commission on Media and the Electorate. 1990. *Recommendations*. New York: The Commission.
Markus, Greg. 1990. "Measuring Popular Individualism." Memorandum to the National Election Studies Pilot Committee. University of Michigan. February 1. Mimeo.
Martin, Joe. 1960. *My First Fifty Years in Politics*. As told to Robert J. Donovan. New York: McGraw-Hill.
Martin, Judith, and Gunther Stent. 1991. "Say the Right Thing—or Else." *New York Times*, March 20, A29.
Mathews, Jay. 1990. "Tide Is Turning Against Big Green." *Washington Post*, October 30, A5.
Matthews, Donald R. 1960. *U.S. Senators and Their World*. Chapel Hill: University of North Carolina Press.
May, Clifford D. 1988. "Pollution Ills Stir Support for Environment Groups." *New York Times*, August 21, 30.

Mayhew, David R. 1966. *Party Loyalty among Congressmen*. Cambridge: Harvard University Press.
———. 1974. *Congress: The Electoral Connection*. New Haven, CT: Yale University Press.
———. 1991. *Divided We Govern*. New Haven, CT: Yale University Press.
Melnick, R. Shep. 1983. *Regulation and the Courts*. Washington: Brookings Institution.
Merelman, Richard M. 1984. *Making Something of Ourselves*. Berkeley: University of California Press.
———. 1989. "On Culture and Politics in America: A Perspective from Structural Anthropology." *British Journal of Political Science* 19 (October): 465-93.
Merry, Robert W. 1991. "Sen. Paul Wellstone and Gadfly Politics." *Congressional Quarterly Weekly Report*, February 2, 318.
Merry, Robert W., and Jane Mayer. 1986. "President Tightens Already-Firm Control of National Agenda." *Wall Street Journal*, March 28, 1, 7.
Merry, Robert W., and David Shribman. 1985. "GOP Hopes Tax Plan Will Help It Become Majority Party Again." *Wall Street Journal*, May 23, 1, 27.
Michel, Bob. 1984. "Politics in the Age of Television." *Washington Post*, May 20, B7.
Michel, Robert. 1989. "Full Repairs for a Broken House." *New York Times*, June 18, E27.
Miller, Clem. 1962. *Member of the House*. Edited by John Baker. New York: Charles Scribner's Sons.
Miller, Warren E., Arthur H. Miller, and Edward J. Schneider, comps. 1980. *American National Election Studies Data Handbook*. Cambridge, MA: Harvard University Press.
Miller, Nicholas R. 1983. "Pluralism and Social Choice." *American Political Science Review* 77 (September): 734-47.
Miller, Warren E., and J. Merrill Shanks. 1982. "Policy Directions and Presidential Leadership: Alternative Interpretations of the 1980 Presidential Election." *British Journal of Political Science* 12:299-356.
Mitchell, Jacqueline. 1990. "More Car Ads Challenge Rivals Head On." *Wall Street Journal*, June 25, B1, B6.
Moe, Terry M. 1985. "The Politicized Presidency." In John E. Chubb and Paul E. Peterson, *The New Direction in American Politics*, 235-67. Washington: Brookings Institution.
———. 1988. "The Politics of Structural Choice: Toward a Theory of Public Bureaucracy." Presented at the Annual Meeting of the American Political Science Association, Washington, September.
Morgan, Dan, and Walter Pincus. 1990. "You Think the Budget's Solved? Maybe So, Maybe No." *Washington Post*, November 11, C5.
Morgan, H. Wayne. 1969. *From Hayes to McKinley*. Syracuse, NY: Syracuse University Press.
Morin, Richard, and Dan Balz. 1989. "Shifting Racial Climate." *Washington Post*, October 25, A1, A16.

Morin, Richard, and Helen Dewar. 1992. "Approval of Congress Hits All-Time Low, Poll Finds." *Washington Post*, March 20, A16.
Morin, Richard, and Paul Taylor. 1990. "Poll Shows Plunge in Public Confidence." *Washington Post*, October 16, A1, A10.
Morison, Samuel Eliot. 1965. *The Oxford History of the American People*. New York: Oxford University Press.
Mosher, Frederick C. 1982. *Democracy and the Public Service*. 2d ed. New York: Oxford University Press.
Mufson, Steven. 1992. "Bushwacking the Reagan Tax Reforms." *Washington Post*, January 19, H1, H8.
Mufson, Steven, and John E. Yang. 1990. "Why Deficit Crisis Is So Hard to Fix." *Washington Post*, October 7, A17, A18.
Muir, William K., Jr. 1982. *Legislature*. Chicago: University of Chicago Press.
Murphy, James T. 1974. "Political Parties and the Porkbarrel: Party Conflict and Cooperation in House Public Works Committee Decision-Making." *American Political Science Review* 68 (March): 169–85.
Myrdal, Gunnar. 1964. *An American Dilemma*. Vol. 1. New York: McGraw-Hill.
Nagel, Thomas. 1987. "Moral Conflict and Political Legitimacy." *Philosophy and Public Affairs* 16: 215–40.
Nathan, Richard P. 1975. *The Plot That Failed: Nixon and the Administrative Presidency*. New York: John Wiley.
National Science Board. 1977. *Science Indicators—1976*. Washington: Government Printing Office.
———. 1981. *Science Indicators—1980*. Washington: Government Printing Office.
———. 1983. *Science Indicators—1982*. Washington: Government Printing Office.
———. 1989. *Science Indicators—1989*. Washington: Government Printing Office.
NBC News. 1990a. February 14. Press release.
———. 1990b. April 16. Press release.
———. 1990c. April 27. Press release
———. 1990d. June 1. Press release.
———. 1990e. September 28. Press release.
———. 1990f. November 2. Press release.
———. 1991a. March 29. Press release.
———. 1991b. May 29. Press release.
———. 1991c. July 9. Press release.
———. 1992. January 6. Press release.
Nelson, Ralph L. 1986. "The Amount of Total Personal Giving in the United States 1948–1982 with Projections to 1985 Using the Personal-Giving Estimating Model." New York: United Way Institute.
Nelson, Steven E. 1990. "Distributive Politics and Representation: Support for Agriculture in the U.S. Senate, 1965 to the Present." Presented at the Annual Meeting of the Southern Political Science Association, Atlanta, November.

Newsweek. 1991. "Opinion Watch." March 11, 50.
New York Times, 1986a. "Key Programs to Be Eliminated and the Reasons for Doing So." February 6, B14.
―――. 1986b. "Reagan Aims Fire at Liberal Judges." October 9, A32.
―――. 1987. "Freshman Attitudes." January 18, E30.
―――. 1989. "Excerpts from Court Decision on the Regulation of Abortion." July 4, 12–13.
―――. 1990. "Cutting the Budget: The Final Package." October 28, A26.
Nichols, Roy Franklin. 1962. *The Disruption of American Democracy.* New York: Collier. Originally published in 1948.
Niemi, Richard G., John Mueller, and Tom W. Smith, comps. 1989. *Trends in Public Opinion: A Compendium of Survey Data.* New York: Greenwood Press.
Nisbet, Robert. 1980. *History of the Idea of Progress.* New York: Basic.
Noll, Roger G., and Barry Weingast. 1991. "Rational Actor Theory, Social Norms, and Policy Implementation." In Kristen Renwick Monroe, ed., *The Economic Approach to Politics,* 237–58. New York: HarperCollins.
Norpoth, Helmut. 1985. "Changes in Party Identification: Evidence of a Republican Majority?" Presented at the Annual Meeting of the American Political Science Association, Denver, August–September.
O'Neill, William L. 1986. *American High: The Years of Confidence, 1945–1986.* New York: Free Press.
Oppenheimer, Joe A. 1973. "Relating Coalitions of Minorities to the Voters' Paradox." University of Texas. Mimeo.
Orbell, John M., Peregrine Schwartz-Shea, and Randy T. Simmons. 1984. "Do Cooperators Exit More Readily than Defectors?" *American Political Science Review* 78 (March): 147–62.
Oreskes, Michael. 1985a. "Poll Finds Most Americans Fearful of Being Harmed by Cuts in Budget." *New York Times,* March 7, A22.
―――. 1985b. "To New Yorkers, Border War with Jersey Has Claimed a Victim: Westway." *New York Times,* September 25, B1, B2.
―――. 1989. "The Television Politicians Rise in Congress, Too." *New York Times,* June 18, E4.
―――. 1990. "As Election Day Nears, Poll Finds Nation's Voters in a Gloomy Mood." *New York Times,* November 4, A1, A14.
Ornstein, Norman J. 1983. "The Open Congress Meets the President." In Anthony King, ed., *Both Ends of the Avenue,* 185–211. Washington: American Enterprise Institute.
Ornstein, Norman J., Thomas E. Mann, and Michael J. Malbin, comps. 1990. *Vital Statistics on Congress, 1989–1990.* Washington: CQ Press.
Ostrom, Elinor. 1991. *Governing the Commons.* New York: Cambridge University Press.
Ostrom, Elinor, James Walker, and Roy Gardner. 1990. "Sanctioning by Participants in Collective Action Problems." Presented at the Annual Meeting of the American Political Science Association, San Francisco, August–September.

Packwood, Bob. 1986. "What I've Learned: The Maverick." As told to Vera Glaser. *The Washingtonian*, December, 97–98.
Palmer, John L., and Isabel V. Sawhill, eds. 1982. *The Reagan Experiment*. Washington: Urban Institute Press.
Parris, Judith. 1979. "The Senate Reorganizes Its Committees, 1977." *Political Science Quarterly* 94 (Summer): 319–38.
Patterson, Samuel C., and Gregory A. Caldeira. 1990. "Standing Up for Congress: Variations in Public Esteem Since the 1960s." *Legislative Studies Quarterly* 15 (February): 25–47.
Pear, Robert. 1985a. "Many Households Get U.S. Benefits." *New York Times*, April 17, A23.
———. 1985b. "Rewriting the Nation's Civil Rights Policy." *New York Times*, October 7, A20.
———. 1986. "Aide in Justice Department Holds That Brennan Has 'Radical' Views." *New York Times*, September 13, 1, 10.
Peterson, Bill. 1985. "Study Says Senators Do Less With More." *Washington Post*, December 25, A13.
———. 1988. "City Council Rules Insults out of Order—Sometimes." *Washington Post*, November 11, A3.
Peterson, Cass. 1988. "$9 Billion Bailout for Nuclear Industry." *Washington Post*, May 21, A9.
Peterson, Mark A. 1990. *Legislating Together*. Cambridge: Harvard University Press.
———. 1992. "The Presidency and Organized Interests: White House Patterns of Group Liaison." *American Political Science Review* 86 (September): 612–25.
Peterson, Mark A., and Jack L. Walker. 1986. "Interest Group Responses to Partisan Change." In Allan J. Cigler and Burdett A. Loomis, eds., *Interest Group Politics*, 2d ed., 162–82. Washington: Congressional Quarterly Press.
Petrocik, John R. 1987. "Realignment: New Party Coalitions and the Nationalization of the South." *Journal of Politics* 49 (May): 347–75.
Phillips, Don. 1989a. "State Delegation Sizzling over One District's Pork." *Washington Post*, October 9, A19.
———. 1989b. "Atwater Snatches Prize away from Democrats." *Washington Post*, November 10, A18.
Piore, Michael J., and Charles F. Sabel. 1984. *The Second Industrial Divide*. New York: Basic.
Pitney, John J., Jr. 1988a. "The Conservative Opportunity Society." Presented at the Annual Meeting of the Western Political Science Association, San Francisco, March.
———. 1988b. "The War on the Floor: Partisan Conflict in the U.S. House of Representatives." Presented at the Annual Meeting of the American Political Science Association, Washington, September.
———. 1990. "Republican Party Leadership in the U.S. House." Presented at the Annual Meeting of the American Political Science Association, San Francisco, August–September.

Plattner, Andy. 1985. "Republicans Walk out in Protest after House Seats McCloskey." *Congressional Quarterly Weekly Report*, May 5, 821–25.
Pole, J. R. 1978. *The Pursuit of Equality in American History*. Berkeley: University of California Press.
Polsby, Nelson W. 1968. "The Institutionalization of the U.S. House of Representatives." *American Political Science Review* 62 (March): 144–68.
———. 1971. "Goodbye to the Inner Club." In Nelson W. Polsby, ed., *Congressional Behavior*, 105–10. New York: Random House.
———. 1981. "The Washington Community, 1960–1980." In Thomas E. Mann and Norman J. Ornstein, eds., *The New Congress*, 7–31. Washington: American Enterprise Institute.
Polsby, Nelson W., Miriam Gallaher, and Barry Spencer Rundquist. 1969. "The Growth of the Seniority System in the U.S. House of Representatives." *American Political Science Review* 63 (September): 787–807.
Portney, Paul R. 1984. "Natural Resources and the Environment: More Controversy than Change." In John L. Palmer and Isabel V. Sawhill, eds., *The Reagan Record*, 141–75. Washington: Urban Institute Press.
Potter, David M. 1954. *People of Plenty*. Chicago: University of Chicago Press.
———. 1976. *The Impending Crisis, 1848–1861*. Completed and edited by Don E. Fehrenbacher. New York: Harper and Row.
Press, Aric. 1986. "Reagan Justice." *Newsweek*, June 30, 14–19.
Price, David E. 1972. *Who Makes the Laws?* New York: Schenkman.
Public Opinion. 1980. February/March.
———. 1984. February/March.
———. 1990. November/December.
Quinn, Robert P., and Graham L. Staines. 1979. *The 1977 Quality of Employment Survey*. Ann Arbor: Survey Research Center, Institute for Social Research, University of Michigan.
Raines, Howell. 1988. "In Britain, Tax Overhaul and a Feud." *New York Times*, March 16, D1, D7.
Ramirez, Anthony. 1990. "From Coffee to Tobacco, Boycotts Are a Growth Industry." *New York Times*, June 3, E2.
Ranney, Austin. 1976. "The Divine Science: Political Engineering in American Culture." *American Political Science Review* 70 (March): 140–48.
———. 1983. *Channels of Power*. New York: Basic.
Rapoport, Anatol, Melvin J. Guyer, and David G. Gordon. 1976. *The 2x2 Game*. Ann Arbor: University of Michigan Press.
Rapp, David. 1987a. "For the Farmer, It's a Question of Necessity." *Congressional Quarterly Weekly Report*, February 21, 303–8.
———. 1987b. "Farmer and Uncle Sam: An Old, Odd Couple." *Congressional Quarterly Weekly Report*, April 4, 598–603.
Rasky, Susan F. 1988. "Accord Is Reached on Base Closings." *New York Times*, October 6, A19.
Rauch, Jonathan. 1985. "Stockman's Quiet Revolution at OMB May Leave Indelible Mark on Agency." *National Journal*, May 25, 1212–17.

Reid, T. R. 1985. "Mall-Adjusted Americans Fuel Amazing Money Machines." *Washington Post*, August 30, A1, A12.
Reif, Rita. 1990. "Christie's Reverses Stand on Price Guarantees." *New York Times*, March 12, C13, C16.
Reinhold, Robert. 1986a. "Oil's Collapse Leads to Rise in Arson." *New York Times*, August 4, A8.
———. 1986b. "Amarillo, Up 36%, Tops Texas Cities in Crime Rise." *New York Times*, August 25, A11.
———. 1988. "With Proliferation of Ballot Initiatives, Suddenly Everyone's Interest Is Special." *New York Times*, November 6, E4.
———. 1991. "Drought Brings Quiet to Farms in California at Normally Busy Time." *New York Times*, February 6, A12.
Reiter, Howard L. 1985. *Selecting the President*. Philadelphia: University of Pennsylvania Press.
Richey, Warren. 1985. "Senate Democrats Dig in Heels for Longer Review of Reagan Judges." *Christian Science Monitor* November 27, 9.
Riddick, Floyd M. 1949. *The United States Congress: Organization and Procedure*. Manassas, VA: National Capitol Publishers.
Riker, William H. 1980. "Implications from the Disequilibrium of Majority Rule for the Study of Institutions." *American Political Science Review* 74 (June): 432–46.
Robbins, William. 1986a. "Farm Belt Suicides Reflect Greater Hardship and Deepening Despondency." *New York Times*, February 14, A11.
———. 1986b. "Surge in Sympathy for Farmer Found." *New York Times*, February 25, A1, A22.
———. 1987. "Limits on Subsidies to Big Farms Go Awry, Sending Costs Climbing." *New York Times*, June 15, A1, B11.
———. 1988. "After a Year of Subsidized Gains, Signs of New Hope." *New York Times*, February 14, E4.
———. 1990. "Down on the Farm, Things Are Looking Up." *New York Times*, October 23, A14.
Roberts, Steven V. 1985. "Tax Debate Might Foreshadow '86 Campaign." *New York Times*, December 20, A32.
Robinson, William A. 1930. *Thomas B. Reed: Parliamentarian*. New York: Dodd, Mead and Co.
Rohde, David W. 1988. "Studying Congressional Norms: Concepts and Evidence." *Congress and the Presidency* 15 (Autumn): 139–45.
———. 1990. "Agenda Change and Partisan Resurgence in the House of Representatives." Presented at the Conference on "Back to the Future: The United States Congress in the Twenty-First Century." Carl Albert Congressional Research Center, University of Oklahoma, April.
———. 1991. *Parties and Leaders in the Postreform House*. Chicago: University of Chicago Press.
Rohde, David W., Norman J. Ornstein, and Robert L. Peabody. 1985. "Political Change and Legislative Norms in the U.S. Senate." In Glenn R. Parker,

ed., *Studies of Congress*, 147–88. Washington: Congressional Quarterly Press.
Ronsvalle, John L. and Sylvia Ronsvalle. 1991. *The State of Church Giving, through 1989,*. Champaign, IL: empty tomb, inc.
Rothman, David J. 1966. *Politics and Power: The United States Senate, 1869–1901.* Cambridge, MA: Harvard University Press.
Rovere, Richard H. 1959. *Senator Joe McCarthy.* New York: Harcourt, Brace.
Rovner, Julie. 1991. "'Pro-Life' House Democrats Break Ranks, Lie Low." *Congressional Quarterly Weekly Report*, December 14, 3640–44.
Royte, Elizabeth. 1990. "Showdown in Cattle Country." *New York Times Magazine*, December 16, 60–70.
Rundquist, Paul S., and Ilona B. Nickels. 1986. "Senate Television: Its Impact on Senate Floor Proceedings." Washington: Congressional Research Service, Library of Congress.
Runge, Carlisle Ford. 1988. "The Assault on Agricultural Production." *Foreign Affairs*, Fall, 133–50.
Russakoff, Dale, 1986. "A Familiar 1040 Bottom Line." *Washington Post*, September 29, A1, A12.
Russakoff, Dale and Anne Swardson. 1986. "Industry to Limit Fight against Tax-Revision Bill." *Washington Post*, August 19, A1, A8.
Sabel, Charles F. 1982. *Work and Politics: The Division of Labor in Society.* Cambridge: Cambridge University Press.
Salisbury, Robert H. 1984. "Interest Representation: The Dominance of Institutions." *American Political Science Review* 78 (March): 64–76.
Salisbury, Robert H., John P. Heinz, Edward O. Laumann, and Robert L. Nelson. 1987. "Who Works With Whom? Interest Group Alliances and Opposition." *American Political Science Review* 81 (December): 1217–34.
Schattschneider, E. E. 1960. *The Semisovereign People.* New York: Holt, Rinehart and Winston.
Schelling, Thomas C. 1978. *Macromotives and Microbehavior.* New York: W. W. Norton.
Schememann, Serge. 1990. "In Bonn's Parliament, Insults Fly in Debate on Unification." *New York Times*, February 16, A1, A8.
Schlozman, Kay Lehman, and Sidney Verba. 1979. *Insult to Injury.* Cambridge: Harvard University Press.
Schneider, Keith. 1986. "Farm Trade Deficit a Record in May." *New York Times*, June 28, 35, 38.
———. 1987. "The Subsidy 'Addiction' On the Farms." *New York Times*, September 13, E5.
———. 1990a. "The Farm Economy Is Fine, and Can Expect More Aid." *New York Times*, February 4, E4.
———. 1990b. "Come What May, Congress Stays True to the Critters." *New York Times*, May 6, E4.
———. 1990c. "Where Farmers Would Take a Hit in the Cause of Cutting the Deficit." *New York Times*, October 21, E5.

———. 1992. "Pushed and Pulled, Environment Inc. Is on the Defensive." *New York Times*, March 29, E1, E3.
Schwadel, Francine. 1988. "Deck the Halls—And Deck the Clerk: Shoppers Get Nasty." *Wall Street Journal*, December 20, A1, A6.
Schwartz, Ethan. 1990. "Well, Excusez-Moi for Watching." *Washington Post*, February 11, G1, G5.
Searing, Donald. 1982. "Rules of the Game in Britain: Can Politicians Be Trusted?" *American Political Science Review* 76 (June): 239–58.
Shabecoff, Philip. 1987a. "After 85 Years, the Era of Big Dams Nears End." *New York Times*, January 24, 6.
———. 1987b. "With No Room at the Dump, U.S. Faces a Garbage Crisis." *New York Times*, June 29, B8.
———. 1988. "E.P.A. Sets Strategy to End 'Staggering' Garbage Crisis." *New York Times*, September 22, A18.
Shafer, Byron E. 1991a. "What Is the American Way? Four Themes in Search of Their Next Incarnation." In Byron E. Shafer, ed., *Is America Different? A New Look at American Exceptionalism*. Oxford: Oxford University Press.
———, ed. 1991b. *The End of Realignment?* Madison: University of Wisconsin Press.
Shanahan, Eileen. 1986. "Finance Committee OKs Radical Tax Overhaul Bill." *Congressional Quarterly Weekly Report*, May 10, 1007–13.
Shapiro, Margaret. 1985. "California Congressman Puts on a Floor Show." *Washington Post*, June 20, A3.
Shenon, Philip. 1985. "Meese and His New Vision of the Constitution." *New York Times* (October 10):B10.
Shepsle, Kenneth A. 1984. "The Congressional Budget Process: Diagnosis, Prescription, Prognosis." In W. Thomas Wander, F. Ted Hebert, and Gary W. Copeland, eds., *Congressional Budgeting*, 190–237. Baltimore: Johns Hopkins University Press.
———. 1985. "The Changing Textbook Congress." In John E. Chubb and Paul E. Peterson, eds., *Can the Government Govern?*, 238–66. Washington: Brookings Institution.
———. 1986. "Institutional Equilibrium and Equilibrium Institutions." In Herbert F. Weisberg, ed., *Political Science: The Science of Politics*, 51–81. New York: Agathon.
Shepsle, Kenneth A., and Barry Weingast. 1981. "Political Preferences for the Pork Barrel: A Generalization." *American Journal of Political Science* 25 (February): 96–111.
———. 1987. "Why Are Congressional Committees Powerful?" *American Political Science Review* 81: 935–45.
Shields, Mark. 1991. "Mood Swings, '91." *Washington Post*, December 31, A17.
Shribman, David, and Ellen Hume. 1986. "Deficit Is a Vital Issue to Voters, Yet Seems to Attract Few Votes." *Wall Street Journal*, October 24, 1, 12.
Silk, Leonard. 1990. "Why It's Too Soon To Predict Another Great Depression." *New York Times*, November 11, E1, E4.

Sinclair, Barbara. 1983. *Majority Leadership in the U.S. House*. Baltimore: Johns Hopkins University Press.
———. 1985. "Agenda, Policy, and Alignment Change from Coolidge to Reagan." In Lawrence C. Dodd and Bruce I. Oppenheimer, eds., *Congress Reconsidered*, 3d ed. Washington: CQ Press.
———. 1989a. *The Transformation of the U.S. Senate*. Baltimore: Johns Hopkins University Press.
———. 1989b. "House Majority Party Leadership in the Late 1980s." In Lawrence C. Dodd and Bruce I. Oppenheimer, eds., *Congress Reconsidered*, 4th ed., 307–30. Washington: CQ Press.
Sinclair, Ward. 1980. "Carter Seems to Have Dammed Hill on Water Projects." *Washington Post*, May 24, A6.
———. 1986. "Many Quit Farming as Credit Crisis Dims Hope." *Washington Post*, June 3, A1, A11.
———. 1987. "Farm Credit System Requires $6 Billion Bailout, Aides Say." *Washington Post*, May 7, E1, E2.
Sinclair, Ward, and Peter Behr. 1981. "Horse Trading." *Washington Post*, June 27, A1, A3.
Skowronek, Stephen. 1982. *Building a New American State*. New York: Cambridge University Press.
———. 1984. "Presidential Leadership in Political Time." In Michael Nelson, ed., *The Presidency and the Political System*, 87–132. Washington: CQ Press.
Smith, Steven S. 1985. "New Patterns of Decisionmaking in Congress." In John E. Chubb and Paul E. Peterson, eds., *The New Direction in American Politics*, 203–33. Washington: Brookings Institution.
———. 1989. *Call to Order: Floor Politics in the House and Senate*. Washington: Brookings Institution.
Smith, T. V. 1940. *The Legislative Way of Life*. Chicago: University of Chicago Press.
Spanier, John, and Eric M. Uslaner. 1989. *American Foreign Policy Making and the Democratic Dilemmas*. 5th ed. Belmont, CA: Brooks-Cole.
Stanfield, Rochelle L. 1986a. "Resolving Disputes." *National Journal*, November 15, 2764–68.
———. 1986b. "A New Era." *National Journal*, November 22, 2822–25.
Stanley, Harold W., and Richard G. Niemi, comps. 1992. *Vital Statistics on American Politics*, 3d ed. Washington: CQ Press.
Starobin, Paul. 1987. "Pork: A Time-Honored Tradition Lives On." *Congressional Quarterly Weekly Report*, October 24, 2581–91.
Steenbergen, Marco R., and Neil A. Pinney. 1991. "Citizenship and Participation: Are There Similar Qualities between Voting and Tax Compliance?" Presented at the Annual Meeting of the Midwest Political Science Association Meeting, Chicago, April.
Steinberg, Alfred. 1975. *Sam Rayburn*. New York: Hawthorn.
Stevenson, Richard W. 1990. "Many Caught, but Few Are Hurt for Arms Contract Fraud in U.S." *New York Times*, November 12, A1, B8.

Stewart, Charles H., III. 1989. *Budget Reform Politics.* New York: Cambridge University Press.
Stimson, James A. 1991. *Public Opinion in America.* Boulder, CO: Westview.
Strahan, Randall. 1990. "Reed and Rostenkowski: Congressional Leadership in Institutional Time." Presented at the Conference on "Back to the Future: The United States Congress in the Twenty-First Century." Carl Albert Congressional Research Center, University of Oklahoma, April.
———. 1968. *Politics and Policy.* Washington: Brookings Institution.
———. 1973. *Dynamics of the Party System.* Washington: Brookings Institution.
———. 1981. *The Decline and Resurgence of Congress.* Washington: Brookings Institution.
———. 1988. *Constitutional Reform and Effective Government.* Washington: Brookings Institution.
Sundquist, James L. 1986. *Constitutional Reform and Effective Government.* Washington: Brookings Institution.
Swisher, Kara. 1991. "A Wakeup Call for Customer Service." *Washington Post Washington Business,* April 29, 1, 22, 23.
Tapscott, Richard, and Fern Shen. 1990. "Abortion in Annapolis: Maryland's Debate Is a Warning to Other States." *Washington Post,* April 4, D1, D4.
Taylor, Paul. 1986. "Negative Ads Becoming Powerful Political Force." *Washington Post,* October 5, A1, A6–A7.
———. 1991. "Is Government Ready for Role in U.S. Business?" *Washington Post,* January 27, B1, B4.
Taylor, Stuart Jr. 1987. "Feuding Erupts Again in a Key Appeals Court." *New York Times,* August 15, A7.
———. 1988. "Court, 5–4, Votes To Restudy Rights in Minority Suits." *New York Times,* April 4, A1, A24.
Teltsch, Kathleen. 1989. "No Rise Is Found In Voluntarism." *New York Times,* November 24, A27.
Thompson, Michael, Richard Ellis, and Aaron Wildavsky. 1989. *Cultural Theory.* Boulder, CO: Westview.
Times-Mirror Corporation. 1987. *The People, Press, and Politics.* Los Angeles: The Corporation.
———. 1989. *The People, The Press, and Economics.* Washington: Times-Mirror Center for The Press and Public Policy.
———. 1990. *The People, The Press and Politics 1990.* Washington: Times-Mirror Center for The People and The Press.
———. 1991. *The People, The Press & Politics on the Eve of '92: Fault Lines in the Electorate.* Washington: Times-Mirror Center for The People & The Press.
Tocqueville, Alexis de. 1945. *Democracy in America.* 2 vols. Translated by Henry Reeve. New York: Alfred A. Knopf. Originally published in 1840. Citations to vol. 1 are to the Vintage Books reprint ed. Phillips Bradley.
Toffler, Alvin. 1970. *Future Shock.* New York: Random House.
Toman, Barbara. 1989. "Will the Telly Turn Britain's Feisty MPs into Milquetoast." *Wall Street Journal,* November 21, A1, A12.

Toner, Robin. 1989. "Congress." *New York Times,* July 4, A34.
———. 1990. "The House Democrat His Colleagues Lean On." *New York Times,* May 5, A20.
———. 1991. "Poll Finds Postwar Glow Dimmed by the Economy." *New York Times,* March 8, A14.
Towell, Pat. 1989. "Savvy Legislator Murtha Moves to Spotlight." *Congressional Quarterly Weekly Report,* January 7, 21–23.
TRB. 1966. "TRB From Washington: Barry's Fabulous Congress." *The New Republic,* October 29, 4.
Treese, Joel D. 1990. "The 'Missing Quorum.'" Report prepared by the United States House of Representatives Office for the Bicentennial. Washington, December.
United States House of Representatives Office for the Bicentennial. N.d. *Aggressive and Violent Acts.* Washington.
United States Senate Historical Office. 1988. *Breaches of Comity in the United States Senate.* Washington, July 29.
Uslaner, Eric M. 1978. "Policy Entrepreneurs and Amateur Democrats in the House of Representatives." Presented at the Annual Meeting of the Midwest Political Science Association, Chicago, April.
———. 1987. "The Decline of Comity in Congress." Presented at the Annual Meetings of the American Politics Group of the United Kingdom, London, January, and the Midwest Political Science Association, Chicago, April.
———. 1989. *Shale Barrel Politics: Energy and Legislative Leadership.* Stanford: Stanford University Press.
———. 1991. "Comity in Context: Confrontation in Historical Perspective." *British Journal of Political Science* 21 (January): 45–77.
Verba, Sidney, and Gary R. Orren. 1985. *Equality in America: The View from the Top.* Cambridge: Harvard University Press.
Vidich, Arthur J., and Joseph Bensman. 1958. *Small Town in Mass Society.* Princeton: Princeton University Press.
Vobejda, Barbara. 1986. "Education Group Warns of Censorship Dangers." *Washington Post,* October 10, A12.
Vogel, David. 1986. *National Styles of Regulation.* Ithaca: Cornell University Press.
———. 1989. *Fluctuating Fortunes.* New York: Basic.
Walker, Jack L. 1983. "The Origins and Maintenance of Interest Groups in America." *American Political Science Review* 77 (June): 390–406.
Walsh, Edward. 1985. "GOP House 'Guerillas' Soften Their Tactics." *Washington Post,* September 30, A1, A10.
Walters, Dan. 1986. "A Different Atmosphere." *Sacramento Bee,* September 10.
Wattenberg, Martin P. 1986a. *The Decline of American Political Parties, 1952–1984.* Cambridge, MA: Harvard University Press.
———. 1986b. "The Reagan Polarization Phenomenon and the Continuing Downward Slide in Presidential Candidate Popularity." *American Politics Quarterly* 14 (July): 219–45.

WCBS-TV and *New York Times*. 1990. June 26. Press release.
Weatherford, M. Stephen, and Lorraine M. McDonnell. 1990. "Ideology and Economic Policy." In Larry Berman, ed., *Looking Back on the Reagan Presidency*, 122–55. Baltimore: Johns Hopkins University Press.
Weaver, R. Kent. 1987. *Automatic Government*. Washington: Brookings Institution.
Weingast, Barry. 1979. "A Rational Choice Perspective on Congressional Norms." *American Journal of Political Science* 23 (May): 245–62.
―――. 1989. "Floor Behavior in the U.S. Congress: Committee Power under the Open Rule." *American Political Science Review* 83 (September): 795–815.
Weisskopf, Michael. 1990. "Shouting Match Erupts between House-Senate Conference." *Washington Post*, September 29, A3.
Whalen, Bill. 1986. "Rating Lawmakers' Politics by Looking into Their Ayes." *Insight*, October 20, 20–21.
White, Jim. 1990. "A Course in Manners Management." *The Independent* (London), April 2, 14.
White, William S. 1954. *The Taft Story*. New York: Harper and Brothers.
―――. 1956. *The Citadel*. New York: Harper and Brothers.
―――. 1965. *Home Place*. Boston: Houghton Mifflin.
Wiebe, Robert H. 1975. *The Segmented Society*. London: Oxford University Press.
―――. 1980. *The Search for Order 1877–1920*. Westport, CT: Greenwood Press.
―――. 1984. *The Opening of American Society*. New York: Alfred A. Knopf.
Wildavsky, Aaron. 1979. "Doing Better and Feeling Worse: The Political Pathology of Health Policy." In Aaron Wildavsky, *Speaking Truth to Power: The Art and Craft of Policy Analysis*, 284–308. Boston: Little, Brown.
―――. 1989. "A World of Difference—The Public Philosophies and Political Behaviors of Rival American Cultures." In Anthony King, ed., *The New American Political System*, 2d version, 263–86. Washington: AEI Press.
―――. 1991. "Resolved, That Individualism and Egalitarianism Be Made Compatible: Political Cultural Roots of Exceptionalism." In Byron E. Shafer, ed., *Is America Different? A New Look at American Exceptionalism*. Oxford: Oxford University Press.
Wilkerson, Isabel. 1986. "A New Breed of Legislator: Too Modern To Be Clubby." *New York Times*, February 25, B1, B4.
Williams, Lena. 1988. "It Was a Year When Civility Really Took It on the Chin." *New York Times*, December 18, A1, A38.
Withey, Stephen B. 1959. "Public Opinion about Science and Scientists." *Public Opinion Quarterly* 23 (Fall): 382–88.
Wolfinger, Raymond E., and Steven J. Rosenstone. 1980. *Who Votes?* New Haven, CT: Yale University Press.
Woodlief, Annette. 1982. "Science." In M. Thomas Inge, ed., *Concise Histories of Popular Culture*, 354–62. Westport, CT: Greenwood.
Wool, Robert. 1990. "The New Tax Package: What Does It Mean to You and Me?" *New York Times*, October 28, F10.

World Almanac and Book of Facts. 1984. New York: Newspaper Enterprise Association.

Wright, Louis B. 1957. *The Cultural Life of the American Colonies 1607–1763*. New York: Harper and Row.

Yang, John. 1989. "Ever-Growing Deficits Establish the Failure of Gramm-Rudman." *Wall Street Journal*, October 3, A1, A14.

———. 1991. "In Hill Encore, Champagne Music Man Fizzles." *Washington Post*, March 12, A19.

Yankelovich, Daniel, 1979. "Work, Values, and the New Breed." In Clark Kerr and Jerome Rostow, ed., *Work in America: The Decade Ahead*, 3–26. New York: Van Nostrand Reinhold.

———. 1981. *New Rules*. New York: Random House.

Yankelovich, Daniel, and John Immerwahr. 1983. *Putting the Work Ethic to Work*. New York: Public Agenda Foundation.

Yankelovich, Clancy, Shylman. 1989a. July 10. Press release.

———. 1989b. October 19. Press release.

———. 1990a. October 22. Press release.

———. 1990b. December 17. Press release.

———. 1991. July 30. Press release.

Yarwood, Dean. 1970. "Norm Observance and Legislative Integration: The U.S. Senate in 1850 and 1860." *Social Science Quarterly*, June, 57–69.

Subject Index

Abortion, 11, 60, 75, 85, 109, 115, 128, 160–62, 167
ACT-UP, 86, 89
Activist mood, 148–50
Agriculture 17, 32, 39, 40, 51, 102, 128–30, 134, 135, 138, 140, 141, 142, 143, 145, 147, 154, 167
Agriculture Committee, 39, 143
American exceptionalism, 16, 64–67, 69, 73, 74, 77, 81, 82, 103, 110, 112
American High, 75, 80, 81
Antiintellectualism, 72
Apprenticeship, 9, 21, 34, 36, 37, 41, 46, 57, 58, 84, 101
Automobile industry, 91–93, 145, 146, 150

Big Green, 147, 148
Boycotts, 23, 32, 33, 60, 85
Budget deficits, 17, 49, 50, 93, 102, 117, 129, 132–34, 137–39, 141, 149, 154, 157, 163, 166

California, 10, 12, 57, 85, 91, 119, 132, 147
Canada, 9, 164
Charity, 16, 66, 70, 86, 88, 93, 96–97, 100–102, 138
Christian Right, 116, 146
Chrysler, 110
Civil rights, 2, 7, 11, 16, 17, 26, 71, 78, 85, 93, 107–9, 113, 114, 115, 116, 124, 128, 153, 157, 158, 160–62
Civil War, 40, 55, 71, 73, 105, 160
Civility, 3, 7–9, 15, 18, 19, 24, 47, 51, 69, 88, 102, 129, 148, 153

Clean Air Act, 145, 147, 153, 158
Cloture, 23, 26, 27, 33
Collective action, 1, 3, 6, 8–11, 13, 19, 24, 26, 38, 40, 51, 53, 65, 66, 68, 72, 78, 89, 102, 127, 135, 139, 145, 151, 162, 163, 167
Collegiality, 5
Committee on the Constitutional System, 53
Communitarianism, 6, 18, 58, 64, 68, 72, 75, 83–84, 88, 93–94, 96–97, 102–3, 108, 123, 125, 127, 129, 135, 137, 139, 143, 148, 149, 151, 157–59
Conference committee, 35, 37, 147
Congressional Budget Office, 138
Conservative Opportunity Society, 23, 24, 31, 32, 50, 52, 53, 101, 113, 121, 125, 144, 162
Core values, 2, 7, 14, 16, 65, 123, 125, 161, 162
Courtesy, 1, 5, 8–10, 12, 13, 15, 21, 23, 24, 27, 32, 41, 43, 46, 52, 58, 83, 88, 90, 111, 124
Cross-cutting cleavages, 73, 125, 132, 162
Culture, 2, 9, 17–19, 26, 63–65, 69, 71, 90, 104, 164

Deliberation, 6, 17, 128, 129, 157
Democratic Study Group, 58, 101
Depression, 73–75, 88, 104, 106, 109, 142, 163
Destructive coalition of minorities, 130, 131, 135
Distrust of government, 10, 68, 94, 96, 97, 122, 139, 143, 149

Divided government, 2, 16, 45, 50–53, 61, 122, 138, 143, 148, 150

Egalitarianism, 2, 12–14, 16, 64, 66, 68, 69, 71–75, 77–80, 83, 84, 94, 100, 104–6, 112, 123, 124, 160–62
Electronic voting, 46–48
Energy, 3, 13, 16, 17, 29, 32, 34, 48, 67, 75, 81, 109, 116, 128, 129–35, 141, 143, 153, 162, 167
Enlightened individualism, 17, 69, 93
Entitlement, 110
Environment, 17, 43, 109, 113, 114, 118, 128–30, 145–47, 153, 161, 162
Environmental Action, 146
Environmentalists, 82, 108, 111, 144, 146, 147, 159
Equality, 64, 66, 68, 69, 71, 74, 76, 78, 83, 84, 108, 109, 160

Filibuster, 26–27, 49, 58, 153
Folk theorem, 11
Folkways, 12, 22, 39, 57, 168
Food for Peace, 150
Foreign policy, 4, 50, 91, 116, 128

Garbage, 128, 132
Great Britain, 9, 55, 159, 164, 165
Great Society, 7, 58, 60, 96, 106, 110, 115, 167

Hard work, 27, 35, 73, 84, 90, 101, 124
House of Commons, 55, 164

Illinois, 10, 110, 142
Individualism, 2, 3, 12–14, 16, 17, 64–73, 75, 80, 83, 84, 93, 104, 105, 106, 112, 123, 124, 128, 161, 162
Inner Club, 5, 53
Institutional patriotism, 9, 21, 38, 41, 58
Interest groups, 16, 17, 29, 45, 59–61, 108, 113, 114, 117, 131, 160

Iron triangles, 60, 114

Japan, 11, 76, 77, 82, 92, 164

Legislative Reorganization Act, 46, 48, 49, 166
Legislative work, 9, 21, 34
Liberalism, 59, 80, 96, 97, 101, 117, 122, 123, 128, 138, 149
Litigation, 60, 85, 105
Lobbyists, 60, 135

Macropolitical perspective, 50, 58
Majoritarianism, 9, 14, 43, 112–15, 118, 125, 154, 164–67
Manners, 9, 83, 89, 164, 165
Media, 2, 36, 45, 53–56, 61, 163
Medicaid, 133, 135
Medicare, 133–35, 137, 150
Medicine, 78, 82, 101, 116
Merchant Marine and Fisheries Committee, 39
Michigan, 10, 54, 92
Multiple referrals, 34

Natural gas, 119, 130, 131, 135, 153
New Deal, 15, 43, 78, 106, 109, 128, 154, 159, 163
New issues, 7, 14, 60, 106
New members, new values, 56, 97, 100
New Right, 115
New York City, 31, 104, 110
Norms, 1–5, 7–10, 12–14, 16–66, 75, 79, 83, 84, 90, 92–94, 96, 97, 100–104, 117, 121, 124, 125, 129, 151, 159, 164–65
Northeast-Midwest Caucus, 31

Partisanship, 14, 33, 43, 51, 91, 107, 116, 122–24, 151
Policy, bad, 6, 15, 18, 128–30, 147
Political action committees, 60
Polyester realignment, 112, 118
Pork barrel, 21, 30, 31, 40, 131, 132, 159
Prayer in schools, 60, 75

Subject Index

Price supports, agriculture, 18, 51, 93, 102, 128, 141–44, 149, 154
Prisoner's Dilemma, 9, 11, 12, 60
Prohibition, 104, 105
Public mood, 96, 97, 101, 102, 122, 127–29, 139, 143, 150, 157, 167

Rational choice, 6, 18, 19
Realignment, 4, 14–18, 21, 23, 30, 40, 42, 43, 63, 66, 72–75, 103–6, 109, 112, 115, 116, 118, 120–25, 151, 154, 158–67, 169
Reciprocity, 1, 4, 5, 8–10, 12, 13, 15, 21, 22, 24, 26–32, 34, 38, 43, 46, 48, 52, 58, 83–86, 88, 93, 96, 97, 100, 101, 102, 107, 111, 124, 129
Reform, 2–4, 16–17, 19, 33, 43–50, 53, 56, 61, 66, 104, 112, 116–18, 120, 121, 125, 128, 133, 158, 160, 165–68
Regular order, 8, 16, 17, 23, 38, 40, 49, 50, 63, 104, 111, 112, 125
Religion, 2, 12–14, 16, 64, 66, 69–74, 78, 80, 81, 83, 94, 101, 105, 116, 124, 161, 162
Repeated play, 10–13
Rules Committee, 8, 167

Sanctions, 6, 10–13, 22, 33, 36
Science, 2, 12–14, 16, 32, 64, 66, 69, 71–75, 78, 81–84, 94, 101, 112, 116, 124, 161, 162
Self-interest rightly understood, 7, 12, 65, 66, 68–70, 78, 83, 93, 96, 97, 117, 127, 128
Seniority, 22, 36, 37, 46, 84, 92, 93, 111, 124
Sierra Club, 148
Social engineering, 2, 13, 16, 65, 72, 74, 81, 112, 118
Special rules, 122, 123

Specialization, 9, 21, 34, 35, 37, 38, 41, 46, 58, 84, 92, 101, 111, 124
Stalemate, 4, 6, 17, 31, 49, 53, 94, 111, 128–30, 143, 147, 162, 169
Stock market, 110
Subcommittee Bill of Rights, 46
Sunbelt Caucus, 31
Supreme Court, 10, 11, 32, 43, 54, 81, 93, 107, 115, 162
Synthetic fuels, 131

Task Forces, 35
Tax reform, 3, 17, 33, 104, 112, 116–18, 120, 121, 125, 158, 160
Teacher Corps, 150
Teamwork, 92, 93
Television, 16, 36, 45, 53–56, 73, 88, 91
Tit-for-tat, 52
Trust in government, 18, 54, 96, 101, 102, 116, 150
Trust in other people, 1, 14, 16, 18, 93–96, 116, 122–28, 138–39, 143–44
Turnout, 91

Universalism, 26, 30–32, 112–14, 124
Unlimited resources, 64, 67, 107

Vietnam, 15–17, 108, 124
Voting Rights Act, 150

Water, 30, 82, 91, 114, 128, 132, 145, 146, 153
Watergate, 15, 53, 84, 108, 124
Ways and Means Committee, 29, 119
Women's Christian Temperance Union, 105

Yeoman farmer, 65, 67

Name Index

Allen, James, 26
Armey, Dick, 31, 145

Baker, Howard, 5, 23, 39, 41
Biden, Joseph, 2, 25
Bland, Richard P., 42
Boren, David, 50
Bork, Robert, 32
Bradley, Bill, 119, 120
Brooks, Jack, 41
Bryce, James, 66, 69, 70, 84
Burdick, Quentin, 31
Bush, George, 52, 81, 95, 134, 138, 149, 169
Butler, Andrew, 41
Byrd, Robert, 32, 39

Carter, Jimmy, 30, 52, 112, 113, 132, 151, 152
Cheney, Dick, 32, 37
Cilley, Jonathan, 40
Coxey, Jacob, 106

Danforth, John, 24
Derrick, Butler, 31
Dirksen, Everett, 4, 161
Dodd, Lawrence, 108
Dole, Robert, 4, 32, 33, 39
Dornan, Bob, 32
Douglas, Paul, 59
Downey, Tom, 33, 89
Durenberger, David, 25

Eagleton, Thomas, 25
Economist, the, 1, 67
Ehrenhalt, Alan, 28, 36
Eisenhower, Dwight D., 52, 108, 140, 150, 151, 154

Fazio, Vic, 36
Fields, Sally, 141
Foley, Tom, 5, 36, 37
Ford, Gerald R., 93, 132
Frank, Barney, 33, 45

Gephardt, Richard, 36, 37, 119
Gingrich, Newt, 4, 5, 18, 36, 37, 54, 115, 122, 136
Graves, William, 40
Gray, William, 36, 37
Griswold, Roger, 40
Gross, H. R., 86, 111, 147, 160

Hart, Gary, 9, 24
Helms, Jesse, 33
Hollings, Ernest, 23, 32, 50, 167
Hoover, Herbert, 42, 107
Hyde, Henry, 33

Inge, Samuel, 40
Inglehart, Ronald, 159

Johnson, Lyndon, 36, 39, 50, 97, 108, 151, 152
Jontz, Jim, 31

Kassebaum, Nancy, 24
Kelman, Steven, 159
Kemp, Jack, 33, 119
Kennedy, Edward, 39
Kinnock, Neil, 2
Kreps, David, 13

LaFollette, Robert, 42
Lange, Jessica, 141
Long, Huey, 64
Longworth, Nicholas, 43

203

Loomis, Burdett, 25, 58
Lyon, Matthew, 40

McCarthy, Eugene, 5, 158
Mansfield, Mike, 4
Martin, Joe, 4
Matthews, Donald, 25, 26, 35, 39, 65
Mayhew, David R., 51, 148, 150–51
Michel, Robert, 4, 5, 22, 24, 32, 33, 160
Miller, Clem, 4
Miss Manners, 90
Mitchell, George, 32, 36, 90
Morse, Wayne, 59
Moynihan, Daniel P., 30
Mrazek, Robert, 31
Murtha, John, 36

Nixon, Richard M., 2, 32, 51, 52, 115, 132, 151, 152, 154
Noll, Roger, 58

O'Neill, Thomas P., 4, 32, 76, 81, 120, 126

Packwood, Bob, 24, 26, 33, 120
Perot, H. Ross, 170
Proxmire, William, 59, 87
Pryor, David, 24

Ravenal, Arthur, 39
Rayburn, Sam, 4, 5, 22, 37
Reagan, Ronald, 3, 17, 18, 23, 30, 51, 52, 55, 76, 77, 80, 81, 95, 97, 105, 112–22, 124, 126, 128, 132, 134, 147, 149, 165, 168
Reed, Thomas, 41, 42
Regan, Donald, 119

Rohde, David, 25, 32, 37, 122, 123
Roosevelt, Franklin D., 43, 116
Rostenkowski, Dan, 38, 120
Russert, Tim, 57

Shepsle, Kenneth, 46
Simpson, Alan, 33, 126
Sinclair, Barbara, 39, 60
Slattery, Jim, 31
Smith, Al, 42, 107
Smith, Steven, 34, 49, 50
Spacek, Sissy, 140
Spaight, Richard, 40
Specter, Arlen, 24
Stanley, John, 40
Stanly, Edward, 40
Stevens, Ted, 33, 126
Sumner, Charles, 40
Sundquist, Don, 33
Synar, Mike, 38

Thatcher, Margaret, 165
Toqueville, Alexis de, 8, 66, 71
Tower, John, 32, 170
Tuck, Dick, 1, 2

Vander Jagt, Guy, 33

Walker, Bob, 12, 33, 61, 115, 160
Washington, Craig, 33
Watson, James, 42
Weicker, Lowell, 33
Weingast, Barry, 46, 58
Wildavsky, Aaron, 64, 146
Wilson, Woodrow, 74
Wright, Jim, 5, 32, 34, 73, 91

Zorinsky, Edward, 39